LAKE BLUFF PUBLIC LIBRARY

3 0401 0008 9015 6

W9-ARM-411

MAR   1999

Essie's Story

AMERICAN INDIAN LIVES

Editorial Board

General Editor, A. LaVonne Brown Ruoff
University of Illinois at Chicago (emerita)

R. David Edmunds
Indiana University

Daniel F. Littlefield Jr.
University of Arkansas at Little Rock

Kathleen M. Sands
Arizona State University

Gerald R. Vizenor
University of California, Berkeley

ESTHER BURNETT HORNE
AND SALLY MCBETH

Essie's Story

The Life and Legacy

of a Shoshone Teacher

UNIVERSITY OF NEBRASKA PRESS

LINCOLN AND LONDON

LAKE BLUFF PUBLIC LIBRARY
123 Scranton Avenue
Lake Bluff, IL 60044

© 1998 by the
University of Nebraska Press
All rights reserved
Manufactured in the United States
of America
⊗ The paper in this book meets the
minimum requirements of
American National Standard
for Information Sciences—
Permanence of Paper for
Printed Library Materials,
ANSI Z39.48-1984.
Library of Congress Cataloging-
in-Publication Data
Horne, Esther Burnett.
Essie's story: the life and legacy
of a Shoshone teacher / Esther Burnett Horne
and Sally McBeth.
p.   cm. – (American Indian lives)
Includes bibliographical
references and index.
ISBN 0-8032-2386-2 (alk. paper)
1. Horne, Esther Burnett.
2. Shoshoni women – Biography.
3. Women teachers – North Dakota – Biography.
4. Indian youth – Education – North Dakota.
5. Off-reservation boarding
schools – North Dakota – History.
6. Wahpeton Indian School (N.D.) – History.
I. McBeth, Sally J.   II. Title.   III. Series.
E99.S4H67   1998
371.1′0092 – dc21
[B]   97-47581   CIP

Contents

Illustrations

Preface

When first I met Sally in 1981, I could have sworn that I had known her all my life. Our mutual interest in the boarding school experience provided the basis for a growing friendship. I remember receiving a letter from her, after she moved to Vermont, in which she requested permission to work with me in recording my life history. I debated at length whether I wanted to be a party to revealing the events of my life, but she was a person who radiated sincerity, and I detected nothing superficial about her. In our working together, I frequently forgot that Sally was not Indian. Her knowledge about our culture and her respect for it, combined with her warm sense of humor and caring ways, helped create a bond between us.

After we agreed on a collaborative approach, I realized that I would have the chance to tell my own story without embellishment. I believe that I have something of importance to share with the educators of American Indians and the public at large. I would like to think that, after I am gone, the value of my educational experiences and philosophies will live on through this life history.

I would argue with any scholar who said that Sally and I could not maintain our objectivity because of our love for each other. We are both too strong and too feminist to let that happen.

The memories that surfaced as we recorded and edited the manuscript brought both joy and sorrow. Sharing the materials and working on my life story with Sally made me more mindful that we are all interdependent parts in the circle of life. Our memories are long—as long as the line of the generations.

I owe a special debt to my family, especially my daughters, Vonnie and Dianne. Sadly for us, Vonnie died on May 28, 1997, but during her lifetime both she and Dianne always supported my endeavors. They traveled with me, especially when they were younger, and endured my assignments to "in-services" concerned with the education of Native American youth. That support is vital to me even now as an elder.

Acknowledgments

For their patience and support I am indebted to my husband, Loney, my stepdaughter, Maggie, and especially to my son, Malcolm, whose persistent question, "When are you going to finish the book about Granny Essie?" inspired me to complete this manuscript. It has been a long time coming.

The comments, suggestions, and advice of my brother and best friend, Alan McBeth, were of singular importance to the completion of this book. He always had time to read one more section and to advise me on grammar, content, and clarity.

To my mother, Muriel McBeth, I also owe special thanks. She accompanied me on my first trip to Naytahwaush in 1987 to care for my then two-year-old-son while I worked, but more than that, she has always been supportive of my dreams and visions.

I also want to thank my siblings—Ray, Karen, Alan, Dean, Casey, Mark, and Glenn—and my dad, Carroll, for their help and support over the years.

Lucie Minsk (Dartmouth College) provided invaluable assistance with the transcription of many of the taped interviews. The interlibrary loan staff at the University of Northern Colorado were also of tremendous help, as were friends in Fargo, North Dakota; Moorhead, Minnesota; Wahpeton, North Dakota; Naytahwaush, Minnesota; and Greeley, Colorado.

I also want to thank my colleagues in the Anthropology department at the University of Northern Colorado: Bob Brunswig for help with the map, Michael Higgins for theoretical insights, and Jim Wanner for critical readings. Friend and kindred spirit Anneliese Walsh assisted with the family tree. Loney Tassi also provided invaluable assistance with the reproduction of the photographs. The Hispanic Studies Department was generous with the loan of their Macintosh printer.

The comments and suggestions of the three University of Nebraska Press anonymous readers are gratefully acknowledged. Lavonne Ruoff's supportive reading and detailed recommendations greatly facilitated revision of the manuscript.

My debt to Essie can never be fully acknowledged; she is truly one of the finest people I will ever know.

This collaborative life history has been funded in part by grants from the Claire Garber Goodman Fund of Dartmouth College (1987, 1988), the University of Northern Colorado Research and Publications Board (1991, 1993), the Minnesota Historical Society (1991), the Newberry Library (1992), and the University of Northern Colorado Graduate School (1997). In turn, proceeds from the sale of this book will be used to support scholarships, in the authors' names, at Haskell and at the University of Northern Colorado.

Some materials from the introduction and chapter 1 originally appeared (in a different form) in "Myths of Objectivity and the Collaborative Process in Life History Research," in *When They Read What We Write: The Politics of Ethnography*, ed. Caroline B. Brettell, pp. 145–62, and are reprinted here with the permisson of Bergin-Garvey, an imprint of Greenwood Publishing Group, Inc., Westport CT (McBeth 1993). Portions of the introduction and chapters 1, 2, 3, and 5 were published in slightly different form in "'I Know Who I Am': The Collaborative Life History of a Shoshone Indian Woman," in *Unrelated Kin: Race and Gender in Women's Personal Narratives*, eds. G. Etter Lewis and M. Foster, pp. 71–85 (1996), and appear here by permission of the publisher, Routledge: New York and London (McBeth and Horne 1996).

SALLY MCBETH

Introduction: Methodological and Cultural Concerns of Collecting and Coauthoring a Life History

The story and life of Esther Burnett Horne, which unfold in these pages, can be understood on a variety of levels. The story of this life has been written down as the record of an oral tradition so as not to be forgotten. This book is a chronology of a life presented in order to preserve its story for future family members. It is a history of Indian boarding schools as seen through the eyes of a student and teacher in that system. It is a story shared and written in partnership with an anthropologist. It is a Native story and a woman's story.

Life histories are stories people tell about themselves. They provide a point of view on the writer's past life. They are situated in a time and place. They have a teller, a listener, and an intended audience. The perspectives are fragmentary, the telling is motivated, and the resulting text is retrospective and reflective.

These characteristics of life histories illuminate the limitations and breadth of the genre, which are an acknowledged part of what life histories are—self-examined lives made public, stories that allow the teller's voice to be heard.[1] A life story is more than a recital of events. It is an organization of experience. Our experiences are not naturally remembered chronologically but rather in the order of their personal significance and the idiosyncratic connection of personal events.

Furthermore, life histories provide a context in which to reconsider anthropological methods and to question the rationale of ethnographic inquiry. These concerns are germane to the formidable issues that currently dominate many discussions within the social sciences and humanities. Current ethnographic writing seeks new ways to represent adequately the authority of informants and to explore methodologies that more accurately legitimize the expertise of the members of the culture being investigated. This effort to share our authority and to acknowledge who the authorities and sources of our data really are is part of a broader questioning of the motives and objectivity of the anthropological endeavor.[2]

Collaboration with members of the culture offers a solution to the problems encountered in the attempt to generate an honest cultural representation of those we seek to understand. This is not to say that the very relationship established between the anthropologist and the life history subject in the collaborative process, as well as audience considerations, does not color the text. The collaborative approach does not alleviate the impact of the power-laden relationships inherent in ethnographic writings, but it does acknowledge them. Horne's role in producing this manuscript reinforces the urgent need for Native Americans to play a stronger role in the research process.

For me the significance of this project resides both in recording the memories and experiences of a Native woman whose life spans most of this century and in experimenting with the collaborative method. An added benefit is the intimacy that has resulted from my listening to stories told to me by my friend and coauthor. The time given to listening, sharing, and reflecting has been integral to the project. The difference in my and Essie's ages and cultural backgrounds faded as we engaged in revealing our lives to each other. I am not the first person to discover that storytelling is an essential part of being human. As a result of spending time with Essie Horne over the years, I have learned anew that lasting bonds are created through sharing stories. I have often pondered the possibility that part of my reluctance to complete this project has been due to not wanting our focused time of working together to come to an end.

The following description of this collaborative project illustrates the strengths and weaknesses of the life history genre. It includes a brief introduction to Essie Horne, the methods I used to collect and edit data, the nature of Essie's and my relationship, issues surrounding the accuracy of memory, audience considerations, a comparison of Horne's life history with other efforts to document and record the lives of American Indian women, and a brief overview of the themes of Essie's life.

ESTHER BURNETT HORNE, COLLABORATOR AND SUBJECT:
AN INTRICATE COMPROMISE

Essie Horne is a mixed-blood Shoshone Indian woman, born in 1909. The recording of this life history began, as do most such recordings, with a friendship. The source of my connection with Essie was a mutual interest in the effects that the boarding school experience had on American Indian youth.

My research interests in Bureau of Indian Affairs off-reservation boarding schools combined with Horne's firsthand experiences as pupil and teacher in this system led to our initial meeting in 1981. I had recently completed research for my dissertation on Oklahoma Indians' perceptions of their boarding school experiences (McBeth 1983a, 1983b, 1984). Shortly thereafter, I moved to North Dakota and became interested in comparing the experiences of northern plains tribal members who had attended Bureau of Indian Affairs or church-sponsored boarding schools with those of tribes from the southern plains with whom I had worked. In Oklahoma I had documented the wide range of positive and negative reactions to the closures of Bureau of Indian Affairs schools, including Fort Sill Indian School in Lawton, Oklahoma; Chilocco Indian School near Newkirk, Oklahoma; and the Concho Indian School in Concho, Oklahoma. When I moved to Fargo, North Dakota, and discovered that the Wahpeton Indian School was also scheduled to be closed, I continued my research by talking to both former and current students of that institution.

In the process of interviewing and collecting data, Mrs. Horne's name was mentioned again and again. Her students at the Wahpeton Indian School lauded her teaching as a highlight of their educational experience. She was one of a group of Indian teachers who had dedicated their lives to mitigating the negative effects of a boarding school education on Indian youth and accentuating the positive aspects of that experience. I read with interest Horne's pro–boarding school testimony as recorded in a hearing before a U.S. Senate Select Committee on Indian Affairs (1982). I received a friendly response to my phone call to Essie Horne and visited her at her home. Given her warmth and our mutual rapport, I found myself looking forward to more and more frequent visits with this now-retired teacher and elder. She was herself a product of Haskell Institute, an Indian boarding school in Lawrence, Kansas.

Essie Horne is also a well-known figure in North Dakota and Minnesota because of her status as a descendant of Sacajawea, the Shoshone woman who accompanied Lewis and Clark on their exploratory trip from St. Louis, Missouri, to the Pacific coast from 1804 to 1806. In addition to devoting her life to Indian children educated in boarding school environments, Essie Horne also labored to keep the memory of her great-great-grandmother alive (Horne 1980, excerpted in appendix C). The oral traditions that surrounded the life of the "girl guide" were recounted to Essie by her grandparents and tribal elders, and she was singularly influenced by the tribal memories of Sacajawea.

Many historians believe that Sacajawea died on December 20, 1812, at Fort Manuel Lisa in South Dakota. She would have been about twenty-four or twenty-five years old. The evidence for this date is contained in written records and accounts that have convinced some historians that Sacajawea died as a young woman.[3] Essie Horne and others have worked to encourage historians to consider Indian oral traditions and the writings of other scholars who believe that Sacajawea lived to be an old woman who died on the reservation and was venerated by her Wind River Shoshone people. Those who hold this opinion believe she was buried on April 9, 1884, at the cemetery on the Wind River Reservation in Wyoming. Sacajawea would have been in her nineties by that time. As a great-great-granddaughter of Sacajawea, Horne believes in the importance of her heritage. Her sense of personal and cultural worth is entwined with her ancestry, and many of her life experiences are understood as a part of this legacy. The epilogue and appendix C provide a more detailed discussion of this controversy.

It was not until I left North Dakota in 1984, however, that the idea of a collaborative life history project with Essie began to take shape. It was the result of our friendship and my belief that Essie had lived convinced of her life's importance. It was apparent that Essie had contemplated the meaning of her past and that she looked forward to the future. She has a remarkable memory and is thoughtful and articulate. She has always believed that the traditions, values, and beliefs impressed on her by her parents and teachers need to be handed down to succeeding generations. We began the project in 1987, and I have made numerous trips to her home on the Chippewa White Earth Reservation in Naytahwaush, Minnesota, and to her apartment in Wahpeton, North Dakota, to continue work on this project. Needless to say, this endeavor became much more involved than either of us could have anticipated in the beginning.

TRANSLATING FROM THE ORAL TO THE WRITTEN: A COLLABORATIVE METHOD

Essie and I began work by taping her life story chronologically, frequently including successive versions of specific events so that we could more easily negotiate the life history. The notion of negotiation in the life history method includes recording incidents and remembrances more than once (Crapanzano 1977). Collecting successive versions of life events is valuable because it aids in the process of editing the transcribed tape, and it also provides insights into how one goes about rendering a narrative that makes the story of a life coherent and meaningful. This tape-recording process was ongoing (intermittently) from 1987 to 1997, but the majority of Essie's story was recorded and transcribed from 1987 to 1989.

In 1989 we began work on a collaborative editing of the transcriptions, page by page. As we worked slowly through each of the five-hundred-plus pages, refining and condensing them, we were daily made aware that our conversations were not easily translatable into written form. The process would take time, and as a former fourth-grade teacher and a woman frequently called on by the community to address educational and cultural issues, Essie was a busy octogenarian.

Essie has many friends and visitors, and the physical distance between our homes meant that our taping and editing sessions occurred only once or twice a year. Essie was concerned that her story be written in a way that she had a hand in creating and enjoyed; she also insisted that her health and still-busy schedule were not conducive to writing her own story. Our diversionary discussions on politics, mothering, growing old, and survival set the tone for the life history and at times became a part of it. We evaluated each step as we proceeded, and we moved toward an appreciation of the complexities of our mutual endeavor.

From the outset, a life historian must concern herself with the fact that moving from interview to published account involves countless decisions. Even though each of these decisions affects the tone and often the very meaning of the final account, few life historians discuss this concern in the context of their work. Collaboration on some level with informants thusly becomes essential to ensure that the presentation of the life respects the individual's experiences and interpretations. It may also offer a technique that will begin to resolve the methodological weaknesses associated with the life history approach.

The partnership method allows the individual recounting a life to do so with less interference, and it allows the subject of the document a role in presenting the text in its final form and receiving authorship credit. Collaboration is also the only means by which some life histories can be written at all. For example, due to her age, arthritis, and busy schedule, Esther Burnett Horne is unlikely to write her own autobiography or to organize and edit the tapes single-handedly, so we have worked together.

When we began the taping, we had not yet discussed the move from spoken dialogue to written discourse or text. Since we were both novices, it never occurred to us to ask, What next? The social nature of our taping sessions was fun and relatively easy, but when we began the editing process, all of the theoretical and methodological problems inherent in the process began to confront us.

The integrated quality of writing contrasts, often dramatically, with the fragmented nature of speaking. In speaking we often string together various ideas without connectives. Transcripts of conversational data frequently appear to be chaotic and unordered compared to written texts. This is not to say that the dialogue is without coherence but rather that each has its own validity and internal consistency.[4]

Essie and I worked on translating and transforming our oral communication into a more comprehensible written form that did not lose spontaneity and informality in the process. This task was both challenging and exceedingly difficult. Spoken language contains many incomplete sentences or sequences of phrases; it is more repetitive, less chronological, more explanatory. Spoken language uses more general vocabulary and more fillers than written language. The coherence of conversation depends on understanding these characteristics in the context of the dialogue, in addition to observing gestures, questions, intonation, tempo, rhythm, and voice quality. Text does not represent oral communication but undertakes an entirely different task.

The editing process was comprised of hundreds of hours of work and play over a ten-year period. Many nuances were certainly lost in the process of translating the way that we talk into the way that we write. There were times when Essie edited out what I thought were important examples of her style of speech, and times when we pulled out the thesaurus to search for a word that had exactly the meaning that both of us believed was important to getting the story into accurate written form. Essie had a clear sense of how she wanted her story to sound. Frequently, a word that I (or the thesaurus) suggested elicited the response, "I wouldn't use that word. It's not common to my speech," and we would not continue until Essie was satisfied. Other times, when we were working directly from the transcriptions, she would say, "I certainly was waxing eloquent on that day—I was so repetitive. It's too long. I want to cut it down." While we worked together and I assisted her in shortening lengthy or redundant phrases, the final decisions were made by Essie. Whereas I believe that much of her warmth and humor and her thoughtful reflections have been lost in the writing process, her literary style has been retained throughout. The decisions made by both of us as we transcribed from the oral to the written required compatibility, trust, and time. Appendix A, "The Editing Process: Examples of the Transition from

Spoken Word to Written Text," provides some illustrations of our collaborative method.

We chose not to include, or even footnote, my questions in the narrative for two reasons. They were intrusive interruptions into Essie's narrative, and since we both edited every page, they were unnecessary. Essie thought that the inclusion of my requests for elaboration and clarification would be a cumbersome addition to the story. She said, "We both interrupt each other; we both sidetrack, stop in the middle of sentences; we slap a mosquito or watch your son fish off the dock and digress into conversations about mothering, mutual friends, and the like. No one will want to check every footnote to discover why we both said what we did, and we have the tapes and transcriptions anyway."

We even experimented with recording the editing process, and when we listened to these tapes, which for us were the preservation of special times, we began to consider the idea of a never-ending narrative. We decided it was much like life itself: We would make a tape, transcribe it, edit it, tape the editing process, transcribe it, edit it, ad infinitum. Essie once mentioned that life's events follow this pattern, as we remember, interpret, reinterpret, forget, and remember again. There were days when the work seemed slow and tedious, and there were days when we reveled in our insights and growing friendship. The process had become much more important than the product, the dialogue more significant than the text.

In addition to the taped interviews with Essie, I also corresponded with and conducted interviews with Essie's friends, colleagues, students, and family members. These dialogues confirmed my emerging understanding of who Esther Burnett Horne is, and they added insights into various dimensions of her life. Interviews with her daughters provided a glimpse of her as a mother. Friends at Naytahwaush and Wahpeton revealed a teasing and joking rapport that they have established with Essie over the past sixty years; they also commented on how much they appreciated Essie's strength and thoughtfulness, especially when they were going through hard times. Teaching colleagues shared with me the respect they have for Essie's dedication to her students. Clergy with whom she has worked expressed appreciation for her abilities to mediate between the white and Indian worlds; they also made note of her spirituality.[5]

The final section of the last chapter of this life history is an exception to our regular method of collaborative editing from transcribed tapes. Chapter 8, "Retrospective," includes sections on activism, education, feminism, grandmothering, Who is Indian?, spirituality, and death. These topics were drawn from portions of the transcribed tapes that seemed to belong in a separate section. The final section of chapter 8, subtitled "The Why? of Recording This Story," was generated by a process unrelated to the transcribed interviews. Essie wanted the finale to explain why she chose to record her story and reveal her life to the public. She chose the sections that she wanted to reemphasize in her concluding statements and selected the wording for them. We wrote this section together but retained Essie's voice and style.

In all, the end result is a truly collaborative project. We do not stand in the traditional positions of informant and ethnographer, in which the informant speaks and the ethnographer writes. Instead, our relationship has cast Essie as coauthor rather than informant. Not only was the nature of the collaboration defined by us both, but the very direction of the project—organization, time frame, and style—was a part of the mutual endeavor.

An additional value of this collaborative method, given Essie's life as the focus of the text, is that it respects her life experiences as she chose to present, explain, and interpret them. The life history, as related in the following pages, is Essie's story, told to me between 1987 and 1997. She chose the chronological ordering; every word on every page has been reread to her so that errors could be remedied or re-remembered events included. Essie joined together facets of remembered experience and self-interpretation as we taped and edited the narrative.

Essie and I acknowledge that our method is an imperfect one, and we do not expect the process with which we experimented to revolutionize the way that ethnography is done in the future; but the method we used will add one more piece to the puzzle of how anthropologists represent and interpret the "other." We believe that our project is important in that it *is* experimental, and we acknowledge that any experiment with dispersed authority is open to varying levels of success. The method is also one from which we learn as we proceed in understanding how people go about creating a narrative that makes sense of a life, both for the subjects and for their audiences.

COLLABORATORS, COLLEAGUES, FRIENDS: THE RELATIONSHIP BETWEEN COLLECTOR AND SUBJECT

The two most-often reported criticisms of the life history method are the intrusive role of the researcher and the accuracy of the informant's memory. What both of these criticisms refer to is the subjective nature of the fieldwork endeavor and, in some cases, the resulting written materials.

The first of these criticisms—the frequently unacknowledged role of researchers and their relationships with subjects—is a pressing one. Life histories, as understood in the work of anthropologists, are usually translated, edited, interpreted, reorganized, and sometimes even rewritten by a collector. While I do not advocate this intrusive method, which violates the integrity of the storyteller's words and style, I also do not believe that it is possible or desirable for the anthropologist to maintain complete objectivity. In fact, it may be that the blending of the subjective and the objective is one of the unique strengths of the anthropological approach.

Since the life history is filtered through the perspectives of the recorder and the interpreter, both must be aware of the consequences of the telling of the life in the presence of another. Through our intensive work together, Essie and I created a close bond of respect and rapport. Although I am not a detached, impartial observer, Essie and I have tried to maintain a certain objectivity. Essie's comments on the subject are revealing. She says, "Our friendship has enhanced the project; we've worked many hundreds of hours together, and I would not have shared my life with you had I not known and cared for you."

Our relationship has matured and changed since we became acquainted in 1981. I was single and childless before beginning this project, and the friendship we shared was one between two women from two different cultures and two different generations. (We are exactly forty years apart in age.) However, when my son was born in 1984 and Essie became his "Granny Essie," a new kinship dimension was added to our relationship. Essie offered me advice about parenting. She, an experienced elder, instructed me in the arts of womanhood and motherhood, as well as in my roles as wife and stepmother.

One component of our rapport was the ease of communication established by getting to know so much about each other. We often engaged in word play, the process of which is not detailed in the text but which is nonetheless critical to the process of creating the text. The dialogue and laughter joined us together as coauthors. Certain verbal cues became the signal to move into a joking and teasing interplay, during which we created and constructed the text of the life history. In the process, we also deconstructed it, laughed at it, played with it, or imagined an exchange of words that was more playful than what we had already written down. A few examples will clarify the complexity and engaging nature of this collaborative process.

Transcription error was a source of much play. In the early phases of the project, I hired a high school student to begin transcribing the tapes. When she couldn't understand a spoken word (all the tapes are in English), she created a substitute. For example, after the death of her father, Horne's mother and five brothers and sisters moved back to Wyoming to the area around the Wind River Reservation, and her mother began working outside the home. The transcription as recorded by this student reads, "My mother received a job as a chambermaid in the Union Pacific Deep Hole. Well, it wasn't exactly a deep hole, it was more like a hotel where the firemen and railroad people stayed and had rooms when they were away from home." So, quips made by me, such as "Your mother works in a deep hole" (rather than depot), became a verbal cue for a break from the sometimes emotional remembering and listening in which we were involved.

Another example is taken from the period when Horne was a student at Haskell Institute in Lawrence, Kansas, an off-reservation boarding school for Indian youth. Ella Deloria and Ruth Muskrat Bronson, two influential Native American teachers at Haskell, produced and directed *A Midsummer Night's Dream* in 1923. Esther landed the role as Hermia and on closing night was given a bouquet of roses by the cast, an event that held a special significance for her.

Years later, Horne and Deloria happened to run into each other at a conference and were reliving some of their Haskell experiences. Deloria went out in the afternoon and upon her return presented Esther with a single rose with a note that read, "This is for my Hermia." The transcriber had not read much Shakespeare but did have a limited knowledge of medical terms. She transcribed the note as reading, "This is for my hernia." While examples of this form of dialogue are included only in this introduction, such interaction was and is an important part of maintaining the friendship and rapport that Essie and I created.

It is impossible to document the values of an interpersonal and inter-cultural friendship. As the time the project was taking to complete lengthened, Essie frequently made jokes about it. "Little did you know that you were going to get involved in such an immense project. You thought Indians were people of few words, but not this Indian"; or, "You asked for my life history and you got it—maybe more than what you bargained for." These were familiar remarks which strengthened our friendship as well as our collaboration.

THE VAGRANCIES OF MEMORY: ACCURACY AND
MEANING IN REMEMBERING THE PAST

The accuracy of memory is another frequently criticized aspect of the autobiographical or life history form. It is important to consider that what is remembered (and why and how it is remembered or forgotten) helps us to understand how storytellers struggle to shape their identity and understand their world.

Truth is highly subjective. What exactly happened in the past may never be understood fully, because the past is remembered differently by different individuals whose perspectives are influenced by timing, culture, insights, agendas, and the past.

It is clear that in recounting a life, human memory selects, emphasizes, rearranges, and even revises past episodes. Therefore, an understanding of the selective process and the strategic decisions involved in remembering can help us understand and discover this essential part of human behavior. Memories reveal truths about experience and serve to locate a person's life in cultural, social, and historical contexts.[6]

As Essie and I began working on the life history, I realized that understanding the limiting factors of memory is of great importance to the method. Memory is a window on what is prized: Essie is aware that as she remembers her past, she interprets it in accordance with her present ideas of what is important and what is not. Remembering and reflecting are, then, creative processes. Life historians can, and certainly do, distort, avoid, or idealize in their life history reports—to themselves as well as to the listener. While questions of reliability, accuracy, and bias may be interpreted as a weakness of this approach, they may also be perceived as a unique strength, for self-interpretation is a part of the human expression and a part of what life histories are.

We come to know about and understand our pasts and ourselves by remembering, for memories illuminate what it means to be human and alive. Through memories we can understand the important happenings of the past either from the perspective of an individual or collectively from community members who may remember the past differently than historians have recorded it. History continues to live and be passed down to succeeding generations as individuals seek to make sense of their lives; as communities try to find pattern in chaos; and as both discover solutions to the universal problems that each new generation encounters.

Memory, then, is central to the life history, since the events of a life are reinterpreted many times over during the life history process. The fascination and frustration of this approach are revealed in this reinterpretation. Not only are events and remembrances of the past discovered and interpreted by the individual who has lived them, but they are also interpreted by whomever is recording them, and later by the reader of the documented life. The reader and writer must recognize that autobiographies and life histories are constructions. They reflect the human need to examine a life and to know oneself and one's past through the insights gained. The truths that they reveal are metaphorically rather than historically accurate. These truths of experience are not open to empirical verification.

AUDIENCE CONSIDERATION: FOR WHOM DO WE WRITE?

The concept of audience consideration is rarely discussed in the life history process. Sometimes Essie and I were both very cognizant of potential readers and of Essie's entering the public arena by recording her life. At other times we abandoned the idea that the manuscript would ever be read by anyone outside the family, and so we worried little about how the outside world might read her life.

Essie seems comfortable with the language of this manuscript. She knows she will be read as a woman and that her ambitions and sense of self are inherent in the "presumption" of her writing her life story at all, even though she did so at my request. She may be unsure of her place as narrator, but she is sure of herself as a Native American elder. She believes that her story may be of some value to educators, historians, anthropologists, and Indian people.

We anticipate that the audience for the completed text will encompass academic and nonacademic readers. Individuals interested in the boarding school experience, in oral traditions, in women's issues, in twentieth-century American Indian life, and in collaborative methodologies may have a particular interest in portions of the completed book. We are also aware that this text will be read by people who know or knew Esther Horne. While this anticipated audience does not directly control our writing process, we admit to a concern for their reactions and criticisms.

In answer to my questions about what she thought community reactions would be to the life history document, Essie said, "It will depend on who reads it. I don't think there will be many negative reactions, but there will certainly be those who will find fault with me for baring myself on the written page and revealing my life to the public. When we live so close to people, they don't see us the way others do. My family doesn't see me as an educator or historian or lecturer but as Mom or Grandma."

TRADITIONS OF LIFE HISTORY RESEARCH:
THE SIGNIFICANCE OF HORNE'S CONTRIBUTION

The life history of Esther Burnett Horne is part of a long tradition of Native

American women's autobiographies. Horne's contribution to this narrative genre is illustrated by situating this collaborative endeavor in the larger context of American Indian women's life histories and autobiographies.

It is important to begin this discussion with a significant distinction made by most life history scholars. Many have argued that there is a basic difference between Native American life stories written solely by the individual whose life is the focus of the manuscript and those written in collaboration with an editor, author, or recorder.

William Bloodworth (1978), for example, uses the terms "anthropological" and "authentic" to distinguish between, respectively, as-told-to and self-authored autobiography. Bloodworth uses these particular terms because he believes that the motivation of the teller is the distinguishing characteristic between these two types. He asserts that anthropological autobiographies are solicited by curious Euro-Americans who seek to document the culture. They are motivated by a historical curiosity and by the desires of authors to enhance their professional careers by publishing these stories in scientific journals. Authentic autobiographies, on the other hand, derive from American Indians' own desire to record and tell the stories of their lives. These published accounts are, according to Bloodworth, examples of "traditional Indian self-expression" (1978, 70).

What Bloodworth fails to acknowledge is that the motives of individuals who decide to record their life stories, whether the endeavors are solo or cooperative, are complex and dynamic. For example, Natives and non-Natives alike may be motivated by the need to chronicle the customs, culture, and remembrances of a fast-disappearing way of life. Their writings may also be responses to white prejudice, unfair governmental policies, and the assimilationist mentality of the white public, among others. To distinguish perceived motives for writing based on ethnicity or level of education limits our understanding of this complex pursuit. In addition, since *written* personal narratives are not an indigenous form, the Euro-American literate tradition has clearly exerted a strong influence on narrative form. As more and more Native people have become literate, one must consider how reading and writing have influenced Native people's desires to record tribal stories and personal experiences.

Esther Horne's life story provides an illustration of this point. Her connections to her past combine written *and* spoken history. She began listening to and recording the Shoshone oral traditions of Sacajawea and then proceeded with an intense investigation of the written history on this topic. This factor connects her autobiography with, and sets it apart from, other contemporary life history projects; that is, through her perspectives on the oral and written accounts of her great-great-grandmother, the reader is provided with insights into how the transition from a preliterate people to a literate culture occurs as well as how what is written may alter or influence oral accounts.

In one of his ground-breaking works, *For Those Who Came After*, Arnold Krupat also distinguishes between self-written "autobiographies of Indians" and collaborative "Indian autobiographies." Unlike Bloodworth, however, he does not dismiss the collaborative approach as less authentic. He says that "the principle constituting the [collaborative] Indian autobiography as a genre [is] the principle of original bicultural composite composition." The collaborative autobiography is, he says, "a ground on which two cultures meet" (1985, 31, 35). Indeed, Krupat forcefully objects to the term "as told to" as "anachronistic, ethnocentric, patronizing, inaccurate, and simplistic because it essentially negates the Native person's role in the complex production of these texts" (Krupat 1994, 176). It might be argued that most Indian autobiographies, whether self-authored or written with the assistance of an editor, provide this common ground, this arena where cultures meet and where white Americans attempt to understand American Indians by reading the published accounts of their lives.

Autobiographical writing must be recognized as legitimate in its many shapes, arrangements, and constructions. In her book *Sending My Heart Back across the Years*, Hertha Wong emphatically states that "self narration is the fundamental act of autobiography" (1992, 6). Therefore, while readers should recognize the differences among the many forms of autobiography, they must also be willing to accept the veracity embedded in each. It is important to recognize that the structures of these personal narratives reflect a diverse range of influences.

In *Keeping Slug Woman Alive*, Greg Sarris reminds us that in addition to the "fundamental questions about what each collaborator contributed to or omitted from the text," what the reader brings to the text is also an important part of the equation of understanding (1993, 87). In addition, he asks the narrators to consider the limits and consequences of their scholarship. His insightful perspectives, those of a mixed-blood scholar, reflect the same questions that Essie and I have contemplated over the past ten years.

TWENTIETH-CENTURY NATIVE WOMEN'S AUTOBIOGRAPHY

An examination of selected twentieth-century Native American women's autobiographies shows how Horne's life history is part of an established collaborative tradition and yet stands apart as a unique contribution to the autobiographical genre.

The value of this assemblage was the recording of the voices of Native Americans' thoughts and recollections on topics ranging from traditional beliefs to the impact of Euro-American ways on their lives. In addition, this genre provides insights into the way the information-gathering was undertaken. A problem with these writings was that they were often unclear as to how the final product was produced. The reader was generally provided with only minimal knowledge of how editors collected data, how the editors rewrote the text, and whether the names given authorship credit reflected the contributions of the life history subject.

Among the many Native American life histories collected during the first half of the twentieth century, most were men's stories. A number of classic Native women's life histories were included as well. For example, Gilbert Wilson ([1927] 1981) collaborated with Waheenee (b. 1839), a Hidatsa woman, and Frank Linderman collected the life story of Pretty-shield (ca. 1858), a Crow medicine woman ([1932] 1972). Truman Michelson published three short autobiographies of unnamed Indian women—one of a Fox woman (1925), one of a Southern Cheyenne woman (1932), and one of an Arapaho woman (1933). All five autobiographies utilized interpreters from within the tribes and notes from which the stories were rewritten. None of the authors, however, provide detailed comments about the editorial decisions made in the production of the texts.[7]

Ruth Underhill published *The Autobiography of a Papago Woman* (b. 1845 or 1846, d. 1936) in 1936. She admits to rearranging the translations and omitting repetitions and unimportant details; she states that Maria Chona's Papago (now Tohono O'odham) autobiography was "an Indian story told to satisfy whites rather than Indians" (1979, 33). Chona's story, then, is a composite of her words translated into English by Ella Lopez Antone and edited by Underhill (cf. Bataille and Sands 1984, 47–68). These examples demonstrate that little attention was paid to recording details of the collection or editing processes during the first half of the century.

During the second half of this century, the continued use of the collaborative method and the addition of many self-written narratives resulted in an explosion of accounts of Native American women's lives. Many women born into traditional families recorded the transitions that a century of American-style education and Christianization, assimilationist policies, and racism had wrought in their lives.

The life histories published from 1950 to the present represent a wide array of styles and forms. Stories emerge of women who are active in tribal politics, of women who have combined the Native and non-Native world into their lives, as well as of women who have actively resisted the American/Canadian system. These narratives also provide great diversity in terms of how much information is provided and how the accounts were collected, edited, or written.

In 1961, Nancy Lurie edited the life story of a Winnebago (now Ho-Chunk) woman called Mountain Wolf Woman (b. 1884). Lurie's work still stands as an exemplary model for collaborative Indian autobiography. The editor provides a candid and detailed explanation of when, why, and how she collected Mountain Wolf Woman's life history. Lurie's stated intent was to document the impact that the intrusion of white settlers and white values had on the Winnebago and to provide some detail on Indian gender roles. Mountain Wolf Woman was the sister of Sam Blowsnake, whose life history, *Crashing Thunder*, was published by Paul Radin in 1926; Lurie believed that her work with Mountain Wolf Woman would also prove valuable as a comparative manuscript. As she states, "Therefore, Mountain Wolf Woman's story takes on particular significance in scholarly terms, since it is the account of a woman from the same tribe as Crashing Thunder" (1961, xiii).[8]

Also in the 1960s, two Hopi women collaborated with two white women and used the "as told to" format. Helen Sekaquaptewa (1898–1974) told her life story, *Me and Mine*, to Louise Udall (1969) and Polingaysi Qoyawayma (b. 1892) worked with Vada Carlson on her life history, *No Turning Back* (Qoyawayma 1964).

The stories of Helen Sekaquaptewa and Polingaysi Qoyawayma are both labeled "as told to" life histories. In her one-page introduction titled "How the Story Came to Be Written," Louise Udall provides a two-sentence explanation of the method used with Sekaquaptewa. "I started writing the events as she told them. I visited her at the Ranch for weeks at a time, and the story grew and grew" (Udall 1969). In her work with Qoyawayma, Vada Carlson reveals even less; she says nothing. Most disturbing is the fact that while Qoyawayma is credited as the author, this life history is written in the third person. The reader is not informed whether a tape recorder was used or if any translation was necessary. No details of the production process were supplied in either of these life histories.

Beginning in the late 1960s and early 1970s, a number of Native American women, none of whom were professional writers, began experimenting with recording their life histories. This genre of self-authored autobiographies by American Indian women had its beginning well before the second half of the twentieth century. With few exceptions, such as Sara Win-nemucca Hopkins's *Life among the Piutes* (1883) and the autobiographical es-says of Yankton (Dakota Sioux) Zitkala-Sa (Gertrude Simmons Bonnin) titled *American Indian Stories* ([1921] 1985), most of these late nineteenth- and early twentieth-century, self-written narratives were written by Indian men.

Lucille (Jerry) Winnie's (b. ca. 1902) *Sah-Gan-De-Oh: The Chief's Daugh-ter* (1969) is one such example of a Native American woman's story. In her introduction, Seneca-Cayuga Winnie states, "My story was not told to a ghost writer and every opinion expressed is mine." Anna Moore Shaw (b. 1898) also wrote her own life story in 1974. *A Pima Past* begins in the third person; Shaw does not explain why she chose to begin the story of her early life in this way.

Irene Stewart (b. 1907) is also given authorship credit for her life history, *A Voice in Her Tribe: A Navajo Woman's Own Story* (1980). However, the foreword by Mary Shepardson indicates that Stewart's story was written as a series of letters to Shepardson, an anthropologist. Shepardson further re-veals that Doris Dawdy, who is the credited editor, edited the letters, re-vised the order, and made changes in spelling and grammar. So while we learn that the story was written as a series of letters and that the letters were edited, we learn little else about the editing process.

I have highlighted these six women's life history narratives (Mountain Wolf Woman, Sekaquaptewa, Qoyawayma, Winnie, Shaw, and Stewart) be-cause all are rooted in similarities of experience. Lucille Winnie and Irene Stewart both attended Haskell Institute; Esther Burnett Horne was a pupil at Haskell from 1923 to 1928. Shaw, Sekaquaptewa, and Qoyawayma all at-tended Bureau of Indian Affairs off-reservation boarding schools; Shaw and Sekaquaptewa attended the Phoenix Indian School; and Qoyamayma at-tended the Sherman Institute in Riverside, California. Mountain Wolf Woman attended a government boarding school in Tomah, Wisconsin, for two years, but the educational system had only a minimal impact on her life. Qoyawayma, Sekaquaptewa, Winnie, and Shaw all were teachers for some portion of their lives. Horne taught from 1929 to 1965. All six women share a devotion to family, community, and their Christian religion; all contemplate and finally resolve the difficulty of moving between the white and Indian worlds; and all reflect on how female gender affects the perceptions of their worlds.

Three Canadian women recounted the stories of their lives in auto-biographical format around this same time. Jane Willis (b. 1940), a Canadian Cree, wrote about her childhood in 1973. *Geneish: An Indian Girlhood* recounts the struggle of Janie, a mixed-blood, to endure the Anglican residential schools she attended for nearly eleven years. Her story, like that of Maria Campbell's *Halfbreed* (1973), recounts instances of Canadian racism toward Native people. Campbell (b. 1940) is much less bitter than Willis. She recounts numerous examples of prejudice and discrimination but is not as harsh as Willis in her condemnation of the oppressive system. The strength and enduring nature of this work lie in Campbell's ability to take responsibility for her own behaviors. Lee Maracle (b. 1950), a mixed-blood Mohawk, wrote *Bobbi Lee, Indian Rebel* in the 1970s. Reprinted in 1990, the book recalls the poverty of Maracle's life in Vancouver, the demonstrations of the sixties, and the beginnings of the Red Power movement in Canada and the United States. These three Canadian women's stories stand in marked contrast to most of the autobiographies considered so far. Their tone is more strident and angry; for the most part, these women pit themselves against the white system and seek satisfaction in their political activism.

The collaborative method of writing Native women's life histories continues to be used into the 1990s. Like the politically charged writing of Willis, Campbell, and Maracle, the best-selling life histories of Mary Crow Dog (also known as Mary Brave Bird), entitled *Lakota Woman* (Crow Dog 1990) and *Ohitika Woman* (Brave Bird 1993), recount her life of poverty, alcoholism, and emerging maturity. Both were written with Richard Erdoes. The reader learns a little of Mary's relationship with Erdoes in the second book, but very little is revealed about his role in the actual writing or editing of either of these life histories. In his "Instead of a Foreword" at the front of *Ohitika Woman*, Erdoes refers briefly to the taping and transcription process as well as to putting the "manuscript together like a jigsaw puzzle" (1993, xiii). Little else is revealed as to how Erdoes went about the task of editing, refining, and rewriting the "mountain of tapes."

This brief review reveals the dilemma over how to distinguish between the many autobiographical genres. The somewhat arbitrary division between self-authored autobiographies and collaborative life histories, while useful, needs to be reexamined, because there are many complex variables to be considered. For example, only rarely is the reader provided with background information on the role of the editor, and the person or persons to whom authorship credit is given is capricious at best.

In his book *American Indian Autobiography*, H. David Brumble poetically describes this phenomenon as he reflects on the popular autobiographies of

Black Hawk, Plenty-coups, Geronimo, and Black Elk. "These are compelling narratives, narratives in which much that is commonplace for the teller is exotic for the reader. These are the narratives that make us feel 'epistemological vertigo' most keenly, that make us feel as though we are seeing the world from a cultural perspective far from our own. This is a heady feeling—so heady that we are inclined to forget all that the Anglo editor had to do to make it seem that way" (1988, 6). Fortunately, the authors and coauthors of recent life histories have begun to correct this omission. For example, the style, tone, and format of Horne's life history is more akin to recently published women's life histories such as *During My Time: Florence Edenshaw Davidson, A Haida Woman* (Blackman 1982), *Sadie Brower Neakok, An Iñupiaq Woman* (Blackman 1989), and *Life Lived like a Story* (Cruikshank 1990a).[9]

Julie Cruikshank's exemplary model, *Life Lived like a Story*, includes traditional stories and songs, reflections, and genealogical and mythological themes in addition to the life history materials. Cruikshank's cognizance of the challenges that anthropologists face concerning cultural representation is evident in the first sentence of her introduction. She notes that "one of the liveliest areas of discussion in contemporary anthropology centers on how to convey authentically, in words, the experience of one culture to members of another" (Cruikshank 1990a, 1). She insists that her collaborators—Angela Sidney, Kitty Smith, and Annie Ned—were responsible for charting the direction that their narratives would take.

The unique kind of autobiography resulting from collaboration addresses "how these women use traditional narrative to explain their life experiences" (Cruikshank 1990a, 2). As different as these more traditional women's experiences are from Essie Horne's, they share common themes. Landscape, myth and legends, everyday events, and the continuity between generations are common motifs in many Native women's life stories (Bataille and Sands 1984; Cruikshank 1990a, 2).[10]

A brief discussion of two recently published life histories will conclude this overview of the variety of processes used to collect Native women's life stories. While different in style from each other and from Horne's life history, *Ellen Smallboy: Glimpses of a Cree Woman's Life* (Flannery 1995) and *They Call Me Agnes* (Voget 1995), published in the same year, both provide important background information relating to how the texts were produced.

Regina Flannery, who takes authorship credit for *Ellen Smallboy*, moves back and forth between her voice and that of Smallboy (1853–1941). Flannery and Smallboy talk to each other and to the reader; the resulting text is warmly conversational in style. Flannery explains that she has pieced together the life of Smallboy from interviews that she collected through an interpreter in the 1930s. Historical context and information on the Cree of the James Bay of northern Ontario are also provided.

In the introduction to *They Call Me Agnes*, Voget supplies detailed information about every chapter. He explains that this personal narrative was recorded in shorthand notes in the 1950s, that he added background details when he deemed it necessary, and that in 1993 he, Agnes (b. 1908), and other family members reviewed the manuscript to double-check details, contexts, and voice. The text not only provides important background information concerning the way the manuscript was put together, but it also provides a comprehensive and intensely personal account of life on the Crow reservation during this century. Nevertheless, Voget retains full authorship credit.

There are, of course, numerous other life histories and autobiographies that form a growing foundation for what promises to be an informative comparative base.[11] Important themes revealed in the published life stories of Indian women include early childhood experiences, the impact of a variety of educational systems, career choices, the importance of family, reactions to government policies, and reflections on achieving elder status. Most important, the reader begins to understand the role that gender plays in how an individual constructs an identity and narrates a life.

Editors of recent life histories, then, are beginning to document the editing and rewriting processes. Horne's story adds a new chapter to the description of the kinds of lives that American Indian women have lived in this century and also provides detail on the collaborative model.

SEARCH FOR MEANINGS IN A LIFE: INTERPRETATION AND REPRESENTATION IN THE LIFE HISTORY

Horne combines remembered experience with sage advice as she constructs a narrative that reveals who she is. We may define the autobiographical act as an interpretation of life that invests the past and the self with coherence and meaning (Bruss 1976). If we so define the act, it becomes clear that by talking and writing about our experiences we express who we are as individuals and members of groups, and we assign meanings to these experiences.

Horne's life history is interesting not only for the events and insights that she shares but also for the narrative motifs that are a part of her story. I believe that these themes and motifs represent one way in which she fashions her identity and assigns meaning to her life.

Many of these themes will be apparent to the reader. A few, however, merit itemization and explanation. My intent is not to provide an analysis of Horne's life, even if I had the training to do so. Rather, I want to provide the reader with some insights into how Horne reveals herself and her place in the world through her story.

Essie's Relationship to Sacajawea

Essie begins her life history talking about her relationship to Sacajawea. This relationship becomes her first theme. She cautions the reader to note that she does not consider herself the great-great-granddaughter of Sacajawea but rather one of many who claim descent from this woman. Horne's life has for the most part been spent away from her tribe and reservation. Remaining conscious and aware of her prestigious ancestry, which she was expected to learn about, respect, and embrace, allowed her to maintain a connectedness to her Eastern Shoshone people and the Wind River Reservation.

Likely, her parents, who left the reservation so that they could marry, understood the importance of this legacy for their Indian children's lives and identities. As a child in Idaho, in boarding school, as a young teacher, and even into her later life, Horne's relationship to Sacajawea provided her not with a quaint reminder of her Native American heritage but with a powerful connection to her culture. This relationship, and the notoriety that accompanied it, provided Essie with a link to her Indian heritage that was recognizable to the Indian and non-Indian worlds beyond the borders of Wyoming.

Essie's commitment to keeping alive the Indian version of Sacajawea's later life further demonstrates the significance of this connection to her ethnic past and tribal identity. Her lectures and writing preserve the memory of her great-great-grandmother and give voice to the primacy of oral tradition in American Indian society.

The story that she and others tell of Sacajawea's later life is an empowering one for the Shoshone tribe and for all Indian people. Essie's discourse emerges as a challenge to and disruption of the writings and voices of historians as she debates their interpretations of the past of her people. It is an opportunity for her to refute the established historical position that Sacajawea died in 1812. In recounting her early memories she says:

> I think it's important to keep on insisting that the oral traditions are very important, that they are truth personified. I was careful to allow the historians their view, and I respected their historical perspectives, but I thoroughly believed what I said. I knew it was true. I knew peo-

ple, whose integrity was beyond reproach, who had known Sacajawea—I'm talking of my grandfather Finn Burnett, and Rev. John
Roberts, who officiated at her burial, as well as the tribal elders. Anyone who visited with these people would not doubt for one moment
that the things they said were true. They had really known her and
really had worked with her and really had been friends with her. I think
it's hard for non-Indians to give credit to the Native American. They're
so used to always stepping on our necks and grinding us down, and of
course there's the fact that what is written is considered more important than what is verbally passed down. I think there is an effort to discredit the Native position and those who side with our views.

Sacajawea is one of Essie's personal metaphors, an interpretive figure by
virtue of which she understands, interprets, articulates, and organizes
many of her life experiences.[12] Essie does not build her life around the memories of her mythologized great-great-grandmother, but she does use Sacajawea's life to make sense of her own.

Metaphor is essentially a way of knowing. As one seeks meaning in life,
specific recurring patterns emerge and become the metaphorical means
through which we come to understand who we are. In addition, metaphors
mediate between the author and reader. Not only do metaphors supply
meanings as autobiographers make sense of their lives, but they also assist
the outsider in acquiring these same insights.

Essie's reflections on her life reveal that much of what she knows about
Sacajawea's life has influenced her sense of self. Sacajawea's role as liaison
between the Indian and non-Indian worlds, her strength as a woman, her intertribal wanderings, and even her physical appearance have come to have a
special significance for Essie. The family ties to Sacajawea provide an underlying organizational principle through which she finds meanings for her life.
Through this connection to her past and culture, she creates an inner har-
mony that reaches across the periods of crisis and turmoil in her life. Furthermore, she disrupts the attempts of many historians who deny that Sacajawea lived beyond her mid-twenties. The ongoing disputes, kept alive by
voices like Horne's, have served to keep the memory of Sacajawea, whose
accomplishments might otherwise have been noted and forgotten, alive.

The Boarding School and Essie's Identity

A second theme that emerges in Essie's account of her life is a growing sense
of self, a formation that extends into her boarding school years. The setting
is the Haskell Indian Institute in Lawrence, Kansas. The years are from

1924 to 1929. Horne was fourteen years old when she arrived at Haskell, and at age twenty she was recruited to teach at the Eufaula Boarding School, an off-reservation boarding school for Creek girls located in Eufaula, Oklahoma.

It would be reasonable to suggest that Essie's identity is pan-Indian rather than Shoshone. Pan-Indian identities are formulated when Native Americans choose to transcend the particularities of their tribal heritage. This may occur in select situations as an adaptive strategy, when an overarching sense of "Indianness" is called for. It is more accurate, however, to describe this pan-Indian dimension as adding another level of ethnicity to Essie's already intact identity. Although Essie grew up away from the Wind River Reservation and the Shoshone community, and although she spent much time in the multinational boarding school setting, she retained a strong sense of her Shoshone heritage.

What she found in the boarding school setting became an important part of her life. She found Indian friends, Indian teachers, an Indian husband, and a future in the field of Indian education. Recollections of this experience include the following thoughts recorded in the summer of 1988, in which Essie displays a recognition of the complexities of the boarding school experience and the ways it affected her identity:

When I think back on the many years that I have lived, so much of what I have learned about Indian cultures, aside from what I know about my own tribe, I learned at Haskell. For me, one of the things that the boarding school fostered was an understanding of different tribes. We were not allowed to speak our own languages or dance our own dances, but by our being thrown together we associated with one another and would talk to one another. We discussed our beliefs, our homes, our food, our arts and crafts . . . our lives! I think of the boarding school as a kind of cultural and historical feast. I was tremendously enriched by my association with people from other tribes.

The schools were trying to take the Indianness out of us, but they never succeeded. Not completely, anyway. They actually ended up putting a lot of Indianness into the Indian, just by throwing us all together in a group. The boarding school may have contributed to the breakdown of the family and may have increased the rate of alcohol abuse. I have read that this may be so; but it also unwittingly created a resistance to assimilation, which might take shape in very subtle or quite rebellious forms. The experience of us boarding school students strengthened our resolve to retain our identity as American Indians and to take our place in today's world.

Federal off-reservation boarding schools like Haskell were only one type of educational facility available for the education of Indian youth. There were also mission schools, both day schools and boarding schools, affiliated with particular Christian churches. Public day schools were also an option in some areas. Still, the federal off-reservation boarding schools were the preferred method of "civilization." The goals of these institutions were no less a wholesale remolding of Indian children's value systems, to be accomplished by removing children from the source of those values—their communities.

In 1886 the commissioner of Indian Affairs succinctly articulated this goal: "The greatest difficulty is experienced in freeing the children attending day schools from the language and habits of their untutored and oftentimes savage parents. When they return to their homes at night, and on Saturdays and Sundays, and are among their old surroundings, they relapse more or less into their former moral and mental stupor" (U.S. House 1886, 100).

The irony of this endeavor to remove Indian children from their families has been noted by Indian students, Indian scholars, and non-Indian observers. When one segregates Indian children from white society, the creation of a unique Indian bonding occurs. This is what Essie calls the "historical and cultural feast." She experienced the assimilationist goals of boarding school education, but she also experienced the unexpected consequences of putting young Indian people from a number of tribes together in a unique all-Indian setting, a setting whose design was to remold Indian students "in the image of the white man."

Gen. Richard Pratt, founder of the Carlisle Indian School, which was the first federally funded off-reservation boarding school and was located in Carlisle, Pennsylvania, was aware of the probable effect of these types of institutions. More than a hundred years ago he noted that "no better means of perpetrating tribalism and Indianism can be inaugurated than a system of schools holding the Indian together" (Pratt 1897, 14). His observations went unnoticed. Few government officials accurately predicted the powerful and lasting effects of this practice; the segregationist system continued.

The 1886 annual report of the commissioner of Indian Affairs talks about this same "problem." The superintendent of Haskell Institute makes a recommendation that parallels Pratt's observation, but he sees the Indian problem from a different perspective. His specific reference to Haskell bears repeating: "It was deemed necessary to establish during the year a stricter system of discipline than heretofore prevailed. A cadet battalion organization of five companies broke up the tribal associations. Size of cadets, and not their tribal relations, determining now place in dormitory and mess hall, also necessitates a more frequent recourse to the English language as a common medium, by bringing pupils of different tribes into closer contact" (U.S. House 1886, 224).

While Haskell personnel were attempting to break up tribal cliques, they were also reinforcing multitribal alliances. By 1924, when Essie arrived, this pan-Indian practice was not only well established but flourished among Indian students who also clung tenaciously to their individual tribal heritages.

The very act of separating Indian children from their white counterparts and placing them in separate schools led to the resistance that has been discovered by nearly every boarding school researcher.[13] Settings range from a Canadian residential school in Vancouver, British Columbia, to the Bureau of Indian Affairs off-reservation Chilocco Indian School near Newkirk, Oklahoma. In virtually every case scholars devote attention to the resilience of Indian children in the often enervating boarding school system. Horne and others provide examples of the forms that this resistance takes.

The camaraderie that developed among the children provided a welcome respite from cultural attacks. In her life history narrative Essie says, "We students nurtured a sense of community among ourselves, and we learned so much from each other. Traditional values such as sharing and cooperation helped us to survive culturally at Haskell, even though the schools were designed to erase our Indian culture, values, and identities."

Older or more experienced students mentored younger ones; they assisted them in accommodating to a new set of rules and values. Cherokee classmate Louise Breuninger's dressing down and subsequent counseling of Horne provides an illustration of this sort of example setting. Horne says that as a result of Breuninger's advice, she began to make her own decisions; she became an independent thinker. She remembered the teachings of her parents who told her always to trust her own judgment and not to be swayed by peer pressure. This was a difficult decision for her—as it would be for any sixteen-year-old.

Chippewa historian Brenda Child says, "And for better or worse, the schools became part of our histories, the boarding school became part of tribal history" (1993, 70). The boarding school experience affected generations of Native American survivors, and the experience engendered contradictory emotions among American Indians. Horne's recollections reflect those of other boarding school students and demonstrate that students were not passive players in what Adams calls "the acculturation drama" (1995, 268). Boarding school students' responses included passive and active resistance, limited acceptance, and a healthy skepticism of the United States government's Indian policies. Sharp images of Indian tenacity, resilience, and sometimes out-and-out rebellion emerge from Horne's story.

Throughout Horne's narrative we learn in detail of the immense power the school wielded through its maintenance of strict adherence to military regimen, work details, discipline, diet, and dress. On the other hand, we are shown how the boarding school engendered creative and successful adaptive strategies on the part of its students. The students expropriated some of the control mechanisms imposed upon them and in fact used the boarding school to strengthen their separateness from the dominant society—a separateness firmly grounded in an orientation to a collective origin. Female resistance to the system may have been more subtle than that of their male counterparts, but it was just as effective.

The boarding school experience was integral to Essie's developing sense of herself as a Shoshone and as an Indian teenager of the 1920s. She recognizes that her life was drastically changed by the death of her father and her subsequent removal to the Haskell Institute in Lawrence, Kansas. The pan-Indian identity that she acquired in the boarding school setting did not replace her individual, female, Shoshone identity. It did, however, add an important new dimension to her sense of self. She found a place in a yet larger sphere of indigenous peoples who shared common values, common fears, and common pride in their heritage.

Master Teacher

A third theme of Essie's life relates to the concept of "master" teacher.[14] Her accounts of this theme begin with her reflections on individuals who influenced her and taught her values and virtues that she incorporated into her life. She stresses how her Indian mother and white father taught their children to respect others and to be honest but mostly to love and be kind. Later, as a student at the Haskell Indian School in Lawrence, Kansas, the influential lessons of Ella Deloria (Lakota) and Ruth Muskrat Bronson (Cherokee) inspired Essie to drop her business major, become a teacher, and work with Indian youth. In my opinion Essie survives with her culture intact in spite of the bulk of her educational experiences, not because of them. Much of this is due to those dedicated teachers who worked to instill in their students a belief that they could succeed as Indian people. Essie talks about her women teachers fondly and compassionately. Her students speak of her in the same way.

Essie herself eventually became a master teacher. Since she was trained in an Indian school, she was expected to support the government's educational system that required students to renounce their culture, values, and sense of community. Essie's teaching, recognized by the Bureau of Indian Affairs of the Department of the Interior with the Distinguished Service Citation in 1966, would not have been approved by this agency in the 1920s, as becomes apparent in her life history. The reason it wouldn't have is that Essie worked to instill pride in her students in the Eufaula Creek Girls Boarding School in Eufaula, Oklahoma, and at the Wahpeton Indian School in Wahpeton, North Dakota. She used their common heritage to inspire, not denigrate them. During our nearly seventeen-year acquaintance, I have witnessed numerous incidents where former students have approached Mrs. Horne to tell her of the difference she made in their lives. She was, they said, a teacher who cared about them as individuals. Her concern for them extended beyond the classroom as she created a home for them within the government's assimilationist system.

Essie was well ahead of her time in her teaching techniques. She used what is today called whole-language learning to teach Indian children more effectively, and her understanding of styles of learning and cultural values is today recognized as an effective educational approach.[15] In addition, Essie taught her students to preserve their Indian ways while effectively negotiating through and around the rules of the dominant society. Her narrative embodies realizations that resist the conventional wisdom about Indian boarding schools and yet reinforce the strengths of Native Americans' ability to resist and adapt.

Essie's ability to find the teachable moment did not end when she officially retired from teaching in 1965. I, for one, have sometimes unwittingly become her student. She has taught me valuable cultural, academic, and personal lessons.

For instance, in September of 1987 we were working together at her home in Naytahwaush, Minnesota, when Essie invited me into her back room to see her family heirlooms: Shoshone beadwork, Hoopa baskets and shell necklaces, and other special items from both the Burnett and Horne sides of the family. I was especially verbal in my admiration of a beaded belt buckle decorated with a traditional Shoshone rose design. The next day Essie said, "Here, Sally, this is for you. I want you to have this." She pushed that buckle across the counter toward me. Surprised, I blurted out, "I can't take that Essie. That's a part of your family's collection!"

I have never seen Essie so mad. She pounded her fist on the counter in reply. "Sally, you never say no to an Indian when they gift you! What has become of your anthropological training?" I was at first embarrassed by my combination of ignorance and my reversion to my personal and familial difficulty in accepting a gift without feeling indebted. Then I noticed a twinkle in her eye as she fought back a hearty laugh. I reflected on my two-fold mistake. First, in admiring the belt buckle so emphatically, I had signified a desire to possess it, to which Essie provided the correct cultural response—a gift of the item. My second error was my ungracious refusal of the gift. Essie used that incident both to teach and tease me, and the buckle is one of my most prized possessions.

Another of my experiences of Essie's method of teaching occurred in the fall of 1989. I was asked to make a short presentation on the collaborative method that Essie and I were using at Moorhead State University in Moorhead, Minnesota. We went out to dinner before the talk. (Essie has family and many friends in the Fargo-Moorhead area.) Essie remarked at dinner, to a full table of friends, "Sally says she's going to talk about hermeneutics tonight. I know I'm old, but why she needs to talk about stool samples—to which I'm sure that word must refer—I don't know. I wonder what vials and petri dishes full of human BM samples have to do with a life history project?" I chuckled at her joke, and she looked back with a wry but warm smile.

I had recently been trying to read essays by Gadamer, Giddens, Foucault, and others, and I had become quite enamored of extravagant words like hermeneutics and dialogic and deconstruction.[16] The night before, I had told Essie that I would be talking about the hermeneutic approach. I explained that hermeneutics meant not only the interpretation of narrative but also a self-conscious reflection on the process of interpretation itself. She asked why I wouldn't just use the word "interpretation" instead. I supposed that I intended to impress my audience (and her) with my new jargonized vocabulary, but after her humorous caution, I opted for a more straightforward approach.

Cultural Broker

A fourth motif that permeates Horne's narrative is that of her role as cultural broker. This theme is revealed in Essie's mediation between the white and Indian worlds but is also made apparent as Essie seeks out connections both with other Indian cultures and to a pan-Indian cultural heritage.

This theme of her mediating role occurs throughout the stories she tells, from the courtship and marriage of her white father and Indian mother to her current position as grandma to many Indian and non-Indian children. Her participation in the Sesquicentennial of the Lewis and Clark journey in 1954–55 and her goodwill trip to Europe in 1966, as described in her life history, also illustrate this theme.

Much historical and anthropological literature suggests that Indian women were able to retain closer ties to their heritage than Indian men and also suffered less acculturative stress. This may be due, in part, to women's roles as mothers and primary socializers and caregivers in the home. These roles may have provided more stability than men's roles as hunters and warriors, which changed more drastically after contact with U.S. assimilation efforts. Other sources suggest that many Indian women were important mediators of cultural exchange as they became convinced that this foreign European culture was here to stay.[17]

I use the term "broker" rather than the metaphor of "being caught between two worlds" because Essie's stories are ones of survival and optimism, not of failure and discrimination. She refuses to dwell on those periods of her life when criticism was directed at her because of her heritage. Essie is not an angry woman. She is proud, strong-willed, and opinionated but not angry. Also, she does not consider herself a "marginal" person, one who must seek her identity somewhere between the white and Indian cultures. She experiences and is a part of both cultures.[18] She is neither immune to nor separate from the roles of Indian women as promoted during the era of which she writes. She is, however, cognizant of her unique position as a mixed-blood, boarding school–educated, great-great-granddaughter of Sacajawea.

One of Essie's goals is the preservation of stories that are being forgotten. In the process of our conversations she provided new stories of survival and strength that are also a part of the theme of cultural mediation. As Horne and I recorded her reminiscences of the life of a twentieth-century mixed-blood woman, it was not to record a "vanished" past but to celebrate persistence and change and survival. One might interpret her philosophies as an indiscriminate acceptance of assimilation. However, what we see upon close examination in the narrative is a woman who accepts the system for what it is: a sometimes flawed, sometimes well-meaning but misinformed construct that is unlikely to disappear in the near future.

In order to make sense of her position as an employee of a government whose goal was to eliminate her culture's traditions, she has come to understand the system well and to laugh at it, and her position in it, with ease, for she knows that she has played a part in sabotaging it. She, like many but not all other Indian people, buys into the system insofar as education, political participation, and socioeconomic opportunities go, but she insists on retaining a unique value system. This cultural ambiguity combines an adherence to Native American traditions, values, and appearances with accommodation to the white world.[19] Even in her adherence to Christianity she adds layers of Indian meaning to her Episcopal beliefs. Mediators like Essie desire to influence positively the dominant society's values as well as to alter that society's negative impressions of Indian people.

The status of her role as broker and mediator has increased with age. Old age does not seem to be a frightening prospect, in part because Indian culture reveres age and learning, irrespective of sex. The wisdom acquired with the passing years is prized by her culture. The emerging self-portrait of this aging narrator is one of a confident woman who is sure of herself in both the white and Indian worlds.

A STORY IN NEED OF HEARING

Horne's self-representation and my cultural representation of her are both integral to the life history as subject and researcher work together to create a story that is satisfactory to their concerns and goals. When I asked Essie about her reaction to the themes described above (her relationship to Sacajawea, her boarding school experiences, and the roles of master teacher and cultural broker), she responded:

I react to these themes as the things that have had a great deal of meaning in my life. First of all, though, I put my family, my marriage and children, my mother, my brothers and sisters, and my extended family first. They are most important in my life. I suppose I talk so much about them because I was robbed of their companionship and the security of a family because of my father's death and my seven years in a boarding school.

But I do react positively to these themes. My relationship to Sacajawea has played an important role in my life; she has had a great influence on me. She has been a role model because of the kind of person she was. Then, of course, my boarding school experiences were positive for the most part, and I found a security there that was important to me. My commitment to teaching is also so important. It was wonderful to be paid for doing something that I loved to do, and, of course, my connectedness to my Indian heritage has been a very very important part of my life. My father and mother gave us strength by teaching us the many positive things about our Indian culture and the many things that Indian people have contributed to the American way of life.

The way Essie Horne chooses to reveal herself holds much for the reader. While she writes about the significance of her gender and the sphere of domesticity linked with the public domain of teaching, travel, and government employment in the 1930s, and she discusses the traditional relationships of daughter, wife, and mother, as well as her unique sense of personal autonomy, she also stands outside of the dominant, Western, white culture. She lives in a world that I cannot fully grasp. It is a spiritual, mythological, and historical world that combines traditional Native American and Western concepts. It is a world grounded in the past but geared to the future of her people. She does not set out to paint a grand portrait of herself, but the canvas of her self-perception allows creation of a clear and idiosyncratic image of a powerful female personage.

Essie is self-reflective about her world and her life. Through her story it becomes clear how cultural and personal meanings inform one another. Stories that she tells of herself as teacher, mother, and grandmother reflect her sense of who she is. She says, "I'm not ashamed of my life. . . . I think that I have fought for my rights as a woman and a mother—continuing full-time teaching even after the birth of my first child. Throughout my life I've had the desire and the discipline and the dependability to get what I wanted; women didn't used to do that. We were supposed to be seen but not heard." Essie's story is one that needs to be heard. What follows are recollections of ordinary life lived under extraordinary circumstances.

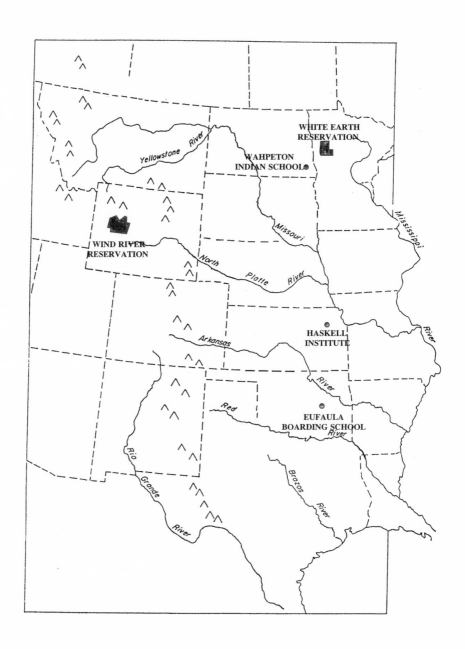

Map of the central United States

xlii

Essie's Story

Esther Burnett Horne's Family Tree
Shoshone Ancestry

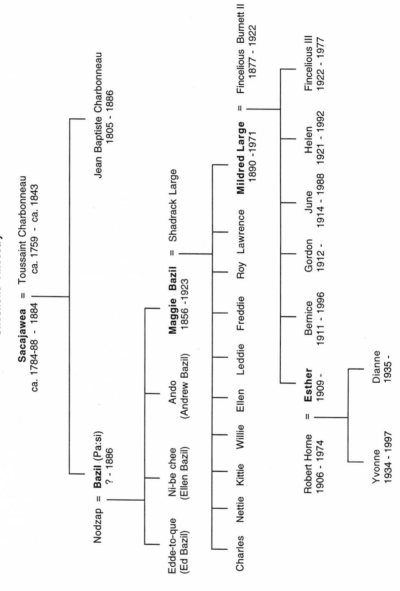

CHAPTER ONE

My Relationship to Sacajawea

One of the illuminating themes of the life history of Essie Burnett Horne is the experience and actualization of many recognized Native American values in the life of this mixed-blood Indian woman. As portrayed in this oral history, the values are lived rather than announced or analyzed. To a large degree, they find their roots in Native American culture, and for Essie they resonate with the values "lived" by her ancestor Sacajawea.

The story of Sacajawea emerges within Essie's more recent history and touches upon the controversies surrounding Sacajawea's later life and the concomitant question of the status of oral tradition versus the written (white) history concerning this memorable Native American woman.

Essie begins her life story by recounting the oral traditions that relate to her great-great-grandmother Sacajawea. Thus, she places herself and her story within the continuum of a history recognizable to both Indian and non-Indian readers and establishes the dimensions of her ancestry and genealogy.

My relationship to Sacajawea is by no means the most important theme of my life, but I will admit that my connections to this well-known heroine have brought me a great deal of attention in my eighty-plus years. From the time I was a small child in Idaho, to the time spent around the Wind River Reservation, to my days as a student and teacher in the Bureau of Indian Affairs boarding schools, the oral traditions of this woman have inspired me to hold on to my traditions. Now as a great-grandmother myself, I understand a little better how the legacy of my great-great-grandmother has influenced my sense of who I am.

I have heard that there are more monuments erected to honor Sacajawea and more geographical features, including a crater on Venus, named after her than after any other person in the United States. Be that as it may, she earned her reputation. Sacajawea is of course the young Shoshone Indian woman who accompanied Lewis and Clark on their now famous expedition from St. Louis, Missouri, to the Pacific Ocean and back. She would have been in her teens at the time she joined the expedition. She carried her first child, Jean Baptiste, with her all the way. He would have been about two months old when the expedition left from Fort Mandan in what is today North Dakota.

For as long as I can remember, my mother and father taught us about our relationship to Sacajawea. I call her "Sok-a-*jaw*-a" in Shoshone. I was corrected by many of my friends who are North Dakotans. "Oh, you mean Sakakawea. You're saying her name wrong." I would say, "No, it's 'Sok-a-*jaw*-a' in Shoshone." As I got older, I realized that there were at least three correct pronunciations. A close Hidatsa friend of mine, Martha Voigt, said that "'Sakakawea' means 'bird woman' in Hidatsa." I said, "'Sok-a-*jaw*-a' means 'someone who pushes the boat away from the land' in Shoshone." Well, we were talking about the same person, but we were using different tribal pronunciations. In 1924 the government settled upon the official spelling and pronunciation as being Sacajawea and coupled it with the Hidatsa meaning, "bird woman."

I am also aware that today most historians prefer the spelling Sacagawea, pronouncing the name with a hard "g." So take your choice: Sok-a-*jaw*-a, Sakakawea, Sacajawea, or Sacagawea—all refer to the young Shoshone woman who accompanied Lewis and Clark on their expedition in 1805.

Both my mother and father told us stories about her travels and about the things that she had done.[1] I can remember my mother showing us roots and berries that could be used for medicine. Then she would tell us that her great-grandmother had used these when she had traveled westward with a group of white men who had gone out to the Pacific Ocean. She said that these roots had saved their lives. We were also told that due to a meat shortage the travelers were reduced to eating dog and horse. Sacajawea refused to eat either of these foods, preferring to subsist on camas and other wild foods. I recall her telling that her great-grandmother, Sacajawea, was a very fine swimmer and that she had saved important papers. I later realized that this incident happened during the Lewis and Clark expedition when their boat was overturned. What reminded my mom of this incident was that she believed she had inherited her swimming abilities from her great-grandmother.

My mother was also fond of relating that my great-great-grandmother had gone clear to the Pacific Ocean—the "Big Water"—and that she had seen a gigantic fish; she told those who gathered around her that she had seen a fish as big as a house. At that time, before the turn of the century, most of the Shoshone people were still living in their tipis at Fort Washakie. Sacajawea's adopted son, Bazil, however, was given a log cabin next to the government agent's house. Our great-great-grandmother lived with him and his family in that house because of her high standing in the tribe. She would tell them that she had seen a fish as big as their house, but they would say, "Ishump," which means "that's a lie. Ishump. No fish could be that big." We now realize that it must have been a beached whale.

My father said that his dad, Finn Burnett Sr., told him that Sacajawea saw quite a number of people in the water and that when she tried to talk to them, they would just dive under. She could never get quite close enough to speak to them. She believed that they must be an odd race of people—a community whose homes were in the sea. She must have been talking about seals! The many stories about her were told with humor and pride. She had been an important person on the reservation, and we were proud to claim her as a relative.

Sacajawea told my paternal grandfather, Grandpa Burnett, that she had been beaten by her husband, Toussaint Charbonneau, and that the red-headed man [Clark] had stopped him. Sacajawea had not married this white man by choice. She and another little Shoshone girl had been taken captive by the Hidatsas while berry picking in the Three Forks area of the Missouri River. She would have been about eleven or twelve at the time of her capture. Later, probably when she was around fifteen or sixteen, Toussaint Charbonneau, a French-Canadian voyageur, won her in a gambling game.[2] According to my mom, the whiskey flowed freely during this exchange. My Hidatsa friend, Martha Voigt, whose tribe also had oral traditions about this young captive, said that her people would probably not have gambled Sacajawea away had they not been under the influence of liquor.

Lewis and Clark met and hired Toussaint Charbonneau while wintering at Fort Mandan in what is now North Dakota. His employment as a translator was conditional on his bringing one of his Snake wives since the expedition would travel through Shoshone Territory.[3] The son of Charbonneau and Sacajawea, named Jean Baptiste, was born at the fort in February of 1805; the expedition departed in April of that same year.

I remember my mother telling me that Clark was very kind to Sacajawea and was fond of her newborn son, Baptiste, whom she carried with her on her back throughout the journey. I also remember hearing, I think probably from my mom's folks, that Sacajawea said that Charbonneau had wanted to sell her body to some of the men on the expedition, but she refused. Perhaps, we thought, "He beat her because she was unwilling to disgrace herself." She would have had the tip of her nose cut off had she committed adultery in our tribe.

Another bit of information that came to us via our oral tradition was that Sacajawea was a sister of Chief Cameahwait, leader of the Shoshones at the time of the expedition. On the westward journey, as Lewis and Clark passed through Shoshone territory familiar to Sacajawea, they met a band of Shoshone Indians. She recognized her tribe because of their attire, and let them know by sign language that she too was Shoshone. As she rushed toward them, she recognized her brother Cameahwait. It was a joyful reunion! Imagine how she must have felt after not seeing her family for five years or more.

At one point on their journey back from the Pacific, they were almost overtaken by a band of Crow Indians on the warpath. They had great trouble getting away from them. Sacajawea always spoke of meeting this war party as one of the greatest dangers they had faced. The expedition had, of course, encountered many other tribes of Indians. Sacajawea's presence, as a woman with a child, and her knowledge of sign language clarified the peaceful intentions of the explorers and alleviated many potential problems.

Sometime after the expedition, Charbonneau and Sacajawea went to St. Louis together. The story is that William Clark had offered to educate Jean Baptiste when he was old enough to be away from his mother. By this time, however, Charbonneau had taken another wife and was abusive to Sacajawea. So she left him in St. Louis and began her migration back home to her Shoshone people. She wandered through many states on her westward journey.

When she got to Indian Territory, in what is today Oklahoma, she passed through Comanche country. Comanche and Shoshone are closely related languages and cultures, and the oral tradition of both of our tribes concur that she settled there for a while, married a Comanche man by the name of Jerk Meat, bore him some children, and then moved on after their children were grown and her husband had died. She left Comanche country in search of her other sons.

You see, Sacajawea had two sons prior to her travels to Oklahoma: Jean Baptiste and Bazil, both of whom she thought might have eventually traveled west and north to their Shoshone homelands in their adult years. Baptiste was believed to have many of the qualities of his French father, and we were told by Granddad Burnett that he had a drinking problem. Bazil was a

4

nephew whom she had adopted, a common practice among Indian people. As it turned out, both Bazil and Baptiste eventually returned to their Shoshone people. This was prior to the Shoshones' confinement on the Wind River Reservation, but both moved with the Shoshones from Fort Bridger to the reservation in 1871. Baptiste would come and go from the reservation; he'd come back for the tribal buffalo hunts, but then he would leave and be gone for long periods of time.

Shoshone oral tradition says that he lived out his old age on the reservation, died, and was buried there. Bazil, Sacajawea's sister's son whom she adopted, was very solicitous of his mother and her comfort throughout her later life. Tradition has it that after many years of travel, at about the age of eighty, Sacajawea returned home to her people in what later (1890) became the state of Wyoming. Maggie Bazil, my maternal grandmother, was Bazil's daughter. We had connections to Sacajawea from both sides of our family. We were biologically related through our mother's side, but my father's side of the family also had a long-standing relationship with her.

My grandfather, Finn Burnett, the frontiersman who later became the agricultural agent or "boss farmer" for the Shoshones, worked with Sacajawea and knew her personally. He said she was anxious to help teach the Shoshones agriculture. She remembered the Mormon wheat fields. She had eaten bread and liked it, and she wanted her people to be able to make T'de Cup—that's how we say "bread" in Shoshone. My great-great-grandmother and paternal grandfather were friends and co-workers and had a great deal of respect for each other.

Sacajawea was more or less a liaison between the Shoshone people and the military. Just as she had served as a symbol of peace on the Lewis and Clark expedition—war parties were never accompanied by women and children—so too did she continue in this capacity in her later life. You see, Fort Washakie was established as a military post to keep the Shoshones where the government wanted them to be: confined on the reservation. We had been a tribe of nomadic people, and the government did not want us roaming around.

Sacajawea spoke English and some French, as well as Shoshone and Hidatsa. She was also fluent in sign language and so was able to help the Shoshones make their wants known to government employees as well as the military. Oral tradition also suggests that she was instrumental in keeping peace between the Shoshones and other tribes. So, that was her great service there. My dad tried to impress upon us that our great-great-grandmother, Sacajawea, was a helper of Chief Washakie.[4] He said that it was very unusual

5

that a woman would be allowed to speak in council, as Sacajawea was allowed to do with and for her Shoshone people. He told us that Bazil and Baptiste were both subchiefs, and we understood that they were the chief's helpers, as was their mother, Sacajawea.

Then he told us, with my mother sitting there and nodding her head in affirmation, that she was like a chief-woman. He was trying to impress upon us the great leadership strength that she had. She was, we thought, one of the first women ever allowed to speak in council. Sacajawea not only helped Chief Washakie but also helped my white grandfather in his teaching of the Indian people. One of Sacajawea's names, Porivo, reflects this status. We were told that she received this name, which means "chief woman," from the Comanches.

She carried papers signed by Lewis and Clark in a leather pouch and sometimes wore her Jefferson peace medal to show who she was and what she had done.[5] Mormon records also indicate that when Sacajawea passed through what is now the state of Utah on her way home, some Mormon elders also saw the papers and were aware of her historical role. The bag with the papers and medal were passed down to Bazil and buried with him when he died in 1886. He was buried in the traditional way in the mountains. Some years later, in an attempt to verify our oral tradition, Bazil's body was disinterred in order to locate the papers and medal. The pouch was found, but the contents had decomposed and were unreadable. Shoshones believed the medal was bad medicine because both Sacajawea and Bazil had died while wearing it. When I inquired about the whereabouts of the medal, my mother said it had been hidden away in a cave. She offered to take me there. Being steeped in our tribal traditions, I refused her offer. No self-respecting Shoshone would be caught dead looking for it. I believe my mother's suggestion was a way of testing the depths of my Native spirituality. Granddad Burnett told me that the pouch and paper remnants had been given to the University of Wyoming.

In addition to the name Porivo, Sacajawea was also known as Bird Woman, Wadze Wipe, Bo-i-nav, and by innumerable other names. This multiple naming was not uncommon among Indian people. The things that so many of our people knew about Sacajawea's life were those things that were passed down through oral tradition.

My mother used to tell us about Sacajawea's power to break up storms. Electrical storms with a lot of thunder and lightning were common in the northern plains and mountains. Quite often, when a storm was approaching, my mother told us that her great-grandmother possessed the power to dissipate those storms. I asked my mother how she did that, and my mom showed me that she would take her arms and talk to the storm in "Indian" and tell the storm to go around, and it would! That may seem unbelievable to some people. In fact, I was sharing this with my son-in-law Bill Barney who had been a history teacher for fifteen years and was a student of Indian history, and he kind of smiled and said, "Essie, be careful who you tell that to." He was saying that a lot of people don't believe that those kind of things are possible, but they are!

My Hidatsa friend, Martha Voigt, had that same medicine to break up storms. We were very very close friends. Back in the late 1970s, Louise Breuninger Peake, a Cherokee friend of mine, and I were visiting Martha in Partial, North Dakota. Louise and I were at the post office, and while we were there the people inside said, "There's a tornado coming." We looked out, and it looked like the funnel was coming right for Partial! Then, all of a sudden, it dissipated. I saw it separate and go away, and I thought to myself, "My friend is working." When we got back to her house, I asked her about it. I said, "You destroyed the storm." She just put down her head.

We believed that Sacajawea had the power to break up storms through medicine that was passed on to her from one generation of our family to the next. She happened to be given that power from way back in time. A lot of people don't understand the concept of Indian medicine. It's both physical and spiritual, like the medicine in a medicine bundle. It's a power that one needs to be taught to use. It is passed down from one generation to the next. In the Indian way, Sacajawea would feed her medicine and pray to it. She would treasure it and do those things that an Indian person who had been given this great honor, this great gift, would do. She would have to take care of it so that the power would stay with her. Should she be lax in her care and respect and honoring of the medicine, then bad things would happen to her. Bad medicine would result.

All of what I have just explained needs to be clarified as it relates to the controversy surrounding the date that Sacajawea died. Some historians believe that Sacajawea died as a young woman in 1812, but how could all that we know about her later life have been fabricated? Because the oral traditions of our people are truth personified, we've always known who we were. The recollections of my grandfather, Finn Burnett, and the Rev. John Roberts, who officiated at Sacajawea's burial, substantiate the oral tradition. James McAdams, an elderly cousin of mine who lived with the Bazil family until he was twelve, knew our great-great-grandmother, too. I picked the brains of these three men, gleaning every bit of information possible, and it all supports the story that has been handed down by my family and the tribe.

Those individuals who do not believe that Sacajawea lived to be much older than twenty-five years accused my grandfather of having read the Lewis and Clark journals, but he never read them! It seems preposterous to suggest that my family and others on the Wind River Reservation had read the journals of Lewis and Clark. The journals weren't readily available, and what motive did we have? Truth and honoring one's word are very important values to Indian people. There is no way that the Shoshones could or would have lied about their knowledge of Sacajawea. Those things could not have been made up. There is no way that a little Indian woman in her eighties or nineties could have fabricated the experiences that so closely parallel Lewis and Clark's journals unless she actually had taken part in that expedition. It could not, as some historians have argued, have been a myth created by the people of my tribe—the account is just too complete.

I've never had any doubts about Sacajawea having come back and lived with her people. The veracity of the tribal elders and of Finn Burnett, Rev. John Roberts, James Patten, James Irwin, and others has never been questioned by our tribe.[6] Mrs. Sarah Irwin, the agent's wife, interviewed Sacajawea and wrote her story in shorthand on legal cap paper. My father remembered the notebook—he said she had recorded more than seventy-five pages, front and back, but that the manuscript burned in an agency fire.[7]

Historians have quipped, "How very convenient that this manuscript mysteriously went up in smoke." My reply to them is that we already knew the story anyway—it has become our history through an age-old method that we believe in: oral tradition. We believe that the spoken word is powerful.

I've often wondered why historians are so quick to dismiss our oral traditions. I've frequently mulled it over in my mind, and I've had many conversations with historians over the years. I recounted our oral traditions to them, and they listened with interest to the logic of my argument but then retreated to the safety of the written word. They closed their minds to alternative explanations. They don't, I think, respect or understand how insistent we Indian people are on being truthful. We all know that so much of what has been *written* is untruthful, false, and biased. Therefore, I do not understand their narrow-mindedness.

The research of scholars such as Grace Raymond Hebard, Charles Eastman, and others also supports the fact that Sacajawea lived to be an old woman among her people, venerated by her tribe. Grace Raymond Hebard was professor of political economy at the University of Wyoming. Her book, *Sacajawea*, published in 1933, is filled with the testimonials taken from the people on the reservation who knew Sacajawea personally. Charles Eastman, a Santee Sioux physician and an author of note, was commissioned by President Calvin Coolidge in 1923 to resolve the controversy of whether Sacajawea died in 1812 or 1884.

He traced back her route from St. Louis to Wind River, collecting and substantiating oral tradition. He collected data from Shoshone elders at the Wind River Reservation, from Hidatsa people at the Fort Berthold Reservation in North Dakota, from the Comanches in Oklahoma where she had married and had children, from the Gros Ventres, from the Mormons in Utah, and from other sources along the trail. My understanding is that copies of this report were channeled to all government agencies that might have some interest in Indian culture and history. It is my belief that the findings of this report were intentionally kept under cover! The research of both of these individuals confirmed our tribe's oral traditions. There never was any doubt in our minds that this woman who lived and worked on our reservation was indeed Sacajawea.

After I first started teaching in 1929, I realized that the oral traditions I had heard about my great-great-grandmother were an important part of our tribal history, as well as of American history. I was aware of the weight that historians attach to the written word, and so I decided that I should obtain a record of these oral traditions. I asked my paternal grandfather, Finn Burnett, and Rev. John Roberts, who officiated at the burial of Sacajawea, to recount in writing some of the things that they had shared with me in conversations since I was a young girl. Their letters, which are dated in 1933 and still in my possession, are valuable documents of confirmation.[8]

I know that there are journal entries from 1811 and 1812 written by travelers in South Dakota who record that the wife of Charbonneau was sick and that she eventually died and was buried at Fort Manuel Lisa in 1812; but those reports do not name the woman. Rather, they describe her as Charbonneau's "squaw." I believe that *one* of Charbonneau's Indian wives died in 1812 but that it was Otter Woman or another Indian wife, not Sacajawea. It is a well-known fact that Toussaint Charbonneau was what was called a "squaw man" and that he had many Native American wives.

I also know that William Clark wrote "dead" on the front of his account book next to Sacajawea's name, but he also wrote "dead" next to Patrick Gass's name. Gass was another member of the expedition who was very much alive at the time; *he* lived to a ripe old age.

I feel this is what must have happened to Sacajawea. Someone who did not really know for sure told Clark that they thought Sacajawea had died. So in his tally of the known whereabouts of the expedition members, he wrote that down. But *we* know that she lived to be nearly a hundred years old because she came back and lived among our people. When I was a little girl, I heard people who knew her and worked with her recount the stories she had told about her journeys; they remembered her pervasive influence on reservation politics. I have no apologies to make about my beliefs. My only wish is to make clear to those who hold that Sacajawea died in 1812 the reasons why I believe what I do and why I will never recant my beliefs.

CHAPTER TWO

Early Life at Home, 1909–1922

Essie's remembrances of her early life in Idaho provide a personal picture of rural America in the early twentieth century. This individual picture reflects the timbre of experience shared by ranchers and farmers across the country during the "teens." Essie's life is a microcosm of the lives of Native Americans all over the United States, Indians dealing with the ambiguous status of being Indian, as well as with the trials of ranchers and farmers everywhere.

Essie's personal accounts of Anglo/Indian perceptions and interactions tell the story of the larger evolving picture of Native Americans integrating into mainstream America while attempting to retain their cultural identity in the face of a national (BIA) policy of assimilation.

The memories here show a family emphasis on education and career growth, as well as on the development of a value system with inherent integrity. Essie might not be *every woman*, but she could be *any woman* of her time, influenced by family relationships, survival of financial reversals, the values of rural life, the impact of World War I, and the experience of family tragedy.

FAMILY BACKGROUND

I began the life history by recounting some remembrances of my great-great-grandmother. Now I want to share the story of my own life.

I was born in 1909, on November 9, and the earliest thing I can remember is being on top of a very tall dappled gray horse. It seems to me I still had on a diaper. I don't know whether this memory is something that I made up, images remembered from what I've been told, or simply the truth. Could I remember being that young? I would have been a year or two old and that would have been somewhere in Idaho, because my mother and father had to run away to get married.

My father, Finn Burnett Jr., was Scottish-Irish and my mother, Mildred

Large, was Shoshone Indian. My name is Esther, but my nickname is Essie. My father named me after one of his old girlfriends. Everyone calls me Essie or, now that I am older, Granny Essie.

In 1871, my paternal grandfather, Fincelious Grey Burnett, joined the Shoshones as they began to prepare to go to their newly created Wind River Reservation.[1] He was stationed at Fort Washakie, Wyoming, and had been sent there to teach agriculture to the Indians after the big treaty was made at Fort Bridger.[2] He was the agricultural agent, or what they used to call "boss farmer" of the Shoshone people.

My grandfather enjoyed life at Wind River and learned to like the Indian people very much, but he was not so sure that he wanted his son marrying an Indian. That would have been frowned upon. A young white male marrying an Indian girl would have been called a "squaw man" in those days. It was just as much beneath the dignity of my mother, as a young Indian woman, to be marrying a white man; she would have lost status in the eyes of her tribe and family. But they cared little about what people might say.[3] They had fallen in love, and they ran away from the reservation and went over into Idaho, and that's where they were married. I remember being told that my folks' relatives attempted to block the mountain passes to keep the couple from reaching Idaho. My dad was fourteen years older than my mom; the two of them certainly received a lot of attention with their elopement. At any rate, I was born in Idaho, and that's where I remember sitting on this tall gray horse.

The relationship between my father's people and my mother's people was mended almost immediately after my parents were married. My father used to go back to visit his parents, but my mother and we children didn't go with him. I think it was simply a lack of money and not ill feelings that kept us from visiting. A favorite story that both families were fond of telling confirms the positive feelings that my white grandfather had for my Indian mother.

It goes like this: One day, probably back in the early 1900s, before Mom or Dad were married to each other, Grandpa Finn Burnett saw my mother walking toward her home on a reservation road and offered to give her a ride. She was young and unmarried at the time, and he knew her and her family well. During the course of the ride he cautioned her. "Millie," he said, "I hope that you're not going to marry one of these young bucks on the reservation but that you'll get an education and eventually marry somebody who can really give you a good life." My mother would always laugh and end the story saying, "I did. I married his son!"

After my mother and father left the reservation to be together, my father worked on a ranch and then later became part owner of a fruit farm in Eden. Eden is in the fruit section of Idaho, and they raised apples, apricots, cherries, pears, plums, peaches, and other kinds of fruit. There was a little packing place right there on the farm where they boxed the fruits for shipping. He was partners with two men who were brothers, Forrest and Clarence Warrington. They became like uncles to us because we were away from our own relatives. One of Forrest's daughters was so nice to me when I was a little girl that I always thought that if I had a daughter, I would name her after that young lady, and I did. My oldest daughter is named Yvonne after Yvonne Warrington, who took the time to make me feel important when I was a little girl.

My father was a slender man, around five-feet-ten-inches tall; he had medium brown hair and really blue eyes. My mother was five-feet-two-inches tall, not much taller than me. When she was young, she was willowy and had very long black hair that came halfway between her knees and her heels. She wore her hair in a single braid most of the time. My mom had severe headaches when she was young, and as a result it seemed like we children had to walk very quietly. If we stepped on the floor real hard, it hurt her head. A doctor in Idaho told her that her thick, long, heavy, black hair might have been the cause of her headaches. So one time when her cousin, who was a barber from Salt Lake, came to visit, she had her hair cut, and we all cried. Since I was the oldest, she gave me the long braid, and I treasured it for years.

Early Sense of Heritage

My mother spoke some Shoshone, but she didn't speak it real well. She grew up during a time when many of our traditions and languages were lost or forgotten. In those days, speaking one's Native tongue was frowned upon, and English was taught as the first language in many homes. This was due in part to policies set forth by the government, but it was also due to the expectation that *Americans* would conform and become a part of the melting pot. Indian people were taught that their culture was backward and uncivilized, and as a result, many parents did not teach their children the tribal language or tribal values. They thought it might prevent their children from attaining their full potential in white civilization. Of course, discrimination against Indians continued whether they spoke English or a tribal language.

My father spoke better Shoshone than my mother did because all of his family had learned to speak the language by living on the reservation. My grandfather would not have been able to work with the adult Shoshones if he could not understand and speak their language. My father's family spoke the "old" Shoshone. You know, the Shoshone that was spoken by the old people a long time ago. Our language is like anything else: it changes with the years. When I was young, if the adults didn't want us to know what they were talking about, they used our Indian language because they knew we couldn't understand it very well.

In Idaho, we were the only Indian people in a community of non-Indians, but because my father became a leader in the community, my mother was accepted by people in the area, at least most of the time. My father belonged to a fraternal order, and my mother was refused membership in the auxiliary because she was Indian. So my father dropped out of the lodge and gave up his membership because of that policy. You see, my father would never have put up with that kind of discrimination. We had a very good relationship as a family. There were six of us children: the four oldest were myself, Bernice, Gordon, and June. The two youngest, Helen and Fincelious Burnett III, were born six years later.

Grandma Maggie Bazil

My mother used to tell an amusing story that she remembered having heard from her mom about our Grandma Maggie Bazil and Grandpa Shade Large. Shadrack (or Shade) James Large was a young man just getting started as a rancher on the outskirts of the Shoshone Reservation. He saw young Maggie Bazil and liked very much what he saw and decided that he would like to have her for his wife. In keeping with the custom of that time, he went to her guardian, our Uncle Andrew Bazil, and asked for her hand in marriage. He was informed that he was expected to give gifts in exchange for Maggie. Shade was non-Indian but decided that Maggie was worth the price. No one can remember the exact amount of goods that were decided upon, but the old folks said that there were some horses, sugar, salt, dry goods, and of course, tobacco. Tobacco is treasured by Indian people because of its spiritual and ceremonial importance and because it is a traditional gift that seals an agreement. So, Shade and Maggie were married.

At that time, cattle and other livestock were trail-herded to central railroad points where they were shipped east. Grandpa Large regularly made these long and sometimes dangerous trips, which generally did not include wives or children. So, the first time Shade left after their marriage, Maggie did too, only she headed back to her people. Well, Grandpa Large figured that there was nothing left for him to do but to take Maggie with him if he was going to keep her as his wife, and she found herself trailing along with him as he trailed the cattle to market. Well, Shade wanted to keep his new wife happy while on the trail, and he knew that one of the things that she loved dearly was hard candy. So, when they'd come anywhere near a settlement where there was a possibility of buying candy or other necessities, he'd give her money so that she could make the purchases.

Maggie thought that he must be a rich man if he could give her money all the time to spend on candy, and in her mind it followed that if he were not rich, he'd not be able to keep her and would take her back to her father. With this in mind, she would make her purchases, and when she got the change, she sewed the paper money inside her clothes to use at a future date, but she threw the change away. I can remember my mother talking about how she'd toss it, a little bit at a time, along the trail as she and Shade herded cattle. Maggie was puzzled that she was never able to make Shade poor enough so that he'd have to take her back to her people. In later years she told my mother that she sometimes wished she knew just where she had thrown the money so that she could go back and pick it up when she needed it.

Maggie and Shade had thirteen children, of whom my mother was the youngest girl. Maggie's cattle-driving days took in only the first year of her marriage; the rest of the years of her marriage were spent on the ranch at Henry's Fork, where Shade also raised mules for the United States Army. I can remember my mother talking about the mule teams that they had, too. When Shade died, Maggie was grief-stricken, and mother was trying to console her in her loss. Maggie said through her tears, "I don't know why I feel so bad . . . I never did like him," but she must have liked him or she wouldn't have borne him thirteen children and stayed with him all those years.

REMEMBRANCES OF CHILDHOOD AND EARLY SCHOOLING

When I was little and my dad owned the fruit farm, we lived in this large two-story white house near Eden, Idaho, that I remember so well. It had a porch all the way around the outside and lots of roses in the yard. We made a lot of caps for our dolls from those rose petals. I remember one of my favorite spots was the upper branches of a Bing cherry tree where the cherries were the sweetest because they were closest to the sun. As I lay there, I would listen to the mourning doves; they sounded so far away. I was so surprised when my father said that they were probably quite close.

An earlier story told to me by my mom was that one time when I was still nursing, my father was tickling my nose with a feather. He laid the feather

15

on my mother's breast, and from that time on I refused to nurse. Since I was not old enough to be weaned, I was put on a formula of Borden's canned milk. This company later had a Beautiful Baby contest. My folks took a picture of me in a fancy white eyelet dress and sent it in, and I won a gold locket. Imagine this little mixed-blood Indian baby winning a contest like that in 1910.

I can remember my folks going to square dances. My father chorded on the piano and somebody played the violin, so he was much in demand for dances. Even as children, we would go along with them in the wagon. We took straw and quilts to make a bed so that we could sleep when we got weary. Sometimes we'd watch our parents dance, and I would sit on the piano bench with my dad while he chorded. Once in a while one of my parents' friends would pick us up and dance with us.

My dad could Indian dance, too. He grew up with the Wind River Shoshones, and his peers were Indians. He spoke our language and learned about our culture. He was a really good Indian dancer and would entertain us by tying a colored cloth around his waist and doing a man's traditional or fancy dance. We children would laugh and try to imitate him.

In addition to dancing, there were other activities that we did as a family on weekends and in the evening. Baseball was a popular pastime in Idaho. Our family often went to games on Sundays during the baseball season. We would pack a picnic lunch consisting of fried chicken, homemade ice cream, and other special foods. This was a time when members of the community got together to visit and socialize. We also went to the county fair every year. I think it was in Jerome, Idaho. My mom would enter pies and cakes and canning, and she won many blue ribbons. We kids would take the big turnips that we grew and would win prizes, too.

One of our greatest thrills at the county fair was riding on the Ferris wheel. There were also games of skill where you threw a ball to knock over wooden figures on a conveyor belt. The prize I always tried to win was a Kewpie doll. I don't know why, but I've always liked them. There is one sitting on the ledge in my bathroom to this day.

We also went horseback riding often. As a little girl I loved horses; I loved to stroke their soft velvety noses, and I rode a lot . . . rode bareback. My mother was an accomplished rider, and she had a little mare that different men we knew would bet that they could ride. None of them ever could ride her. She would buck them right off, but she would let me ride her. I remember riding her very fast and just lying low on her neck, hanging onto her mane, and it felt so good just having the wind blow around the side of my face and to be moving across the ground so fast.

As a family, we always had large vegetable and flower gardens, which we all had to help weed and harvest. When we raised pigs, we would put our table scraps in a slop pail to feed to them. Occasionally, a sheepherder taking his sheep out to pasture would pass by our place with his flock, and we would ask him to give us a bum lamb. These were lambs that had lost their mother and so needed to be nursed with a bottle. One of our pet sheep was named Sammy. He and our German shepherd, Bishop, became good friends. Bishop protected Sammy from coyotes and other varmints when he was outside of the fence. We used to hitch the two of them to our wagon, and if Bishop saw a rabbit, we'd get a very wild ride. Sammy eventually became lamb stew because of his mean disposition. A sad bunch of kids refused to partake of *that* stew.

A donkey showed up at our gate one day. We begged our parents to let us keep Jenny. My dad was unable to find her owner, so she became another pet. Poor little thing: as many of us that could fit would pile on her back from head to tail. When she got tired, she'd put her head down, kick up her heels, and scatter kids in all directions. Sometimes we'd use Jenny to herd our cows. On one occasion when I was herding our cattle, I thought I heard a rattlesnake. No matter how hard I kicked Jenny, she refused to move. She stood absolutely stock still; when I finally looked down, there was a rattlesnake crawling near her feet. She had more sense than I and knew better than to move around. Finally, the snake crawled away, and I was so glad to get home safely.

When I was about five years old, we kids were climbing trees in the yard. Being the tomboy that I was, I was pretty high up in a tree when I came eye-to-eye with a huge cecropia worm. I was climbing up the trunk of the tree, and I held on tight, but I couldn't get down quick enough! I was smart enough not to let go my grip, but I bark-burned my belly as I slid down. Ever since, I've had an aversion to green worms. Even thinking about them or recounting this story gives me the chills. My family and my friends tease me about this fear. Every four or five years we have an infestation of army worms in our lake country, and I almost go into hibernation during this period. I call my friends to sweep off the porches and stairs and to caulk the doors and windows because those little worms are so green and ugly. Although these army worms are only the width of spaghetti, and one to two inches long, they're still green, and they trigger this phobia.[4]

My mother used to receive a monthly farm magazine called *Comfort Mag-*

azine. One of the stories that we used to look forward to was about Cubby Bear. This little bear did all kinds of exciting things, and I remember being so excited when that magazine would come in the mail. We had a phonograph at home, too, and occasionally Dad would order a cylinder record for it. He sent away to either Sears Roebuck or Montgomery Ward; we used those catalogues not only for ordering merchandise but also as toilet tissue at the outhouse. One of his favorite records was "When You and I Were Young, Maggie." He would play that over and over again. When we asked him why he played that so many times, he would say, "Well, that's the name of your oldest aunty, my sister." I suppose that he was lonesome for his home and family. My favorite song was called "Lame Deer." It was a love song, sung by a young Indian brave to his sweetheart, Lame Deer. All I can remember was that the chorus went, "Lame Deer, My Pretty Lame Deer. . . ."

Indian Legends

Our mother and dad used to tell us Indian legends, but I've forgotten a great many of them. I do remember that the coyote was the trickster in our tribal scheme of things. Sometimes he was good and commendable and taught us traditional Indian values, and other times he was a scamp. He loved to play tricks on people. My father often jokingly called us an "old coyote" to tease us about things that we were doing that he didn't like. The owl also figured into our tribal tales. Because it could foretell your death or that of a family member or relative, we were told not to listen to the owl if it hooted near your dwelling.

And then there were the little people, the nimimbe. They were comparable to elves or leprechauns. If you could catch a nimimbe, or if you could just touch one, you'd be set for life. When he was grown, my oldest brother Gordon had a dream about the nimimbe. In his dream they were peeking in his bedroom window; he was just ready to grab one when my sister-in-law woke him up. He became violently angry at her, because if he had touched a nimimbe, he would have had good luck for the rest of his life.

We believe that some of the nimimbe reside in the mountains and reveal themselves in the gurgling of the mountain streams. These little water people also inhabit the sinks in the foothills of the Wind River mountains in the Crowheart area. Sinks occur where the water runs along from a creek and all of a sudden drops down into the bowels of the earth and comes out way down someplace. I've always been interested in those little water people in the mountains, because I used to spend a great deal of time up there, and when I would hear the gurgling streams I would think to myself that the nimimbe were probably talking about me as I passed by.[5] My mom also used to tell us that if we lied, a dragonfly might sew our lips shut to keep us from lying again.

Early Education

Some of the other early things that I can remember were what my mother and father taught us children. There was no school where we lived in Idaho, so when we were school age, my father obtained textbooks, and we had regular instruction in reading, writing, and arithmetic. My mother, who only had a sixth-grade education, was the teacher most of the time, with my father serving in the capacity of helping to formulate the curriculum. The next thing I can remember about our education was that all of a sudden a teacher came to live with us. Evidently, there were now [1918] enough children in this little community in Idaho to qualify for a teacher. My father cleaned out our granary, got some desks, and made a school. We were living in Perrine Siding, Idaho, near Twin Falls. We went to school in the granary for a number of years. Our teacher, Miss Durfee, not only provided us with quality education but also challenged us to learn more. She and my mother used to make candy at Eastertime. I thought that was so great: all those different colors and fancy candies.

Sometime after that, we started attending a public school. One of the things that made public school in Idaho less difficult for us four Indian children was that my mother and father worked very hard to instill in us the fact that we had a great deal to be proud of as Indians. They told us that what was American was, in essence, Native American. My mother told us a lot about the native foods and quite a bit about the medicines that Indians in the Americas were responsible for introducing to the Europeans. So many things that seem popular now were actually old and a part of the traditional teachings. As I think back on it, I see that here was this white man, my father, married to a young Indian woman, teaching his part-Indian children and his Indian wife to be proud because they were Indians. Rather than trying to take the Indianness out of us, he always reminded us that our ancestors had given so much to the American way of life.

The public school was a one-room schoolhouse that went from first to eighth grade. There was a wood stove that the teacher had to keep stoked. She would cook stew or soup on top of the stove and that was our hot noon lunch. We also brought sandwiches that mother packed in little syrup pails or little lard buckets. One day the lid on the stew must have been on too tight and a great deal of steam collected and popped the lid off, and the stew flew off the stove and hit the ceiling. Somehow that event has remained with me after all these years.

Another thing that happened in that school is that a group of us children got together to try to make things a little bit more exciting. Three of us caught a gopher, and we tied that gopher's leg to the teacher's desk. Of course, when school started, she jumped up and yelled because she saw the gopher. We thought it was funny until it came out that the three of us had played that trick. She reported us to our parents, and my father gave me one of the few spankings I ever got from him, and I had to apologize to the teacher for what I had done.

It was also when I was at this school in Idaho that we got "the seven-year itch." A lot of families in the community got it that year. We never knew where it came from, but my mother used to keep her big boiler on the stove full of hot boiling water, and every time she'd wash our clothes, she'd boil them real hard in the boiler for a long time to kill the germs. She made us change our clothes what seemed like all the time. We were required to bathe more than just on Saturday, which is what we were used to. It seemed like she boiled our clothes for quite some time until the "itch" went away. Maybe that sticky sulfur salve helped, too. I never did know if it was called the seven-year itch because it lasted so long or because it came around every seven years.

When I was attending this public school, I remember that I used to write stories in a notebook, just to read for my own pleasure. I didn't intend that anyone else read the stories, but I did share them with my best friend, Thelma. The teacher saw us reading and giggling and asked to see what we were reading, and I reluctantly gave her the notebook. She read the stories and told my mother that she felt I had a great deal of creative ability and that perhaps my mom should try to have the stories published. I don't know what became of those old stories. They were mostly love stories. Some were about cowboys, and others were about Indians; some were about my great-great-grandmother. Boy meets girl, those kind of romances.

As a child I was an avid reader. I had such a thirst for knowledge, a desire to know all kinds of things. I loved poetry and I loved fairy tales and I read the stories of B. M. Bower, Jack London, Gene Stratton Porter,[6] and Zane Grey. These were in my dad's library, along with Robert Burns's poetical works, Longfellow, and others. *Freckles* and *Girl of the Limberlost* (Gene Stratton Porter), *Call of the Wild* (Jack London), *Riders of the Purple Sage* (Zane Grey), and other titles were favorites, especially for the descriptive passages of the terrain. I probably was not more than nine or ten when I was reading all of these books that my dad had.

I am so grateful to him for opening up those literary horizons. He wanted us to have a well-rounded education, and to him this included an appreciation for our non-Indian *and* Indian heritages. All through my life I have also tried to teach my children and my students to have a deep appreciation for their own heritage, as well as that of others. Related to my love of reading, I remember the traveling libraries of the Idaho schools. These libraries were large hinged boxes filled with a variety of books. They came to the school on a monthly basis; new books could be checked out and the old ones checked in. They were very much like the bookmobiles of today, and the arrival of new books was an exciting time for me.

The only time that I ever really told my folks an intentional lie was when I wanted to know the answers to a lot of questions. I came home from school one day and told my parents that I *had* to have a set of encyclopedias in order to complete my homework assignments. My folks knew that that was a lie. My father was on the school board, so he investigated this story and was told that I did not need a personal set, because I could use the encyclopedias in school. I wanted to bring them home so that I could have them at my fingertips to read anytime I wanted. My parents taught us the importance of being truthful; I think that's why the impression of telling the lie about needing the encyclopedias stuck in my mind. My mother impressed on us that even if you took a common pin from somebody without asking for it, you were stealing. My father and mother taught us that self-control was the best control, and that good behavior should come from within ourselves. My mother would tell us that Indian people were taught to be brave in their mind and in their body and in their innermost.

My love of reading also got me into trouble a second time. One of my household duties was to make the beds, but I would frequently take my book along and become so engrossed in the story that I would neglect my work. After my mother caught me doing this a number of times, she said, "The next time this happens, I'm going to burn your book." I never dreamed that she would actually burn a book, but the next time it happened, she did. She burned the book, *A Girl of the Limberlost*. I saw my favorite book go up in flames. My mom lifted the stove lid and threw in the book, just like that.

But I had a very close relationship with my mom. That is, we talked about a lot of things. I don't know whether it was because she was fourteen years younger than my father; I think she was sixteen or seventeen when she got married. We could laugh, you know, and talk to each other so easily about mother-daughter things or girl things . . . girl talk. We had security as a family. We children could feel the deep affection that our parents felt for one another and the love they had for us. I look back, and I can't remember any real anger or yelling or swearing at each other. I think back on those times with a great deal of fondness; things got worse after that.

Domestic Activities

At home we were always busy. My mother was an excellent seamstress. She made her own clothing: shirts and trousers for the boys and dresses for the girls. She gleaned the material for this clothing from two of my father's sisters, who were stenographers for the Bureau of Indian Affairs in Wyoming. They would clean out their family closets once or twice a year and send us large boxes of cast-off clothing. My mom would alter some for herself and dad and remake the rest into clothing for us children. I don't believe she had any formal training in home economics, but we would look through Sears Roebuck and Montgomery Ward catalogues and select styles of clothes that we liked. My mother would cut patterns out of newspaper and make our clothing. She would add some ribbon, some braid, and some pretty buttons, and we had clothing as nice or nicer than the rest of the kids in the community.

I think we believed that since we were the only Indian children in a non-Indian social setting, it was necessary for us to be dressed on a par with our peers. One Easter I thought I had one of the prettiest dresses I've ever had. Mom made Bernice and me beautiful dresses with grosgrain ribbon sashes, out of white curtains that we had gotten in the box from these aunts.

It was this Easter that I had my first menstrual period. When we got up to leave the church service, my father noticed blood on the back of my new white dress. He took me gently by the shoulders and whispered, "You have blood on the back of your dress; don't be frightened. You've just become a woman; your mother will explain this to you." I was forever grateful that my father was sensitive enough to take charge of the situation. He took off his suit coat and put it around me.

One of my biggest wardrobe disappointments is that my father went to town one time and bought us new shoes. He got us what they called Buster Brown shoes that came over the ankle and laced. I didn't like those shoes because they looked too much like boys' shoes. I wanted little patent leather slippers that had a bow on them and a strap across the ankle, but like many families, we didn't have the money to spend on those kind of extravagant items. My mom wore clothing in the style of the day; she used to wear long-bib aprons that came up over the shoulder and tied in the back.

Homesteading

One of my father's friends, Robert Holmes, embezzled a lot of money that my father had given him to build us a house and invest in the sugar-beet business. I remember being taken by my father to the town of Eden, Idaho, and being shown the house that we thought was going to be ours. I was impressed by the number of windows and the large glass doors. When Dad showed the house to Bernice, Gordon, Mom, and me, he said, "This will be our home someday," but of course, that was never to be. After our family lost our money, it was necessary for my father to start all over again. He took up homesteading in the area, and we moved to our new place using hayracks and wagons and lived in a tar paper shack that Dad and his friends built. Our lifestyle changed radically: our quarters were cramped and simple. I guess this would have been around 1916 to 1919, because I was probably seven to ten years old.

The land that we were homesteading was near some buttes, and I remember playing on them with my sister Bernice and my brother Gordon. My mother said that prickly pear flowers were good to eat, and I loved the color and texture of the flowers. So Bernice and I collected a lot of prickly pear cacti in the aprons that we used to wear, and of course we had the little spines just sticking all over ourselves. When we came in, my mother was aghast. We showed her what we had picked, and she told us to take off our aprons quickly so that she could try to get those little spines out of our skin. I remember that she peeled the prickly pears, but I don't remember eating them or what they tasted like.

Sometimes we ate steamed cattail roots and frog legs and other wild foods that our family collected. In our exploration of the buttes, we also discovered sago lilies. My father told us that he thought they were made into starch. Later on in my lifetime, when I saw a sago lily logo on a starch box, my mind went back to that time.

My mom regularly took butter, cream, and eggs to town to exchange for staple foods at the local store. She baked bread and did a lot of canning. All of us children would haul water in buckets from the creek for her when she was cooking. We stored potatoes, carrots, onions, and apples in the root cellar, and my folks cured their own ham and bacon.

We had fun as a family, too. There was a good-sized beach along a creek that we could run along. One day, we disturbed a bees' nest, sand bees, and they swarmed after us. We ran and screamed as the bees stung us around the head and on the arms. When we got home, my mother rushed us back to the creekbed where there was muddy leaf-mold, and she scooped and plastered that on our stings to relieve the pain and swelling. My mother also would collect silver sage to put in our pillows if we had a bad cold. She'd put a handful in the pillowcase that we slept on to clear up our respiratory problems. Sage is commonly used by the Shoshones as a medicine, as well as for purification in some spiritual ceremonies.

My dad raised wheat on our homestead. When the grain was ripe and ready to harvest, a separator and the thrashing-machine rig would move onto our place. Neighboring farmers got together and helped one another with the harvest; the women of the family where the thrashing was being done would spend days preparing the food to be served. My mother was an excellent cook, and the workers liked to come to Millie Burnett's place to eat; her pies had a reputation throughout the county. At the end of a day's work, when the horses were unhitched from the hay rack, my father would allow us to ride the horses to the barn. One time when I was riding them in, the bottom of the barn door was left open, and the horses ran right into the barn. I had the presence of mind to lie flat on the horse's back so that I was not decapitated by the top half of the barn door, which was closed. My folks looked on in horror and were relieved that I was not hurt. I remember that instead of getting a scolding, I was complimented for having been wise enough to duck.

There seems to have been no end to interesting happenings on the homestead. One of our cows gave birth to a calf out in the field; she wasn't a very wise mother, because she dropped her calf on the side of the irrigation ditch and the calf drowned. My father pulled the calf out of the ditch and brought it in for burial. From that point on, the mother cow followed my father around. When he went out to pasture, she followed him, and when he was in the corral, she would get as close to him as she could. When he would come into the house, she would stand outside and look in the kitchen window and bawl, calling him to come outside so he could be with her. We jokingly called Dad the cow's calf. We also owned a mean gander goose that would waylay us when we went out to slop the pigs; if he caught us out there, he would flog us with his wings and pinch us with his beak.

The first Christmas at the homestead, my mother told us that we weren't going to be able to have Christmas gifts that year. That was the first time we realized that there was no Santa Claus. We didn't have any money to buy gifts, but Forrest Warrington, my father's old partner, had become a storekeeper. He had a bag of wormy peanuts that he gave our family. Mom sorted through them very carefully, and we had a peanut cake and she even added peanuts to the icing, and that was one of our Christmas treats. We had been told many times before Christmas that there would be no gifts, so imagine our surprise on Christmas morning to discover that Clarence Warrington, the other former partner of my dad's, had brought each of us a present. Mine was a twenty-four-inch doll with a pink dress and dark curly hair with eyes that opened and closed. We had such a happy life despite the tar paper shack and lack of money.

Values

My parents used to talk to us about what we would like to do when we grew up and had jobs of our own. Two of my father's sisters, Aunt Eva Burnett and Aunt Ida Greene, were stenographers who worked for the Bureau of Indian Affairs in Wyoming, and Dad would ask us if we would like to be stenographers or maybe teachers. We used to play school, and as the eldest of course, I was always the teacher; but I didn't have a great desire to be a teacher when I was little. I used to think that I would like to be a stenographer.

We had a lot of discipline in our home. My father was a person who liked to be on time, and he insisted that we be on time. He was fond of telling a story about his Shoshone friend whom he was to meet at a certain place at a certain time. When my father got there, he thought, "Well, I'll just sit down and wait." Just as he started to sit down, somebody touched him on the shoulder, and it was his friend. I asked my dad, "How could he be on time? Did he have a watch?" "No, he can tell time by the sun and the shadows." I have repeatedly heard this business about "Indian time" being any time. I say, "No. Indian time is being *on* time." This would have been a matter of survival for Indian people. If they agreed to meet at a certain time to escape from an enemy or move camp or hunt buffalo or have a ceremony, they had to be on time.

Some of our people, too, have gotten the idea that Indians didn't discipline their children. My mom would have disagreed with that. Indian children were taught to obey by example, and they were taught to be quiet. There again, it would have been a matter of survival. If you needed to sneak by an enemy camp or avoid scaring your prey away, silence would have been paramount. A crying child or people making noise or not paying attention would have been dangerous for the whole community. The way we disciplined our children was through touch and firm but gentle words.

WORLD WAR I, THE FLU EPIDEMIC, AND FATHER'S ILLNESS

I know that I was quite young, only five years old, when the First World War began, but it was a frequent topic of conversation in our household when it broke out in 1914. My father was anxious to do his part for the war effort, but because of his disability, he couldn't enlist. When he was a young man, he was climbing through a barbed-wire fence, holding his hand over the gun barrel, when the gun discharged accidentally, severing the middle fingers on his left hand.

During this time, as the war escalated, we learned that the Germans were the enemy and the Kaiser was their leader. I can still visualize caricatures of Kaiser Wilhelm and the racist songs intended to arouse hatred against the Germans.

There was a German settlement near our farm, and my folks had been good friends with a couple in the German community before the war broke out. They continued to bring us homemade cheese during the war, but other neighbors were suspicious of them, and so the visiting was curtailed. There was an unfounded fear that these supposed "enemies" might poison our water or be involved in some other kind of subversive activity. The German community was the object of constant surveillance. Our family had a difficult time understanding the unfounded discriminatory slurs and actions directed at these American citizens of German descent.

The war ended in 1918, the same year that there was a terrible flu epidemic, and all of our family except my dad came down with the flu, as did most of the people in our farm community. People were suffering from high fever, nausea, diarrhea, painful coughing, fever blisters, and other flu-related symptoms. My father cared for us by keeping us cool and comfortable with wet compresses, mentholated chest rubs, and sponge baths. He emptied our bed pans, supplied our meals, and nursed us back to health. It must have been hard on Dad to see us all so sick and to take care of a family of four children and a sick wife.

Many people became unconscious for long periods of time; I was one of them. The last thing I remember before going into a coma was that my new socks were hanging over the foot of my bed. When I woke up, they were gone. I thought I had been asleep for a short time, and I couldn't imagine who had taken my socks. Mother said, "You've been asleep for several days, and I took your socks down to wash them." When I awoke from the coma, water tasted so good. The first solid food that I ate was a roast beef sandwich. I was starved for solid food, and I remember that there was butter on the bread and hot roast beef in between the slices.

During our illness, we were in constant fear that one of us was going to die. We were one of the fortunate families; so many people *were* dying: friends and their children, and sometimes whole families were wiped out. It was a traumatic and frightening time for the community. We did what we could to alleviate the illness, the pain, and the sorrow of friends and neighbors. It seemed like it wasn't much after that, that dad took ill.

We didn't know that my father had a brain tumor until he had a seizure while he was operating the milk separator.[7] That was the first time that we knew that he was in ill health. He got increasingly worse with frequent seizures and finally was hospitalized. The doctors at Twin Falls, Idaho, operated on him, but at that time so little was known about brain operations that the surgery was unsuccessful. The tumor was malignant, and he died shortly thereafter, in 1922.

The period surrounding my father's illness and death was a very traumatic time. Somehow, that period remains both crystal clear and foggy in my memory. We had depleted our stored foods, eaten our chickens, and consumed nearly all of our canned goods. We experienced the indignity of opening up the door and finding boxes and baskets of food on the steps. I must have been about twelve or thirteen years old at the time, and I felt so helpless at not having any food, and that my dad was sick and I couldn't do anything about it. We were all scared and sad. Finn, the youngest of us children, never knew our dad, because he was born after my father's death. I remember that the birthing took place at home. The midwife must have come during the night, because in the early morning of June 22, 1922, I heard this baby crying, and that was Finn. Helen was only eighteen months old, and so there were two little ones in the family at that time, and my mother was left widowed with six children.

More responsibility fell on Bernice and me to take care of the two youngest children. It was a chaotic time. We were scared and frightened and felt hopeless and insecure. Our grief at losing our father was overwhelming. His death seemed so sudden; we were just beginning to get back on our feet financially when our family unit was shattered.

CHAPTER THREE

Life in Wyoming and at the Haskell Indian Institute, 1923–1929

After the death of her father, Essie's family moved to Wyoming to be with relatives. Her account of growing up with a single parent echoes the plight of many families who were left in the same situation due to a parent's death in World War I. Although this move brought Essie into greater contact with her extended family, she and her siblings experienced what she deems "poverty and neglect."

The deterioration of the family situation triggered the enrollment of three of the Burnett children (Essie, Bernice, and Gordon) in Haskell Institute, an Indian boarding school in Lawrence, Kansas. Essie's recounting of this schooling reinforces the positive experience many Native Americans had at these educational institutions. The role the boarding school played in the (accidental) development of pan-Indianism is also illuminated through a glimpse of Essie's experience.

The picture is painted, from a personal and individual perspective, of the growth of self-assurance and independence of "Indian School" students. Ironically, this is coupled with the school's attempt at military-type discipline as part of its assimilationist mission.

Again, there is a personal picture of growing up, immersed in the very different values of two cultures, neither one excluding the other. Essie recalls exceptional teachers who influenced her, and mundane as well as exceptional events in this facet of the life history. The "jewel" here is a young life filled with the normal pains and joys of growing up. The "setting" is a (by today's standards) highly unusual multinational, multicultural boarding school which brought together peoples of many Indian nations and cultures.

WYOMING AND THE RESERVATION:
A FRAGILE SINGLE-PARENT FAMILY

After my father's death, my father's brother, Uncle Bill Burnett—an optometrist in Casper—and my mother's sister-in-law Aunt Effie Large—the wife of my mother's oldest brother—were delegated to move our mother and her family of six children back to Wyoming. The two opposite sides of the family were concerned about our welfare, and so our life began in Wyoming. We lived with Aunt Effie and Uncle Charlie Large in Green River, Wyoming, just off the reservation for a short time until we got a place of our own. Uncle Charlie was an engineer for the Union Pacific Railroad. Through his efforts, my mother secured a job with the Union Pacific Hotel as a chambermaid, and we children were left to fend for ourselves.

My mother was grieving and, I believe, searching for the companionship and love that she lost when my father died. Her new companions were so different from my dad. They were unschooled; they drank and partied and were loud and raucous. Mom wasn't really making enough money to support us. The apartment we lived in was small and not in the best part of town. We weren't very well dressed and didn't eat very well either. My mother worked a great many night shifts and was not home much, and so we were left alone. The apartment became cluttered and dirty. We were undisciplined and would wander around and do pretty much what we wanted to amuse ourselves. We did have permission to charge groceries to Mom's account at the store, but that didn't last long, because the first time she went to pay her grocery bill, she discovered that we had charged candy and watermelon and all kinds of junk food.

Because of this lack of supervision and stability, when we enrolled in school in Wyoming, it was very difficult for us. We hadn't had any problems in the Idaho Public School system, but the picture really changed in the Wyoming schools. We were discriminated against, and I never felt like I fit in. Kids would call us names because we didn't dress very well and because we were Indian. Aunt Effie, who was not Indian, said she wasn't going to have any part of her family identifying themselves as Indian because the discrimination was so blatant. She and Uncle Charlie, who was Shoshone, didn't even enroll their kids as tribal members.

There were other ethnic groups in Green River, too: Italians, Chicanos, and Asians. We were all treated pretty shabbily. I didn't fail academically, but the transition was a rough one for me. I was not very happy in Green River. We had very few friends, except for our cousins, the children of Aunt Effie and Uncle Charlie.

In spite of the hard times surrounding our uprooting from Idaho to Wyoming, the joy of meeting my father's relatives positively offset some of these negative feelings. When I met my white grandfather, Finn Burnett, for the first time, he hugged me and kissed me and told me that he loved me. Aunt Eva and Aunt Ida, my father's two younger sisters, were also genuinely glad to see us. I had a real warm feeling for them. We also visited our Indian relatives, and they were glad to have us back. It seemed good to be part of an extended family.

We heard more stories about Sacajawea, too. Granddad Burnett said, "You look a great deal like your great-great-grandmother; you're about her size. She was a small woman and quite light-skinned for an Indian." I must have reminded him of Sacajawea, because he often said that she was happy and of good humor with dancing eyes. I always felt that I knew more about how she looked by my own looks than I did when I saw some of the statues of her. Finn Burnett Sr. would reinforce how Sacajawea looked by making reference to the statue of her astride what might have been her favorite horse. He always said that this sculpture by Henry Altman looked most nearly like my great-great-grandmother.

Some of my mother's relatives took us to the Indian graveyard where Sacajawea, Bazil, and Baptiste are buried. I gathered some wildflowers, including Indian paintbrush, and laid them on their graves. I had a feeling that my great-great-grandmother was looking down on me and was happy that the flowers were for her. I have always felt a close kinship with her. My mother and father regularly spoke of her truthfulness and courage and inner strength. They spoke of the courage of Indian people in general, and I strove to be like her. I really *tried* to be like her in telling the truth and having the strength to do the right thing at the right time. This has been an ongoing commitment throughout my life.

Economically, our family was not doing so great. What little savings my mom had from my father's insurance policy had been invested by my Uncle Bill Burnett in Teapot Dome stock.[1] This oil reserve scandal robbed us of our pitiful inheritance. I can remember how beautifully Uncle Bill and Aunt Lillian were dressed when they came to the apartment to tell my mom that the money that they had invested for her future had been lost. I can still envision the diamond rings, fur coat, and family jewelry that looked so beautiful to us poor kids, and I can remember the bitterness of my mother's tears at having lost so much. My father's side of the family were quite well-to-do. I did not know until several years later that my paternal grandfather had asked my mother to let him adopt us after my father's death but that she had refused.

After Uncle Bill's visit, our poverty and neglect became more and more apparent to the Burnett side of the family. Things *had* fallen apart—our family no longer had a mother and father, and we children were left to take care of ourselves and hadn't fared so well. The wheels were set in motion through the Wind River Indian Agency to enroll us at Haskell Institute, a BIA non-reservation boarding school in Lawrence, Kansas.[2]

HASKELL: 1924 TO 1929

The Arrival

As we clung tearfully to our mother, she reminded us, "If you run away from school, you'll go *back* faster than you came home." It must have been heart-wrenching for her to say this, but it was her way of protecting us from the dangers that she knew we would encounter if we ran away. It sounded harsh to us, but she had our best interest at heart. We knew she meant what she said because it was a rule in our family to keep your word. It was harsh discipline, but it was a discipline of love. The three youngest kids—June, Helen, and Finn—stayed with Mom, while Bernice, Gordon, and I boarded the train for Haskell. I remember that it was a long, long way. The conductor attended to our needs and remarked, "Millie told me to take good care of you kids, and I will." Mother knew most of the trainmen because of her job with the Union Pacific Railroad.

The conductor showed us points of interest as we traveled through the flat, treeless plains. It might have been much more frightening had we not known that someone on the train was responsible for us, and the conductor seemed to have taken that responsibility very much to heart. As he walked back and forth tending to his own duties, he would joke with us and ask how we were. I was not terribly scared. We ate our meals in the dining car; the flower on the table and the concern of our fellow passengers made us feel quite sophisticated as we began our journey into the unknown.

We were worn out and disheveled from our travels and leery of what new changes were about to take place. In those days they tagged the new kids the way they tagged their baggage, so we arrived at the train station with identification tags pinned to our clothing. Haskell school personnel met us at the train and took us to campus. One of the first places they took us was to the dormitories. I have a vivid recollection of the long row of white cots on the sleeping porches in the dormitory at Haskell; they reminded me of the crowded hospital ward where my father died.[3] I was grief-stricken and frightened, and I can still visualize myself standing there, feeling lost and alone. I was surrounded by images that transported me back to the last time I saw my dad before he died, and I thought, "I hate this place; I will never be happy here." I wondered which direction my home was.

A couple of older Shoshone girls from Wind River sought us out soon after we got there; they were kind of like big sisters to us, and we felt a little better. Knowing there were other kids from our reservation there made us feel more at home, even though we didn't know them personally. Relatives of ours had also been students at boarding schools. Uncle Charlie had gone to Carlisle, and Uncle Roy's claim to fame was that he played football with the great Jim Thorpe and had pictures to prove it.[4]

At Haskell we were required to bathe several times a week. I remember that when we checked in our soiled clothing, and checked out our clean clothing, we had to have our body inspected by dormitory personnel to make sure we didn't have impetigo or pediculosis—what they called infestation with lice. They put some kind of chemical treatment or solution on our hair every so often to make sure we didn't get lice. I did get lice one time at Haskell, and I can remember Bernice fine-combing my hair to get them out and picking through my scalp to remove the nits. We both cried through the ordeal. In time, I got more used to Haskell and the other Indian students there and began to adjust to this strange environment.

Socialization

One thing that boarding school life *did* provide me with from the very start was a larger vocabulary. There was a "slanguage" common to Haskell, the usage of which made us feel like we were a bonded part of the group. Old students would try to trip new students up by giving them the wrong definition of a word. One of the slang terms common to Haskell was KALE, which meant money, but someone might tell you that KALE meant toilet or orchard or bakery. We also used *uncle* to mean a girl's boyfriend and *aunt* to mean a boy's girlfriend. "Chape" meant "shape," like "What a great 'chape'!" You might embarrass yourself by using a word in the wrong context, which was a hilarious thing to do, but you learned not to be too ashamed about it. You tried to take the ribbing with grace. If you didn't, your life could become unbearable, but if you did, you were *in*.

Indian kids came to Haskell from all over the United States and represented a myriad of tribes. I don't remember any intertribal hostilities. We were curious about one another's tribal culture and language. We'd discuss the kind of dances or ceremonies that each tribe had and learn about each other's traditions. We would also compare notes as to how students would say common items such as sugar, salt, or bread in their language. Again, one might play the trickster and relate the wrong meaning of a word. Creek students, for example, would tell you their word for bread. You might try to show off your new-found knowledge of the Creek language to other Creek friends only to have them laugh hilariously because the word you uttered didn't mean bread at all. It might just as easily be a body part or a bit of profanity. I was really surprised the first time that I learned that the Comanches and Shoshones spoke the same language. I was on the way to the hospital, and I had to go by the gym. There were a couple of Comanche boys, who were on the football team, talking to me and teasing me in Comanche as I walked by. I understood them because it sounded like Shoshone to me. When I asked them how they had learned to talk Shoshone, they said, "Didn't you know that Shoshone and Comanche are closely related dialects?"

I also am still carrying around an eagle feather that was given to me when I was a sophomore, by a Ponca friend from Oklahoma. She was leaving and said, "Always carry it with you. It will protect you." I have it still. I feel the spiritual strength of that feather. To me it's the manifestation of the Great Spirit—a link to the Creator. We had a lot of respect for each other's culture and talked a lot to each other about our customs and traditions. We students nurtured a sense of community among ourselves, and we learned so much from one another. Traditional values, such as sharing and cooperation, helped us to survive culturally at Haskell, even though the schools were designed to erase our Indian culture, values, and identities. The intent of these schools was to take the Indianness out of the Indian, supposedly to make our transition into white culture easier.

The Military Routine

All of the boarding schools had military discipline; we had to drill in formation before breakfast. This was certainly foreign to anything we had ever known before. We rose at 6:00 A.M., combed our hair, brushed our teeth, and got dressed in our everyday clothes. We had to be in formation by 6:15 A.M., five days a week. We were divided into companies by grade and sex; the company officers—captain, lieutenant, sergeant, major—were students who were responsible for drilling the companies. There was competition between the companies not only in the drill exercises but also for good citizenship—meaning good behavior—especially in our detail. There was a group called "the awkward squad" by the staff, and actually all of us! They were those kids who couldn't master the technique of marching, and they needed extra drill. They were teased—good-naturedly. This was all a purely military thing, just like the armed forces.[5] If I had not had two little girls to care for during the Second World War, I'd have been a natural in the WACs or WAVES.[6]

The military regime became an integral part of our daily lives, and demerits were a part of this system. We were given demerits for sloppy detail work, loitering in the halls on our way to class, crawling out on top of the dormitory to sun, sneaking around to meet the boys in the orchard or bakery, going to the Shack without permission, or swearing. Boys and girls would sometimes meet in the apple orchard for visiting and socializing. I never did that—not so much because I didn't want to but because I didn't have the nerve. The punishments were pretty harsh. I remember a girl getting pregnant and having to be sent home. The school kept those kind of incidents pretty quiet, but we kids knew most of the secrets.

The Shack was a little off-campus store closely supervised by school personnel who sold food, soft drinks, candy bars, and gum. You could also have film developed there, but your photos would be scrutinized by the Haskell personnel. Company officers would hold random white-glove inspections. The boys would inspect the girls' quarters and vice versa.

I became a commissioned officer by working my way up through the ranks. One had to demonstrate leadership skills, maintain a superior academic record, and be knowledgeable about military organization. It became a matter of honor for me to be able to discipline my best friend or a relative. It was not easy for me to hand out demerits, and it often created hard feelings. I realized that we officers were being used by the school, but like student governing bodies today, we were aware that we were being taught self-discipline. While we were encouraged to compete as individuals and to vie with other students for privilege and favor, we also managed to maintain a sense of responsibility to our fellow students. This responsibility to community is a part of the Indian way. The intention of military drill may have been to break down tribal values of cooperation, but we found other avenues through which we expressed this strong sense of group responsibility. We nurtured a sense of community among ourselves, which helped us not only to survive the boarding school experience but to grow in it and learn from it.

Occasionally, student officers would get so caught up in their own ego trips that they would try to throw their weight around in order to get even with someone whom they had a grudge against. Haskell terminology for someone who acted in this way was a *suitcase*. Nevertheless, it was an honor to be chosen as an officer, and most of us had great pride in the military. You had to work your demerits off by doing the most disgusting tasks, such as cleaning the toilets or the showers or polishing the assembly hall. You could also have your privilege of going to town or to the movies revoked if you had accumulated too many demerits.

After morning drill we went to breakfast, which usually consisted of bread and corn syrup, peanut butter, oatmeal, cooked dried fruit, and a cereal beverage. Detail followed breakfast, and each student was assigned to a group whose job was to clean areas on the campus like the assembly hall or toilets, or to prepare or serve meals, wash dishes, do the laundry, sort and mend clothes, help with the baking, and all kinds of other chores. Even the lower grades formed tot companies, whose duties were to pick up litter on the grounds.

Students rotated from one detail to another in order to learn an assortment of "trades," eventually focusing on a career program by the junior and senior years. Girls in high school might study nursing, home economics, normal training, or business, to prepare them for graduation. Boys might be assigned to the paint shop, blacksmith, dairy, bakery, masonry, power plant training, business, or normal training.

The boys who worked in the bakery sometimes brought their girlfriends or other chums a fresh loaf of bread. That was always such a treat—to share fresh-baked bread! We also had a teacher for home ec who taught us to make pies; we made them right in the class. We would have so liked to have a pie to eat, or to share with our friends. The teacher must not have been aware of the kinds of food we ate daily—she frequently just let those pies go stale. Once in a while, we'd manage to abscond with one of those pies and treat some of our friends to the wonderful taste of a hand-made pie. I always thought that was cruel of that teacher—not to give the pies to the kids who had made them.

The detail work that we all had to do was preparation for our later training, as well as a way to keep the government boarding schools self-sufficient. The work of the students kept the school running.[7] We had dairy cattle, to supply the school with milk; some pigs and cows for fresh meat; an apple orchard for fresh fruit; and gardens with tomatoes, corn, watermelon, and other vegetables. During harvest, big baskets of tomatoes for us to eat were available in the back of the dormitory. I ate so many one time that I got a terrible case of hives; my eyes were swollen shut when I woke up the next morning—a reaction to eating all of those tomatoes.

The washing machines and dryers were electric, industrial-type machines, not like the hand crank machines that boarding school students had to use in the early 1900s. Today, I guess I think of our details as a source for broadening our horizons. I learned to use a mangle and extractor while working in the laundry. Years later, while doing my washing in the laundromat in Mahnomen, Minnesota, that had an extractor, a woman said, "I wish I knew how to work this thing." I said, "I'll show you how." She was amazed that I knew how to do that and said, "Where did you learn to do that?" and I said, "I learned to operate one of these in a government board-ing school in Kansas." The skills I learned have been beneficial to me all through my life. I make an effort to soften the point of view that government boarding schools were hellish places with harsh discipline and beatings. My recollections are that in general we were pretty happy; by and large we were like one big happy family.

There *were* those kids who just could not cope with boarding school life and, in an effort to escape, would run away, hoping to reach home. We called this going AWOL. Some went AWOL as a lark, simply to see how far they could get before they got caught. This was a serious infraction of the rules, and the punishment was harsh. Runaways were restricted and not allowed to go to town for a long time. If a boy and girl ran away together, they might be ex-pelled. I used to hear stories of AWOL kids getting locked up in cells prior to my time at Haskell, but that did not happen while I was there.

The belt line was a more common punishment for going AWOL, and it was a serious disciplinary measure. A company would be lined up in two long lines facing each other. The students would remove their belts and strap clothed offenders on the rear as they dashed through the line. Some were such good runners and such good dodgers that they defeated the purpose of the punishment. I was never aware that any great harm was done to the cul-prit who went through a belt line. Some students who were flailing the of-fender did not put much force back of the belt, perhaps just enough to im-press the employee and officer in attendance.[8]

Once, when I was an officer in charge of the tot company, I asked Grace Thorpe to wash her hands and face, but she told me to shut up and then ran away from me.[9] I chased this six-year-old all over the assembly room and had I caught her, I would have given her a good spanking. She and I have laughed about that incident many times since. By the time that I left Has-kell, I had obtained the rank of major and was sometimes responsible for drilling the whole platoon of companies on Sunday afternoon when towns-people from Lawrence would visit the campus and watch us go through what was called a silent manual, or silent drill. We were trained so well that we could drill without any commands being given. It must have been an in-teresting sight to see us Indian kids marching around in military formation.

Really, much of the student-to-student discipline was in the form of guid-ance and counseling. My husband-to-be—whom I met at Haskell—and I used to talk about the military regime in the boarding school. We were grateful for that military experience because it taught us self-discipline for our later lives. That's what it did for us. It may not have done that for everybody, but we both knew that self-control was one of the strongest of the Indian values.

All students at Haskell were required to wear the same articles of clothing. Girls' everyday garb was a plain, short-sleeved, light blue dress that we called a "hickory." They were made simply so that they would go through the mangle easily. Boys wore plain light blue shirts and dark pants. This clothing was used for work and school. There were advantages in dressing alike. Those of us who didn't have money to buy nice clothes never had to feel inferior to those who could. You might think that most of the Indian kids who attended boarding schools were pretty poor, but that was not always the case. Tribes such as the Osage and Quapaw of Oklahoma were quite wealthy because they received large per capita payments for the oil that was on their reservations.[10] Mary Rose Big Horse, an Osage roommate, had Saks Fifth Avenue clothing. She was very generous and lent us dresses to wear to boy-girl parties where we were allowed to wear our own clothing. She would say, "Here, wear this dress," and we would. When her mother came to visit her, I remember that her mother wore long braids, moccasins, and a bright-colored Pendleton shawl. She had a black chauffeur and a black limousine. Except for the parents of the Osage and Quapaw students, there was very little visiting—Kansas was just too far away for most parents to visit very often, and the twenties were a rough time for the whole country.

On Sundays we wore military uniforms. Girls wore navy blue skirts and capes and white middy blouses with ties, overseas caps, plus dark hose and shoes. Boys wore khaki-colored army uniforms and drilled with surplus army rifles.

At night we wore government-issue nightgowns—flannel in winter and cotton in summer. I have this very clear recollection of falling back asleep one day after wake-up call; I'd stayed up late the night before to complete my homework assignments. In a hurry to get down to breakfast, I tied my nightie up, and threw my dress over it. While waiting in line in the dining hall, the string came untied and my nightgown flopped down below my dress. I got a thorough dressing down for not being properly attired in the dining hall, but my only punishment was going without breakfast that day.

The Physical Layout

The physical layout of the campus and buildings was quite beautiful. In my 1928 annual I wrote:

In all this world of buildings rare
Few of them to this Castle compare

It may sound a little corny to refer to my dormitory as a castle, but many of the buildings on the Haskell campus were ivy-covered, and they became our homes over the years. Five or six girls would share a room. Everyone had a drawer, and we shared tables to study on. We kept our clothes and night-gowns there but slept on large sleeping porches. I think it was the fresh air factor—it was believed to be healthier to sleep where air could circulate than in a confined room.

The girls' dormitory was on one side of the campus, and the boys' on the other. They were separated by a large expanse of lawn that had a bandstand and a sidewalk down the middle, which we called the demarcation line. The lawn was a no-man's-land except for Sunday afternoons when we could visit with our boyfriends and listen to a band concert, or have a watermelon so-cial. We all really looked forward to those afternoons, which were one of the few times that the girls and boys were allowed to be together. I think that the school feared that a girl might get pregnant without constant supervision, which did sometimes happen. In addition to the dormitories, there was a chapel, a gym, a home economics building, a dining hall, a kitchen, a hospi-tal, campus housing for the faculty and staff, a print shop, a carpentry shop, and other trades buildings.

There were two dining rooms: the Prevo for grades one through six, and the Big Dining Room for the older students. The boys ate on one side of the dining room and the girls on the other. We were assigned seats by company. It was the responsibility of the girls to serve the food, clear the tables, and wash the dishes. The dinner meal was served at noon. Employees super-vised the students whose "tour of duty" was to work in the kitchen. The cooking for the hundreds of students was done in enormous steam vats. The staple fare during my first years at Haskell in the twenties was meat, po-tatoes, bread, and gravy. We had fresh fruit and vegetables in season, but we did not receive a well-balanced diet—it was top heavy with starch. There were times that we had gravy that was sour because it had been warmed over so many times. Some of our food, such as the corn sugar and dehydrated po-tatoes, was surplus from World War I. The quality of our food affected our health. Boils and pimples were common afflictions, which seems sad in an agricultural state like Kansas, where vegetables and fruit were in such abun-dance. Poor student health provoked government investigations of the BIA schools, and home economists were hired to develop more nutritious diets.[11]

There were rats at Haskell. At night particularly, we'd hear them running up and down the stairs. They were rather large—you could hear them lop-ping from one stair to the next—and they were heavy! I don't remember anyone being bitten by a rat, but they gave us the creeps nonetheless. There was a lot of joking about the rats. We'd say that they must be carrying little shovels on their backs as they worked in the yard. Or we'd joke about them sweeping and mopping the stairs, saving us from work the next day. One idea that the school had was to get rid of the rats by putting ferrets in all of the buildings. I don't know if they were just let loose in the buildings or what. I don't know what ever became of them. Maybe they ate all the rats and got fat and lazy.

Academic Instruction, Sundays, and Health

Academic instruction took place in the afternoon. Our classrooms were typ-ical, with desks and blackboards and with a mixture of boys and girls in the same class. The standard high school curriculum included the same kinds of subjects that one would have had in the public schools—like history and math and English and physical education. Our instruction was very intense; the teachers' missionary zeal stemmed from their purpose, which was to take the Indianness out of the Indian in preparation for life in the dominant society. The textbooks seemed to be up-to-date; there was a good library; there were study halls, and we had an abundance of homework. Nine o'clock meant lights off and into bed. In order for us to keep up with our homework, we would often tack a towel over the glass transom of the door so that the night matron would not see that we were burning the midnight oil.[12]

The BIA schools were not accredited at that time, but they made use of state curriculum guidelines. My personal evaluation is that I received a very good education at Haskell. Some argue that the curriculum left much to be desired, but I had attended public schools before I went to Haskell, and I felt that some of the BIA teachers were more effective in challenging and mo-tivating students than any teachers I had in the public schools. Or, maybe I was simply fortunate to have had some excellent teachers in my years at Haskell.

After our academic classes, we had a short free time, probably less than an hour, to relax and visit, and then back to detail again in preparation for sup-per. Some boys might attend football, track, baseball, or basketball practice before our evening meal. This was a lighter meal of sandwiches, fruit, milk, and sometimes cake or cookies. Meal clean-up followed, and then there was time for extracurricular activities or homework before our 9:00 curfew.[13]

Haskell students were required to attend church on Sunday morning. We designated a church preference on our applications, and that was the church we were to attend. I don't believe that anyone was allowed to stay away from Sunday services. Members of our family went to the Episcopal church, so I attended Episcopal services while I was at Haskell. We wore our military dress clothes and were transported to church in an army truck. I also enrolled in a Bible history class taught by a professor from the University of Kansas. It was not a required class, but a big drawing card was that Bob Horne, a California Hoopa student of whom I was quite fond, was signed up for it, and that was a way I could socialize with him more.

Throughout my years at Haskell, several students came down with tuberculosis. In my dorm, two girls were diagnosed as being in the last stages of TB. They were not hospitalized but rather were sent back to their cots in our room until arrangements could be made to send them to the Sioux Sanatorium in Rapid City. I have often wondered why they were not isolated in the hospital. They were our friends, and we felt sorry for them because we didn't know if they would get well or not. Later in my life I had exploratory surgery to ascertain the nature of two large masses, one in my lungs and one in my throat. It was discovered that they were not cancerous but rather were healed tubercular areas. It's quite possible that I was contaminated while rooming with these two tubercular-infected students.

Matrons, Teachers, and Normal Training at Haskell

When I first got to the boarding school, I was a follower. I racked up my share of demerits by getting into a great deal of mischief. I was really seeking to belong to a group, and one way of doing that was through resisting the structure imposed on us there. A case in point was the result of a photo that was processed and came back through the Shack, and which ended up on the matron's desk. My chum, Rose La Framboise, and I had decided to pose as flappers with rolled-down hose and hiked up hickories.[14] We rolled up white papers to look like cigarettes and stuck them in the corner of our mouths so that we would appear to be worldly, and then we got a friend to photograph us in this pose. Not only did the matron, Miss Ritter, confiscate our treasured pictures, but we were also made to march around the flagpole for a couple of hours with a broomstick over our shoulders. That was our punishment to work off the demerits that we received for that prank. We were interrogated and scolded by Miss Ritter, who believed that we had sneaked some cigarettes into the dorm. I felt ashamed because the boys were making fun of us, and Sunday sightseers from Lawrence also peered at us as they drove by in their cars. I wasn't ashamed of what I had done but was ashamed of my punishment and also that who-knows-how-many employees had been invited to view the photo.

Once, too, when I was a freshman or sophomore, some of the girls who worked in the kitchen said that they had heard that if you mixed ginger with water and drank it that you could get drunk. So we all tried that, but all we got was a real hot stomach, and we were very uncomfortable. One time, though, the brother of a friend of mine from Oklahoma got us a bottle of beer, and so we stayed home from dinner one evening and divided that bottle of beer. We felt quite wicked and worldly to be drinking beer, and to get away with it, although I did feel a little ashamed afterward. Those were a few of the things that all kids do when they are trying on life, and we were no exception.

It was through the efforts and interests of a number of school personnel that I began to understand the importance of the values that I had been taught by my parents: to look within for the strength to make my own decisions, and to be responsible for my own actions. Without parents around, we learned to work hard and be responsible for our decisions and actions. Many of us were mature beyond our years but still retained the ability to play and joke and tease. This combination is so typical of Indian people.

My company commander, Louise Breuninger talked to me about my behavior and counseled me about my association with the troublemakers.[15] Because I liked and respected her so much, I tried to live up to her expectations, and I did an about-face. I began to make my own decisions. I began to do the right thing at the right time in the right place. Dorothy Kate, the YWCA secretary, made a special effort to reinforce the importance of being independent. I was impressed by her enthusiasm, and she became a friend. I would visit her apartment, and occasionally we attended vespers together at Kansas University.

Significant Teachers: The Decision to Become an Educator

Two teachers at Haskell who had a profound impact on my life were Ella Deloria and Ruth Muskrat Bronson.[16] They stood apart from the others as far as I'm concerned. Ella Deloria was Standing Rock Sioux and a graduate of Columbia. Later in her life she worked with Franz Boas—a very well-known anthropologist. She taught girls physical education and drama. Ruth Muskrat Bronson was Cherokee and a graduate of Mount Holyoke. She taught English. They both had such a wonderful sense of humor. They taught non-Indian subject matter but had a very strong respect for Indian culture, and they were clever enough to integrate it into the curriculum. They taught their students to have a healthy respect for themselves as individuals and a pride in their heritage. They taught us about Indian values and kept them alive in us. They respected and encouraged us to voice our opinions in and out of the classroom, and they had the ability to draw out our creativity. When Ruth would tell us to have pride in who we were, she'd say, "Indians are people, too. Don't forget that." This phrase became the title of a book she wrote in 1944.

Ruth and Ella listened to us. They were interested in what we thought about the subject material and interested in our lives. They taught us that we could accomplish anything that we set our minds to. Their positive attitudes and pleasant dispositions convinced us that they must be right; but they also taught us not to believe that everything we learned was the truth. They pointed out biases in what we read and taught us how to disagree without being disagreeable. They taught us how to defend ourselves, as Indian people, without getting angry or defensive. This lesson has been invaluable to me throughout my life.

They taught us to be receptive to new ideas and not just to dismiss someone's views because we didn't share them. This was especially true in American Indian issues. We learned that we didn't always know as much as we thought we did. Ella and Ruth taught us about generosity and about sharing—what goes around comes around. The kindness that you show to others comes back to you. We Indians have been criticized for our giveaways, but there is so much joy and satisfaction in giving.[17] Students at Haskell had a great deal of respect for these two, probably because they came from the same background as us. They were Indian, and so we knew that they understood us, just as they understood where we came from and what our needs and beliefs encompassed. They were both well-educated Indian women whose desire to help Indian youth led them to commit and dedicate their lives to us.

Ruth was a very fine teacher. She loved literature and so shared with us her joy in that subject matter. She had a quality in her reading voice that made the words come alive, and she had a great imagination, too. I remember that she had a habit of sitting in her chair, with the chair tipped back, and we always thought that one of these days she was going to tip back a little too far and fall. Of course the day came when the chair went out from under her. Her legs went up in the air, and she came crashing down onto the floor. We didn't know if we should laugh or not because we didn't know if she had been hurt. Some of the boys rushed up to help her to her feet. Once she got over being so startled at the whole experience, she started laughing really hard. So we all had a laugh at her expense. That was the kind of teacher she was.

Ruth always tried to make the subject matter come alive for us, and she always tried to bring some of our culture into the literature that she taught. When she taught Longfellow's "Evangeline," she wove in some of the history and even some of the legends of the Indian people who lived in the different areas that Evangeline moved through in her wanderings. Of course some of this was present in the text—I remember references to the Shawnee and other Indian tribes. She related certain passages to ideas that were present in our own oral traditions, and related the exile of Evangeline's Acadian people from the Maritime provinces to Louisiana to parallel stories of our own Indian people. So, without breaking the continuity and beauty of the story, she was able to sneak in a bit our history. It made the readings so much more relevant to our understanding of who we were.

Both Ruth and Ella loved literature, and one of their extracurricular projects was a student production of *A Midsummer Night's Dream*. We had studied this play in one of their classes, and we were excited about being a part of the production. The boys and girls who auditioned for the play worked hard to be chosen, because it was a chance to socialize with each other and to be on-stage. Interpretive dance was integral to this 1927 Haskell production. I was awkward in the regular physical education activities but loved interpretive dance because of the opportunity for self-expression. While we were practicing for the Butterfly Dance in the play, I became so engrossed in my interpretation that I was unaware that I had fluttered down to one end of the gym while the rest of the troupe had gone the opposite direction. I was rudely jolted back to reality when my best chum, Rose La Framboise, began to laugh hysterically. Days later, whenever she would look at me she'd dissolve into giggles.

I starred as Hermia and will always remember the thrill of that acting experience, as well as being presented a dozen long-stemmed roses by Ruth and Ella for my efforts.[18] Movie stars and prima donnas were the only people who I believed could be the recipients of this honor; it was as though I was being recognized as a real star. These two dedicated and selfless Indian teachers not only inspired me as a student, but we also became good friends and kept in touch after I left Haskell. Years later, in 1965, I saw Ella at the Episcopal National Advisory Committee on Indian Work at the Seabury House in Evanston, Illinois. She left the conference for a short time and later presented me with a red rose saying, "This is for my Hermia."

43

Ruth, in particular, was concerned that Bob Horne—my boyfriend—and I not lose track of each other. She hoped we would eventually marry and encouraged us to stay in touch with each other.

Another teacher who broadened my horizons for a lifetime was Miss Stella Robbins. She was the music teacher who gave me an appreciation not only of great music but of the background of the great composers. As part of my normal training, I chose not to take piano lessons from Miss Robbins, because she had the reputation of spanking hands if you didn't hit the right keys. I defeated myself by not taking advantage of this opportunity, because there were many times in my teaching career that I wished I knew how to play the piano. She was a compassionate woman, however. One spring I was the lead female soloist for the Easter cantata. I was to step out from the chorus for my solo, but I froze. I couldn't utter a single sound. She was aware that I was afflicted with stage fright, and she covered up for my dilemma by moving right on with the program. She never once alluded to this incident. I have often thought, "How very nice, how very kind." When my own students had problems expressing themselves, I tried to follow her example by showing a similar sympathy for them.

Very objectively, I didn't sense any discrimination among the employees at Haskell. That is not to say that some teachers did not have more empathy for their charges than others, but by and large they were a dedicated lot. I have the fondest memories of my Haskell teachers. They seemed to care about me and the other students there; they knew that they were our family, as well as our role models.

I really didn't intend to be a teacher. Two of my father's sisters were Bureau of Indian Affairs stenographers, and I thought that's what I would like to be. Our father held those two up as individuals who were professionally successful, and I aspired to be the same. When it was time to choose a vocation in my junior year, I chose to go into the business department. There was an overflow of students who had chosen business; too many for the spaces available. There were three of us who the department felt could catch up after they weeded out the weaker students, so they put us in the Normal Training Department. When it came time to take my place in the business department, I refused to switch. The head of the business department, W. T. Johnson, was a bit unhappy over my decision, but I had found my niche. I discovered that I wanted to be a teacher. I aspired to work with Indian youth, giving them the same nurturing and consideration that Ella and Ruth had given me.

Part of the training included methods and psychology classes and practice teaching. We did our student teaching in the lower grades, one to eight, at Haskell, so we had our classes right there to teach. For me, it was an opportunity to work with Indian kids, which is what I wanted to do. Miss Katherine Bargh was our student-teacher supervisor. She was a stickler for detail and perfection, giving special attention to our teaching and methods and our rapport with students. Miss Bargh is partially responsible for my success as a teacher.

HASKELL EVENTS

Other events throughout the year also created a pleasant atmosphere at the school. For example, there was a Halloween carnival every October. The rooms in the school building were decorated with goblins and witches and other weird Halloween decorations. Each classroom housed a different activity—like fish ponds and ring-toss and sponge throw. There was a house of horrors in one of the large rooms. We had all of the stuff like peeled grapes and coffins, and people jumped out at you. This was our entertainment for Halloween night—we got to stay up late and run around and throw all inhibitions to the wind. The teachers, of course, were our chaperones with a missionary zeal.

Christmas was even more exciting. We decorated our rooms and there was competition between the boys' and girls' dormitories. The boy officers judged the girl's room and vice versa. We used crepe paper and construction paper, silver icicles, and whatever else we could scrounge. There was a big tree in the assembly room that the students would decorate. Christmas was a joyous time of anticipation for us. Haskell was our home away from home, and everybody stayed on campus during the holidays. There were kids from all over the United States, including Alaska.

There would have been a great number of unhappy kids if some had gone home while others who couldn't afford to leave had had to stay. We were with our "school family" of friends. We missed our biological families but created our own holiday atmosphere. There were special events that replaced the academic routine for the holiday week—intramural games, club parties and movies, special assemblies, and Santa Claus with his special treats like candy and nuts, apples and oranges. Sometimes students exchanged Christmas gifts; one year I was the recipient of a box of chocolates that came from an unknown admirer.

I remember having so much fun one year after Christmas. A bunch of us girls spied some left-over Christmas candy in the home economics room when we were putting our sewing projects away. We discovered a bucket full of "pillar chocolates"—these were shaped like a cone—a little bit like a large candy kiss. We were elated! We filled our bloomers full of the candy and then snuck back to our rooms. It was not a very sanitary thing to do, but we didn't care! We shared the chocolates with our friends. They were mighty good, those "pillar chocolates."

At Christmastime, when some kids received large packages from home, we didn't receive any. I remember that my aunts—my father's sisters—did send us a fruitcake one Christmas; and then my last year at Haskell, when Finn and Helen and Gordon and I were there, we received a large holiday package. This was after my mother had remarried. We must have had the biggest box of anybody; it was filled with clothing and toys and even a doll buggy for Helen.

Sports and Saturdays at Haskell

The Haskell football team was nationally renowned for the excellence of its athletes. Although we were a high school–junior college, we played colleges like Oklahoma City University, University of Detroit, Loyola University (New Orleans), and Morningside College. During football season, and even throughout the rest of the year, football was an event of top priority for the students. We were a winning team and were enthusiastic supporters of the team's efforts. A home game brought many visitors from the surrounding area and as far away as Oklahoma. Most of the student body attended and got carried away in the excitement of the game.

A "gridgraph" was used to watch the progress of the games played away from home. I don't know if these were used anywhere but at government boarding schools, but a diagram of the playing field was projected onto a screen in the auditorium where we all gathered at game time. There was a movable light projected onto the graph of the field, and as plays were excitedly announced over the speaker system, the light—emblematic of the football—moved to demonstrate what plays were being made. The crowd went wild! We yelled feverishly and got just as excited as when we were watching our team play at home. I never did know how they received news of the plays, but I suppose it was by telegraph or telephone.

In an effort to keep the football players in good academic standing, especially when they had to be off-campus, some of us girls volunteered to help them with their assignments. It was a combination of hero worship, supporting the team, and resistance to the noncooperative boarding school system. They were expected to maintain excellence in their schoolwork in addition to excellence on the playing field. I remember how big Tiny Roebuck was, and how Miss Loretta Hurley grabbed him by the ear and got after him for not having his English assignment completed.[19] He could have picked her up and thrown her over his shoulder, but he had respect for her, and she was an excellent teacher. Football wasn't the only sport that we excelled in. Haskell's cross-country track team also established some enviable records. Our 1927 team was undefeated. They, too, competed against formidable universities. Basketball and baseball were also popular. During my tenure there, girls did not participate in athletics outside of physical education class.

It seems like boys had more freedom than girls. In addition to doing our homework, we girls would spend a lot of our spare time reading; I think I read nearly every book in the library. We wrote letters and played some board games. I remember getting into trouble one time because we had a Ouija board. We weren't allowed to play cards, either. There were no pho-nographs or radios in our dorm rooms at Haskell. Some of the girls knew how to do the Charleston, but we usually just danced in our rooms. We'd spend what little spare time we had visiting and singing together. "Janine" was a favorite song. There were never boy-girl dances at Haskell while I was there, but different departments like the Normal Training Department or the Officers Club had parties, and we could invite our boyfriends or girl-friends.

Our weekends were different. On Sundays, the high school kids would have watermelon socials when the weather was good. We'd walk around and around the bandstand in the center of campus, just visiting with each other. When the weather was bad, and in the winter, we stayed inside or had club get-togethers. We rode to town on the streetcar on some Saturdays, accom-panied by chaperones. If we had money, we could go to the movies. Some of us who worked odd jobs, such as housework or babysitting for the school employees, had money, and some of the students got money from home. I would share some of my earnings with Bernice and my brother since Mom didn't usually send money to us.

We didn't hear from home very often; sometimes it would be months at a time. My mother had not gone to a government boarding school, so she didn't seem to realize how important letters and packages were. I used to write home rather often, asking for money and talking about what we were doing at school, wishing that I could come home. I missed my mom so much, but she was not a person who wrote many letters. So, when I did re-ceive a letter from her, I really treasured it. Bernice and Gordon and I would read it over and over. Of course, Gordon was on the opposite side of the campus, and it was hard to get used to not being able to talk to your brother whenever you wanted. It was good at least that Bernice and I were together. Bernice did not stay at Haskell for more than a couple of years. She couldn't adjust to the school. She was so homesick that she was physically ill much of the time, and they finally sent her home. My mother did come to see us one time during my high school years. She got a pass from the Union Pacific Railroad, and she brought Finn and Helen with her to visit us. June was staying with an aunt at that time, so she didn't come to Haskell.

The Outing System and Summertime

Since the intent of the BIA system was to Americanize the Indian, we stayed at school twelve months out of the year. In the summer, the girls attended a YWCA camp called Lakeview for about two weeks. The boys attended a different camp. We had regular camp activities: arts and crafts, swimming, nature study, skits, and what have you. Those were happy times and a break in the routine. The remainder of the summer back at school followed the regular routine but with more leisure time. Our jobs were different, too; we might cut corn from the cob and put it on flats to dry for winter use or can foods for fall use.

If you were sixteen years old or older and had been a good citizen, you could be included in the summer outing program.[20] This gave us the opportunity to work and earn money during the summer months. We'd go to towns like Kansas City, Missouri, and Topeka, Lawrence, and Kansas City, Kansas. Our supervisor, Ruth Muskrat Bronson, located places of employment and introduced us to our prospective employers. She briefed them about our rules and regulations, and she checked on us once a month.

I went outing in Kansas City, Missouri, for two summers when I was a junior and a senior. The first summer I worked for a practical nurse and helped her take care of two infants whom she was boarding in her home. The next summer, 1928, I worked for a doctor and his wife as their downstairs maid, and I lived in my own private maid's quarters. I received thirty dollars a month wages. Half of that money was mine to spend as I saw fit, and the other half was sent back to school to be put in my account for spending during the school year. It was a wonderful and rewarding experience to have my own money to spend. The doctor's wife entertained at bridge every now and then, and she had cranberry glass goblets and other fancy dishes. I was petrified when I had to wash them, because I was afraid I would break one. If we broke something, we had to pay for it out of our wages.

This doctor and his wife had a black laundress; she came upstairs and, seeing my dilemma, offered to help me with the dishes. Afterward, we were eating lunch together and talking when the woman of the house came into the kitchen and informed me that I was not allowed to eat with the laundress, and she sent her back to the basement. That incident saddened me, because I had been raised to be kind to everyone and not to be discriminatory. I did eventually break something belonging to this woman. I broke a cranberry glass goblet, and I was afraid to tell her. When I did tell her, she thanked me for telling her and told me that I didn't have to pay for it. I wondered if she'd have done the same for the black laundress.

Ruth Bronson came to Kansas City once a month on our day off to meet with those of us who were in the outing program. If we had any problems with the person who was employing us, or if our employer had any problems with us, these could be resolved. We were always glad to see her; she brought us news from the campus and of our friends who were participating in the outing program in other areas. She always took the time to listen and give advice. Her enthusiasm and charisma made us laugh and gave us confidence in our abilities.

During my senior year, I accompanied Ruth Muskrat Bronson and other students to participate in programs that we presented to schools, to church groups, and to service organizations. Instrumental and vocal music, and talks relating to our Indian heritage, were a part of the programs we presented. This was my first exposure to public speaking. While on these tours, Ruth arranged for us to stay overnight in people's homes, to eat and to socialize with them. She took us beyond the confinement of the boarding school. Both Ruth and Ella wanted us to learn to survive in a variety of environments. They wanted us to be proud of who we were as Indian people and as boarding school students but also to be comfortable in explaining our identity to the non-Indian world. I suppose one could say that this was a "safe" way of being Indian, that is, according to the expectations of white society. But for us it was not this way. With Ruth and Ella as our Indian mentors, these excursions became an expression of our Indianness that may not otherwise have been possible, given the poverty and discrimination so prevalent on most reservations.

Way back then I was speaking about my relationship to Sacajawea. *The Kansas City Star* interviewed me and took my picture in a beautiful white, beaded buckskin costume that Ruth had loaned me for the occasion. The newspaper article appeared while I was in Kansas City, Missouri, working as the maid. I became an instant celebrity to my employer and was treated more like a star than a maid. My employer liked to show me off and introduce me to her friends, saying, "This is that pretty little Indian girl whose picture was in the newspaper." I was simultaneously embarrassed and flattered at the turn of events. I felt a little uncomfortable, but it was a definite boost for my ego.

A SUMMER AT HOME: 1928

When we finished high school at Haskell, the government paid our fare back home. I spent part of that summer in Kansas City but went home during the latter part of the season to be with my mother, who was still living in Green River. Helen and Finn were living with Mom and Bernice at home. She had moved from the apartment where we lived when Bernice and Gordon and I had gone away to school. My mother and Bernice were working at Y-Bings, a Chinese restaurant, at this time; they would have liked me to work there, too, but I chose to stay home and take care of the children and do the housekeeping. I cleaned the house thoroughly and wanted to keep it that way. I insisted that the children play outside, except for meals and to go to bed. I didn't want them messing up my clean house. My mother had to talk to me about how important it was for our house to be a home. She said to me, "Essie, it's their house! They need to live in it." I guess that the rigors of my Haskell training were not always in line with my mother's ideas.

After this incident, we had a rather pleasant summer except that we didn't know what had happened to June. A great sadness hung over our family, because we believed that June had been kidnapped. My mother had allowed her to spend time visiting with an acquaintance from Rock Springs, Wyoming. After several weeks of not hearing from this woman, my mother became very apprehensive and tried to get in touch with her; but she and her husband had left the state and taken June, who would have been about twelve years old, with them. Mother notified the police, who assured her they would locate June, but they never did. When I returned from Haskell, I immediately went to the police with a plea to help find my sister. They said they were aware of the situation, but my intuition told me that they hadn't done and weren't about to do much in the way of tracking her down. I really thought they didn't take me seriously because I was just another bothersome little Indian kid. It was a couple of years before I saw June again.

As it turned out, June had been taken to New Mexico by this woman and her husband. She was married by proxy to this woman's brother-in-law. I don't know exactly how this transpired—it's all quite strange. Be that as it may, June was pregnant at the age of thirteen. Her "husband" was convicted of embezzling money and sent to prison. June returned to Rock Springs, Wyoming, to live with her husband's mother, who was really quite nice in spite of her black sheep son. June wrote to me, and I went to visit her during a summer vacation. She seemed to be pretty happy with Grandma Moss, who took good care of her and the baby. I remember Junie asking why everyone at the hospital was so interested in the birth of her Buddy. I said, "Junie, you were a baby having a baby."

While Haskell was fashioning me into a respectable young woman of the twenties, there were still times when my more adventurous side came out. A friend of Gordon's owned a little racing car that he called "the bug," and he was always trying to get Bernice and me to go for a drive with him around the Green River Palisades. Steve's father owned the biggest pool hall in town; it was on the other side of the tracks, in a red-light district. Bernice and I were reluctant since Steve had the reputation of being a daring driver, but Gordon kept coaxing us to take a ride until we finally agreed. Steve did not start speeding until we were on our way back home. The Palisades road is twisty and windy with steep banks on the river side of the road, and Steve was driving that car as fast as he could. We had just come off of the last curve when the car rolled and luckily threw all four of us out of the vehicle.

I thought we were going to be killed and was very grateful that we weren't all broken up in pieces. I slid through the gravel and dirt and sagebrush for a few yards, and my left thigh was quite badly torn up, but nobody else was hurt too badly. I was so mad at Gordon, I said, "I knew this was going to happen, but you wouldn't listen to me!" I never did tell my mother. I was afraid that I'd be sent to the hospital and miss out on returning to school. I doctored it myself and kept it clean, but it festered and got infected just the same. Later that fall, Miss Ritter noticed that I was limping and sent me to the nurse at school. The infection was so bad that it did not clear up quickly, but I was not going to chance not returning to Haskell, which had become my home by then.

RETURN TO HASKELL

I had already made up my mind to go back to Haskell for junior college, even before I returned home that summer. My growing concern for Finn's and Helen's welfare led me to spend my summer formulating plans to take them with me when I returned to Haskell. The situation at home had worsened since I had been away at school. Finn and Helen, who were about five and seven years old, were at loose ends. While Mother and Bernice were at work, there was no one at home to care for them. Meals were irregular, and they were neglected. They had to scrounge for food, and I was worried about them. I pleaded with my mother to allow them to accompany me. I promised they would be well taken care of and receive a good education. I knew that it was difficult for her to care for them while she and Bernice were both working. Allowing me to take them with me would relieve her of worry. She finally conceded and paid their fare.

When the three of us arrived in Lawrence, I simply called the school to have them send someone to pick us up. The superintendent, Mr. Clyde M. Blair, was not expecting this entourage. I introduced him to Helen and Finn and said they were my little brother and sister. I told him I had talked my mother into letting me bring them to school because I wanted so badly for them to obtain a good education. They did not have completed applications from the tribe, but he let them stay and did the paperwork with the agency to get them enrolled. I had worked for Mr. and Mrs. Blair, cleaning their house, so they knew me real well. Years later, Mr. Blair told me he would never forget the image of me standing there holding the hands of those two little children. He said, "I would have moved heaven and earth to honor your request."

Finn was only five years old, and it must have been a real challenge to the school personnel to fit a child so young into the boarding school scheme of things. He stayed in the girls' dormitory and was cared for by the matrons and myself for a while. The personnel pampered him, and the three of us were allowed to spend many hours together. I knew they were lonesome for Mother and for home and that they didn't know me too well. They seemed to adjust quickly, however, to the new routines. Heralding back to many of the harsh tales rampant about the boarding schools, this occurrence is an example of the compassion and concern that was present among many of the employees.

The boarding school provided a safe environment for me. The reason it was such a positive experience was that I had security there. You see, I had security in my home until my father died, but after that we were never sure of where our next meal would come from. We didn't always have as much to eat as we needed, and we weren't eating very healthy food. My mother was grieving, and there wasn't much security in our house. She wasn't home much, and we were left to pretty much fend for ourselves. We would hear fighting or yelling or drunken arguments outside the apartment and were frightened of what might happen to the six of us.

I think, too, that the sense of community at Haskell was very strong. Among Indian people this is very important. We had a pride in our school and in our teams, and we had such a strong school spirit. We were so proud to be associated with Haskell. Most of us who are alumni of Indian boarding schools feel a great pride and sense of belonging to a unique and special group of people—people who we keep in touch with and who have become part of our extended families. Even though boarding schools took children away from their homes, families, and communities, we created our own community at the school. We were proud of our accomplishments and proud that we had retained so much of our Indianness. Critics dismiss boarding schools as assimilationist institutions whose intent was to destroy Native culture. While this may be a true generalization, the students and teachers at Haskell will forever be an integral part of who I am as an American Indian.

CHAPTER FOUR

The Move to Eufaula, Oklahoma, and Marriage, 1929–1930

Leaving Haskell brought home to Essie the real security of the boarding school and the sense of family developed there. Her memory of beginning to teach in an Indian school emphasizes her commitment to add to the positive experience Indian children would have at boarding schools. In many ways this is like a multitude of stories of a first job and the need for an emerging professional to prove herself in an initial situation. Here, of course, the story is complicated by the fact that a new teacher is one of very few Indians actually teaching other Native Americans.

Essie's story is not solely that of proving her own value in the cultural setting in which she finds herself. It exemplifies the larger story of Native American emergence into the mainstream culture without a concomitant loss of the Indian culture.

Essie's story is also the story of pan-Indianism, an unplanned child of the BIA. As a teacher of Indians, Essie was exposed to a variety of Native American cultures outside of her own, as well as to the style of Anglo supervision and administration. It's the story of a young adult secretly keeping her cultural heritage alive and of a young woman marrying her high school sweetheart—an Indian from thousands of miles away.

EUFAULA CREEK GIRLS BOARDING SCHOOL:
FIRST TEACHING EXPERIENCE

There was a great need for teachers in the Bureau of Indian Affairs schools and few qualified personnel to fill them. Soon after my arrival back at Haskell, I was recruited to take a position at a boarding school for Creek girls in Eufaula, Oklahoma. It was called the Eufaula Boarding School. Miss Ritter, the head girl's adviser, had a going-away party for me before I left. That would have been in February 1929. She invited Helen and Gordon and Finn to her apartment in the girl's dormitory and made a delicious meal; I've often thought how nice that was of her. It was not something she had to do, but she knew that I was leaving my family behind and that we were all sad to be parting. That was her way of making the parting less traumatic, and I shall always be grateful for her thoughtful concern and kindness.

Leaving Haskell was very traumatic, particularly because I was leaving security. The notion existed that Indian students went to the boarding school and became so secure in their environment that they didn't want to be pushed out of the nest. I don't really think that was true for the majority of the enrollees. It certainly wasn't true of me. Like anyone leaving security, we were ambivalent and apprehensive about the unknown, but part of our training had been to meet and welcome challenges. I was hired to teach the first and second grades, but my preference would have been to teach fourth to sixth grade. Traveling to Eufaula, Oklahoma, by train was uneventful, although I continued to worry about Finn and Helen, who had just arrived at Haskell.

Miss Elmira Morley, the superintendent at the Eufaula Boarding School, and Lucille Carpenter, a former fellow Haskell student, met me at the depot. Seeing a familiar face softened the lonely feelings. At Eufaula I roomed and boarded in what was commonly known as The Club. This building housed unmarried employees. At this Creek girl's boarding school, all the personnel were female, including the principal, Miss Amanda Eld, and Miss Morley. They were austere looking and very straight-laced, but later I came to appreciate having begun my career under such strict and exacting bosses. We had to sign out to go off-campus and sign in on our return. The deadline to be back in our quarters was midnight. An infringement of the rules resulted in our being called to task. These rigid rules surprised me, because I was under the impression that I had left these harsh disciplines behind.

Shortly after my arrival, Lucille Carpenter overheard a conversation between Miss Morley and Miss Eld about me. They remarked, "Miss Burnett won't last very long; she's just a baby." I suppose they dismissed me as being incapable of doing the job because I was young, and I was very young looking. I was, in fact, nineteen years old. Lucille and I decided that we would make them eat their words, and we did! I worked very hard to be an outstanding teacher. I was the only Indian teacher, and I was not going to be a failure. I was not going to let my alma mater down; I was not going to let my Indian people down; and I was not going to let my family down. I wanted both sides of my family, both the Indian and non-Indian, to be proud of me. I had a lot of energy and a strong desire to succeed. Part of that was the way I was raised, and a great deal of it was my Haskell education, especially the teachings of Ruth Muskrat Bronson and Ella Deloria. I wasn't afraid, and I didn't feel inferior to the other teachers. My classroom and my students were testimonial to my success, and I suppose I felt that way all of my life.

My classroom at Eufaula was a very large room situated above the laundry. I had about thirty-five first- and second-graders about evenly divided as to number. Once in a while we felt the vibrations of the laundry machinery below us, but it didn't bother us a great deal. Fortunately, most of my students were quite normal first- and second-graders.

There was a mixture of bright and motivated learners, as well as reluctant participants. Some of the students were overage, that is, they were ten- or twelve-year-old second-graders, having begun school late. A few students came to our school with a limited knowledge of English, having grown up in homes where Creek was the first language. These girls required more attention, and due to the large class size, I had to be creative in discovering a solution to help these and all of my students out. I initiated the practice of peer tutoring: children helping children. Those who were bilingual (Creek and English) came to the aid of those who spoke no English at all. They translated the children's needs to me and encouraged them to become more proficient in the English language. This cooperative educational effort was a success, and my horizons were broadened in this first teaching experience. I had constantly to monitor and praise the efforts of the teacher-learner team, so as to avoid overbearing or bullying behavior, which was rare but did occur.

My introduction to Creek Freedmen occurred at the Eufaula Boarding School. There were some students in my classroom who appeared to be of black ancestry. I checked their applications and noted that they were listed as Creek Freedmen. When I inquired of Miss Eld what this meant, she told me that they were the offspring of former black slaves of the Creek Indians. After emancipation they had become enrolled members of the Creek tribe with all of the rights and privileges of their Indian owners.

Another of my students, Eulalah Weaver, had black features and red kinky hair. The principal told me that this girl was an octoroon, and when I asked what this meant, she said it referred to someone of one-eighth Negroid ancestry. I have always wondered why we are so intent on dividing up the human species according to blood quantum. I don't remember that there was any fighting or quarreling among the students who were all Indian, mixed-blood, or black.

One of my first trials and tribulations was Janey. She was an overeater and would stuff herself and then come to class and regurgitate all over the floor. After several of these sessions, I discussed her problem with the school nurse, who asked the food service to regulate her food intake. We were finally spared not only the clean-up but the sickening odor and disruption.

One of the most embarrassing experiences of my life occurred at the Eufaula Boarding School. Our principal always wore a white silk dress to Sunday dinner. On these occasions, I was on my best behavior, trying to be prim and proper and mindful of my table manners. My first Sunday meal turned into a disaster. I was trying to carve my steak when it sailed off my plate across the table and landed in Miss Eld's lap. A look of disbelief came over her face, and then she became livid with anger. I was speechless and terror-stricken, and I apologized profusely. "Some people are really clumsy," she sneered as she mopped the gravy off the front of her dress with her cloth napkin. I offered to have her dress cleaned—it was the only way I knew to right this wrong. She refused my offer, and I thought, "Well, I have reinforced her impressions of me as an unschooled Indian." I can laugh at the memory now, but at the time, I was not sure if I would ever live it down.

On another occasion, after a particularly delicious meal in the club, I walked into the kitchen to compliment the cook. Miss Morley really called me on the carpet for that; she summoned me to her office and stated, "Miss Burnett, we do not associate with or talk to the colored cooks, and I ask you to refrain from this practice in the future." This baffled and saddened me. These discriminatory instructions from Miss Morley were part of my orientation to the proper behavior expected of Eufaula employees. I chalked up her remarks to ignorance and to the part of the country that we were in.

My supervisors would also have been dismayed if they had learned that one of my most enjoyable off-campus activities was Creek Stomp Dancing with former Haskell acquaintances. We held these dances in a secluded wooded area, beginning in the early evening. The dance took place around a large fire; the lead dancer chanted and the rest of the dancers, male and female, answered. I vaguely remember that some of the dancers wore turtle-shell rattles on their ankles, shawls, and various kinds of costumes. There were large numbers of dancers in the circle.

Although I'm Shoshone and they were Creek, I felt a really strong kinship with them. Through the intertribal network at Haskell, we had learned each other's culture, and we developed a healthy respect for each other's vision. Had I been caught engaging in this "heathen" activity, I quite certainly would have been fired. The aim of the Indian Service was to divorce our people from our heritage and to assimilate us into the dominant culture. I was not in sympathy with this endeavor, and I taught my Creek students to have a pride in themselves as individuals and a respect for their heritage. I tried to follow the example of Ruth and Ella, my Indian mentors at Haskell. My relationship to the Bird Woman seemed to follow me to Eufaula, and even though I didn't discuss it, I was regularly introduced as Sacajawea's great-great-granddaughter. This connection made my Indianness more palatable to my white employers. I am proud of my heritage but dismayed that most elements of our culture and traditions were held in such low esteem.

My first paycheck was eighty dollars—that was a month's wages! This seemed like a small fortune to me, and of course the dollar went a great deal further at that time. The first item I purchased with my paycheck was a new dress and matching accessories. For the first time in my life, I felt very adult, very sophisticated, and very rich. The second thing I did with my money was to send gifts to my siblings, who were still in boarding school at Haskell. I remembered the years of not receiving many letters or packages from home, and I made a pact with myself that Finn and Helen and Gordon were not going to be in the same situation.

MARRIAGE

Bob Horne had been my high school sweetheart at Haskell.[1] He left Haskell six months before I did, to take a position in the power plant at the Wahpeton Indian School in North Dakota. This was, to use a trite phrase, a case of "absence makes the heart grow fonder." We corresponded and our letters grew more torrid. We had an understanding before he left for Wahpeton that we would get married in a couple of years.

When I was on outing in Kansas City, Bob had come to visit me a couple of times. Since he was on outing on a farm in Topeka, Kansas, the distance was not so great. On one of our dates we went to see the film *Ramona*, which was a love story.[2] I wish I could remember the words of the theme song, because they were Bob's proposal to me. This was one of the first times we had been together off-campus. As we sat together, he tenderly placed his arm around my neck, and I rested my head on his shoulder. He squeezed me and whispered the words of the love song that was being shown on the screen. He said, "I love you and I want you to be my own." That was his proposal of marriage to me. I thought it was quite an original proposal, so the song "Ramona" has always had a special place in my heart.

Not long after I moved away from the confines of Haskell to Eufaula, Bob wrote saying he had sent me a diamond engagement ring and that I should receive it by Valentine's Day. February 14 came and went, and still no ring. I was perplexed and thought, "He can't be joking about something so serious and meaningful!" He said that he wasn't, so we decided to have it traced. We waited and waited, but the ring could not be found. Then one day, I got a phone call from the Eufaula Post Office, asking me to come down. There was a young black woman sitting in the postmaster's office holding a small package.

The postman said, "Miss Burnett, this young woman has the same name as you do." He relieved her of the package and turning to me said, "Do you recognize this handwriting?" "Yes, that's my fiancé's handwriting and address." The postmaster asked the other Esther Burnett why she would keep a ring that she didn't think belonged to her, and she said, "I thought somebody was playing a joke on me." Be that as it may, I finally received my ring and later teased Bob about his short engagement to the other Miss Burnett.

That next summer, Bob and I took our vacations from our respective jobs, he from Wahpeton and I from Eufaula. That would have been August of 1929. We met in Kansas City, Missouri, intending to spend some time together visiting Haskell and seeing some of our old friends. But as we talked about September and the beginning of a new school year, the thought of being separated again was unbearable. We were afraid we might lose each other and that our feelings for each other might change, although we were very much in love.

So, we decided that we would get married in Kansas City and then return to our places of employment. We thought that being married would help us feel close when we were miles apart. I wasn't very keen about being married by a justice of the peace, and I insisted that we be married by a minister. We decided to ask the justice of the peace if he could find a minister to perform the marriage ceremony. So that's what we did; we were married in the office of the justice of the peace, but a minister was there to hear our vows. So I was satisfied; I really felt married then.

I bought a special salmon-colored dress for my wedding; if I hadn't spent so much money on that dress, Bob wouldn't have had to hop a freight back to Wahpeton. We stayed at a hotel in Kansas City for about a week on our honeymoon, and then we went to Lawrence, Kansas, to visit some of our friends at Haskell. One of the first people we went to see was Ruth Muskrat Bronson, and she said, "I am so thrilled that you got married. Where are you staying?" Ruth was an incurable romantic and often cautioned us not to lose track of each other.

We had a feeling that she felt a great joy in seeing that her matchmaking had paid off. She said, "I'm going to Oklahoma to visit John (her husband) for a couple of weeks, and I want you kids to stay in my apartment and spend the rest of your honeymoon there." So we did. We didn't have any wild parties in Ruth's apartment, and it was nice not to have to go to a hotel but rather to be on campus where we had fallen in love and where we had shared so many happy memories and exciting times.

After our honeymoon, we were pretty low on money, and it was time to return to work; but before we left we went to see our old Haskell superintendent, Mr. C. M. Blair, to tell him we were married. He congratulated us and said to Bob, "And now what are you going to do? Here you are married and Essie is teaching in Oklahoma and you're working in North Dakota." "Essie," he asked, "are you going to quit your job and go with Bob?" I said, "No, I want to continue teaching." He thought that was kind of unusual, but he said that he would do all that he could to arrange it so that we could be together. Mr. Blair called Wahpeton to tell them that Bob and I were married, and he asked if there was any possibility of my being employed there.

There happened to be a fourth grade teacher at Wahpeton who was anxious to transfer to a school where she could teach the lower grades. The two schools were sympathetic to the newlyweds' dilemma and so agreed to allow us to exchange positions. I returned to Eufaula in mid-August and worked until mid-February, when final arrangements were made for my transfer. By that time, Miss Eld had decided that since I hadn't destroyed any more of her dresses, that I must be okay, and she was sorry to see me go. Both Miss Morley and Miss Eld were complimentary about my rapport with my Creek students and with my performance in the classroom. I was sad to be leaving my students and new friends and the state of Oklahoma but excited to be joining my beloved.

Before I left Eufaula to go to Wahpeton, Miss Eld, the principal, and the nurse, Mrs. Powell, had a farewell party and a wedding shower for me. The teachers were all there, and they brought gifts. Miss Eld gave me a lovely lace buffet set; I was very pleased to receive that from her, because I was never sure if she had forgiven me for soiling her white dress with my steak. I also received a carving set—a reminder from my peers to be more cautious when I cut my meat.

My mother was very unhappy to learn that I had gotten married so soon after graduating. I'm sure that she felt that this was the end of my professional career and that I would settle down and become a housewife. She and my father always had dreamed that we girls would continue our schooling until we became professional people.

CHAPTER FIVE

The Wahpeton Years, 1930s–1950s

Pursuing her career as a teacher of Native American children, Essie moved to North Dakota to be with her new husband and began teaching at the Wahpeton Indian School. She was the only Indian teacher at the school, and she strove to bring the positive side of boarding school life to her students. Again, the boarding school experience as revealed in this personal testimony confounds the long-held opinion that these schools were completely destructive institutions.

As a teacher, Essie became more of a parent figure in a constructed family of students who spent all year at the school, just as she had experienced the familial support of Haskell as a child in the school family when she was a student there.

The anti-Indian sentiment of earlier times was on the wane during this period of the life history. New attitudes are in evidence in Essie's ability to reinforce the values of the Indian nations represented by her students. Her teaching expands its multicultural emphasis and encourages students to remember and describe their "other" homes on the reservations. Indian cultural identity is valued. American activities are engaged in, Indian style.

Essie's life includes continuing education in diverse Native American studies, where her experience of and ultimate acceptance by mainstream population is a cameo of the larger society's evolving reevaluation of Native Americans individually, as well as of their cultures generally.

This continuing education for Essie is not entirely formal. Her ongoing education with and advocacy of Native American cultural values show up in her exposure to more Native Americans in visits to her husband's Hoopa relatives in California, attendance at Sun Dances, a visit to the Indian village at the 1933 World's Fair, trips to the Southwest, the development of Indian clubs at the school, and many other activities.

This section of the life history gives a view of the experience of the Depression in a boarding school and how a strong woman could succeed in the radical experiment of keeping her job while raising children. Essie's experience of World War II as a Native American seems virtually identical to that of any other American. Men volunteered; women went to work, learned self-sufficiency, and survived rationing. Families lost relatives and suffered with their returned soldiers over the traumas of conflict. Everyone had to adjust after the war.

The decades from the 1930s to the 1950s saw immense changes nationally and internationally. Against this background, the perception of Native Americans by the majority culture, as well as by Indians themselves, was also changing radically. Essie's experiences give a picture of this time from one woman's perspective, but it is a viewpoint that also provides a glimpse into the larger worlds beyond it.

THE EARLY PERIOD, 1930–1934

Introduction to Wahpeton

My introduction to the students and staff at the Wahpeton Indian School was at the Sunday evening assembly program. When Bob and I walked in, it felt like the whole group turned as one to stare at us. As it turned out, many of the older girls had a crush on Bob and were curious to see what his new wife looked like. While there were a number of Indian people on the school staff, I was the only Indian teacher. Bob's position at the school was as power plant fireman, and we lived in the old cottage that had been used for shoe repair.

There were two bedrooms; Bob and I had one, and another employee had the other. We shared a living room, kitchen, and bath. We didn't cook in our place except for on weekends. That first year, our place became a gathering spot for young Indian employees. For Sunday evening get-togethers, we all took our turns providing a main dish for our evening meal. Occasionally, we would cook our Native American specialties: Irving Shepard, a member of the Tlingit tribe, would make clam chowder; I would cook fried pheasant, and others would cook frybread. It tasted so good. We were the only young married couple on campus, and we became close friends with other new and old Indian employees.[1]

On my first day of teaching duties, the principal accompanied me to my classroom. There were about three dozen fourth-grade students, pretty evenly divided between boys and girls. When the students were settled, the principal said to me, "Mrs. Horne, if there is any foolishness in this room, or if you have any trouble with any of these students, just send them to the office." He meant what he said. I just as definitely said, "Yes, I will!" The size of the students amazed me.[2] I had been teaching first- and second-graders, and these were fourth-graders, many of whom were teenagers. Some had started school late, and others lived too far from a school to attend on any regular basis, so in those days this was a common occurrence.

The Bureau of Indian Affairs course of studies was comparable to that used by the public schools. The subject matter included reading, penmanship, English, math, geography, history, and science. I talked to the kids after the principal left, and I said, "We're all Indians in this room. So let's make our classroom the best classroom at Wahpeton. We can do this if we help each other. If you will help me and if you will be responsible for your own behavior, we'll be successful."

Gene Tunney, a Turtle Mountain Chippewa, was one of the first to challenge my discipline in the classroom. "Gene Tunney," that was the nickname by which everyone called this boy. He was big, and he was a school boxer. Gene Tunney was the name of a famous prize fighter of that time, and this student was built like him and acted like him. There were rules and regulations about asking to leave the room, having your assignments done on time, and that kind of thing. He was making a point of not finishing his assignments, and when I got down on him for not handing in his homework, he said to me, "Mrs. Horne, what are you going to do about it?"

I replied, "Well, why are you asking me what I'm going to do about it; what are you going to do about it? Would you like to go to the principal's office? You can either go talk to Mr. Wallon about it, or you can decide that you are going to be a responsible member of this group." Students weren't generally anxious to go see the principal because he was a tough disciplinarian and would intimidate them physically and verbally. Tunney looked at me for a long time, deciding how he would respond. He had to decide whether cooperating would rob him of his macho image.

Somehow, and I don't know exactly why, he decided to turn over a new leaf and become a responsible class member. Maybe he had never considered that there might be reason to be proud of an all-Indian classroom. Fortunately, not only did he become responsible for himself, but he also made sure that no other boys gave me problems. Given his size, all he had to do was glare at potential troublemakers and they would settle down. I think that I gained his respect by not backing down from his bullying style, and we both developed a mutual respect for each other.

Besides being responsible for our own classroom, teachers were also assigned study hall duty in the evening. On one occasion during study hall, I noticed a recent enrollee taking something out of his hair and putting it in the pencil tray on his desk. Being the curious person that I am, I wandered around in back of him and discovered that he was picking lice out of his hair and carefully placing them in the pencil tray. We both watched them crawl around for a while. Needless to say, he was sent immediately to the boy's adviser to be cleaned up.

On another occasion, one of the inkwells was full of gook, and it soon became apparent that someone had spit snuff in the inkwell. I found out who the culprit was and informed the principal, who brought this twenty-one-year-old eighth-grader to my room to apologize. He said he was sorry, and then Mr. Wallon the principal said, "Do you know what your mouth reminds me of when you chew Copenhagen? It reminds me of a chicken's butt." We were both thoroughly embarrassed. I felt that this remark by the principal was very unprofessional, certainly more so back in those days than now; but I shan't ever forget it.

Occasionally, a student from Wahpeton would run away from school, but it was not a frequent event. Mr. Wallon was a strict disciplinarian, and the children were afraid of him. One time in the early 1930s, three of the older eighth-grade girls went AWOL, and Mr. Wallon went out with his car to find them. Next thing we knew he was driving on campus "trotting" those young women behind his car. He had tied them at intervals on a heavy rope, which was attached to his vehicle. The staff couldn't believe their eyes, and as soon as the superintendent got wind of this, well, he terminated that principal's services immediately. While this kind of disregard for student welfare might have been tolerated in the early days of the boarding schools, it was not an accepted disciplinary measure at this time. We all were shocked at his insensitivity and were glad to see him go.

About this time, an educational specialist from the BIA's Washington DC office discovered that there was an Eastern Shoshone teaching at the Wahpeton Indian School. He thought I should be transferred to my own reservation, since I was one of the only government service Shoshone teachers at that time. He sent a written directive through Superintendent Carl Stevens to notify me of an impending transfer from Wahpeton to the Wind River Elementary School in Fort Washakie, Wyoming. I said I wouldn't go. I said it wouldn't be fair to the students *there* because many were related to me in one way or another. It would be difficult for me to be impartial—parents and kids alike would have expected special treatment. It would also have been unfair to *me*. My acceptance or rejection would not have been based on my abilities or skills but on how well I could manipulate the system. It would have been a political nightmare.

As a product of the boarding school, I had a deep-seated desire to continue teaching at the Wahpeton Indian School and to instill in these kids a sense of their dignity and worth as individuals. I wanted to continue to integrate Native American materials into the curriculum. While I knew that I could do this at Wind River, I had a special place in my heart for these Indian kids who were far away from home. I wanted to provide them with the same security and sense of self that my Indian teachers, Ruth and Ella, had instilled in me.

This argument didn't satisfy the BIA hierarchy, and they sent a specialist out to Wahpeton to try to change my mind. When I explained to him how I felt, he was sympathetic to my concerns. He had experienced the same dilemma when he returned to his small midwestern hometown to teach. His close relationships with the townspeople created disciplinary and academic problems in his first position. It was finally decided that I could stay where I was in Wahpeton.

There were about four hundred students at Wahpeton, and by this time students went to school all day. Our classes were very large—usually at least thirty students were assigned to each teacher. Once I had a class of fifty-two students, and the classroom was so crowded that I had bruises on my legs from bumping into the desks. I had the students work with and help each other. A proficient math or reading student tutored a classmate deficient in that area. In class we discussed the strengths and weaknesses of each other to prevent students from stereotyping one another as stupid or smart.

Summers at Wahpeton

Students also stayed at Wahpeton for twelve months out of the year at that time. Parents who were unable to care for children during the school year did not have any easier time during the summer months, so the rule was that our students stayed year-round. In the summer, we made frequent visits to the nearby Minnesota lakes, and I particularly remember Sunset Beach on Otter Tail Lake as a favorite of the kids. We transported the children to the lake, and the kitchen personnel prepared a great picnic lunch for us to take. Activities for the outing included softball, sack races, three-legged races, the fifty-yard dash, and other competitions. We'd also rent boats and swim and have a great time.

Some students took academic classes in the summer if they were weak in a particular area. We also had big gardens, Holstein milk cows, pigs, some grain fields, and so forth. The students and staff were expected to help out with the farm chores. So, during the summer, it was our duty to supervise and assist students in the planting, weeding, and harvesting of the gardens. The kitchen and dining room personnel were in charge of canning the garden produce, and the older girls and teachers helped with this endeavor. The huge vegetable gardens were used as a teaching tool. We sold some of the produce to local townspeople and worked side by side with the students, pulling weeds, hoeing, harvesting, and canning. I became even more adept at cleaning and cutting chickens, a skill I had learned in home economics classes at Haskell. One time the head cook at Wahpeton offered to teach me how to clean and cut chicken, but I said, "I already know; I learned that at Haskell." She was Indian too and had gone to a boarding school, so she challenged me to a chicken-cutting contest; much to her surprise and mine, I won! That feat certainly gained me some stature at Wahpeton.

Another thing, too, that we teachers did in the summertime was to sand the desks and tables in the classroom and whitewash some of the walls. We felt fortunate if we were requested to mend library books because it meant that we might not have to assist with the sanding. The hand sanders were heavy and hard to handle; I hated that sanding. In this particular era the Wahpeton Indian School was like an island unto itself because of the farm, the dairy, the bakery, the laundry, and all of the other things that contributed to our self-sufficiency. This was both good and bad for the school: We felt proud that we were surviving on our own, but we were also isolated from the surrounding community.

Poverty and the School Family

The isolation of the boarding school in the 1930s was also magnified by the fact that there was not a lot of visiting by parents during this time. The economy was so bad, and the students' parents so poor, that few could afford to visit their children with any regularity. The personnel at the school, therefore, had to work to create a home environment for the students. One of the ways that I tried to do that was through my fourth-grade art class. I encouraged my students to draw scenes related to their home environments. The scenes that they created really did two things. They gave the students a chance to reminisce about home and express their thoughts and feelings concretely on paper, and they provided me, the teacher, the opportunity to gain insight into their lives and broaden my horizons about the varied tribal cultures that Wahpeton students represented.

There were tribes from North Dakota, South Dakota, Minnesota, Nebraska, Iowa, Montana, and Wyoming, including Sioux, Chippewa, Cree, Blackfeet, Gros Ventre, Mandan, Hidatsa, Arikara, Mesquakie, Winnebago, Cheyenne, and Shoshone. When BIA supervisors came along, I was very adept at sweeping the Indian components under the table, so to speak. The philosophy of the boarding school was still to assimilate Indian children into mainstream American culture.

The creation of these reservation scenes evolved into a lot of after-school visiting in our room. We talked about differences in tribal regalia, dance, and language, and learned about each other's tribal cultures. We listened to a set of phonograph records of Indian music collected from all over the United States and Canada, and we got lonesome for home.[3]

We felt comfortable together because of our shared history and heritage, and we talked about pets and siblings and life. We visited about our homes and relatives, and frequently about folks we knew in common. I had gotten to know a lot of Indian families from across the United States through my friends at Haskell, and this created a bond between the students and myself. I tried to make Wahpeton a home away from home for these students, who attended the boarding school for a variety of reasons. Some lived in isolated areas that were too far from the public schools for them to attend; some were children in crisis; while others were there out of economic necessity. Many were incredibly shy, perhaps because of an unpleasant discriminatory experience—common during this period.

Few students had telephones in their homes, and so they had no idea how to use a phone. There were *so* many experiences that teachers would assume were familiar to their students, but all too often our Wahpeton kids had no idea what we were talking about. It was important that *all* teachers not assume that most students shared in a mainstream cultural knowledge.

Having an occasional Shoshone student and being in the northern plains area again made me feel as if I was close to home. But North Dakota is not Wyoming, and I did hate the flat, flat land at first. When I saw the clouds, I tried to imagine they were mountains or hills. Kansas had some rolling hills, even around Lawrence, but not North Dakota. As far as your eye could see for miles and miles, it was flat. The mirages created by this landscape were interesting and fascinating to me during those first years in North Dakota. We'd be traveling along and think we were coming to water, and here it was only a mirage on the road. I had never seen mirages before. The first few winters were frightening, with those plains blizzards and all. Of course I was used to snow from Idaho and Wyoming, but here it got cold and stayed cold, and the snow piled up and the temperatures moved down. After several years, I got used to the winters and became fascinated with the beauty of the plains and the waving wheat.

You know, some of this time encompassed the Dust Bowl Days and there were no jobs.[4] The reservations, already pockets of poverty, were hard hit during those years. If you didn't live through it, it is hard to imagine. The first summer I was in Wahpeton, in 1930, dust and dirt drifted like snow around fence lines, and we had to wet sheets in the bathtub to put on the windows of our quarters to keep the dust from sifting through the frames. Many people became afflicted with dust pneumonia, which occurred when too much dust got into their upper respiratory systems. The grasshoppers ate the foliage off the trees and even ate the ivy off the buildings. Grasshoppers were just lying on tree limbs in the dust, having eaten up nearly every bit of vegetation. At least we were employed.

On the reservation, life was particularly bleak and depressing during this time. Bob and I kept in touch with a lot of our friends from Haskell, many of whom had returned to their home reservations. I kept in touch with Rose La Framboise, who had gone back to her home at the Turtle Mountain Reservation in northern North Dakota. Bob and I went to visit her around 1930. We were all saddened by the living conditions there. She was living in a log cabin with a dirt floor, and some of the windows did not have glass in them. I remember that she had tacked some cloth across them to keep the elements out. The economy was so bad then. There was no way for anyone to make any money, and there were no jobs except for a few part-time positions on ranches or farms. It was so hard for me to see my best friend, Rose, in such poverty.

Health Care

During my first ten years at Wahpeton (1930–40), there were few serums to combat the spread of disease, and we had many flu, chicken pox, and measles epidemics. There was a small hospital at the school, and we had traveling doctors to perform surgeries such as tonsillectomies. There were also contract doctors from the town of Wahpeton who could be called in the event of a medical emergency. We also had a nurse and an assistant nurse stationed right at the school. When there were more kids in the hospital than there were in the classroom, one of the dormitories would be turned into a hospital and the teachers were required to become medical assistants; the nurse would tell us what to do. Students who were very ill would be taken to the hospital in downtown Wahpeton or in extreme cases to Fargo. I can only remember a few deaths during my teaching time at Wahpeton.

Tuberculosis was still relatively common. Generally, students who contracted TB would be sent to the Sioux Sanatorium in Rapid City or Ah-gwah-ching near Walker, Minnesota. We watched our students carefully for any signs of abnormal health so as to avoid a breakout of these enervating epidemics. Being a teacher in the bureau in those days required a great deal of ingenuity and the learning of practical skills. We had to be disciplined and dependable. Those kids relied on us to be there when they needed a nurse, a parent, a friend, or a confidant. I always tried to be loyal to those students—we were like family.

Incidental to health care issues, I started smoking when I was twenty-four years old. I had what I thought was a severe cold, and so I went to see the local doctor in Wahpeton because I couldn't shake the symptoms of this cold. He asked me, "Have you ever had hay fever?" I said, "No, but I used to laugh at a fellow teacher in Oklahoma because she sneezed all the time!"

Tests he gave me determined that I did indeed have allergies that caused hay fever. He said, "Now mind you, I'm not prescribing this, but some of my patients who have hay fever get relief from smoking mentholated cigarettes." I thought, "I'll do anything to get relief!" He was right; it did help. The mentholated cigarettes not only gave me relief, but they also caused me to become addicted to them. I smoked for many years until I realized that smoking was hazardous to my health and those around me.

The Uniform

There was still some military regimen at Wahpeton—we still had company formation—but marching and military uniforms had become passé by about 1929. Everyday clothing was still provided by the government. Girls still wore blue "paper-doll" shaped hickory dresses that were flat so they would go through the mangle easily, and boys wore plain blue shirts. Gradually, these gave way to variation in color and style. Much of this was a result of the influence of Dr. Willard Beatty, director of education of the Bureau of Indian Affairs from 1936 to 1951. He had a deep respect for Native American culture and believed not only that Indian children need not lose their culture but also that it could be perpetuated in the boarding school setting.

This was what I had always believed and secretly taught. I taught about Indian place names and states in geography, about the Trail of Tears and President Jackson, and about Lewis and Clark and the assistance provided by Sacajawea. I wanted our young people to have a pride in themselves as individuals, as American citizens, and as tribal members of sovereign nations. So, Beatty's ideas reinforced my teaching style. We were now encouraged to include American Indian materials in the curriculum, and so we began to combat the negative stereotypes of Indian people so pervasive in school text-books.

School Activities

We had quite a good football team at Wahpeton; our students were older than the average high school students, and on occasion they even played the State School of Science (a college located in Wahpeton, North Dakota) or other nearby junior colleges. There were other activities for the students, such as Boy Scouts and Girl Scouts. I organized the first Indian girl scout troop in the United States at the Wahpeton Indian School in about 1931. The reason I chose to organize a girl scout troop rather than a camp fire girl troop was that my great-great-grandmother, Sacajawea, was pictured in the frontispiece of the girl scout handbook. She was described there as the greatest girl scout because she was believed to exemplify the qualities of courage, strength, and truthfulness so important to the girl scout program. As I studied the motto and laws of the Girl Scouts, I thought to myself, "You know, these parallel our Indian values." I thought I could use this activity to advocate a positive model for the Indian girls. The towns of Wahpeton, North Dakota, and Breckenridge, Minnesota, both had camp fire girl organizations, but soon our Indian school girl scout program became so well known in that area that those cities changed over to girl scouting. We financed our girl scout troop's dues and activities by doing needlework using Indian designs and then selling them in the community.

Christmas was a very exciting time at the Wahpeton Boarding School. We made half-gallon-sized bags from white netting, and before Christmas all of the teachers met in the library to fill the Christmas treat bags for the students, employees and their families, and guests. On Christmas Eve, Santa and his helpers passed the bags out at a school assembly after a short Christmas program. The packages that came in for the children from home were kept in the dormitory in a special locked room; they were catalogued, and any child that did not get a package from home was furnished a nice gift purchased by the staff from government funds. All of the gifts were beautifully wrapped and tagged by the dormitory personnel. It was so important that all of the children receive a nice gift.

At Eastertime, boiled eggs were sent to the classrooms to be dyed and decorated. The teachers and students dyed the eggs, and then they were sent back to the dining room to be a part of the Easter meal. The employees and the students were our family at the Indian school; and since we were family, we relied on each other in ways that most people wouldn't associate with the boarding schools. Holidays, weekends, and summers were especially important times for us all.

Summer School

During the second summer (1931) that I was at Wahpeton, I enrolled at the Valley City State Teachers College for some courses. I did not realize that I was one of the first Indian students to attend this school and a curiosity to the faculty and administrators. I guess there were some college personnel who believed that Indian people were not as intelligent as white people, and they watched my performance very closely to monitor my progress. I made straight AS and so was able to uphold the dignity of my race. One of the classes I took was the History of North Dakota, and when we studied the Lewis and Clark expedition, I became a sort of instant celebrity because of my knowledge of and relationship to Sacajawea, which I shared with the class. I told them about her coming back to our people and about her travels through the plains. It was, in fact, the history professor of this class who informed me that my academic performance was being scrutinized. We eventually became quite good friends due to our mutual interests in North Dakota history and the travels of Lewis and Clark.

I stayed in the dormitory on campus at Valley City State, and the first time Bob came to visit me, he was driving a big black Auburn car. We had discussed the buying of this car previous to my enrolling in summer school, and Bob knew that I was very much against our purchasing it. I thought it was too big and looked too much like a car that only the very wealthy would own. I was furious with him and wouldn't even ride in it, but he had brought my best girlfriend, Marjorie McDougall, a Chippewa, along, and the two of them eventually convinced me of what a good buy it had been. I never did feel quite right about that car; riding in it embarrassed me.

TRAVEL BACK HOME

In 1931 we went to visit my mom and Bernice in Wyoming and Bob's family in California. We made the trip in the Auburn car, and we were almost ashamed to be driving such a luxurious-looking auto, especially when we were passing people whose dilapidated vehicles were packed with all of their belongings. We passed truckload after truckload of people who were heading west out of the grasshopper-infested, dusty plains to what they hoped would be a better life. Values were different then, too. You could and would pick up anyone who was in need of a ride, with no fear of anything bad happening; it seemed like everyone sensed being part of the struggle.

My mom had remarried, and Bernice was married, too. Victor Higginson was my stepfather's name. My mother was noted for her creation of thunderbird quilts; sometimes I think of my mother's life as being like a patchwork quilt. She lived through so many changes in her eighty-plus years. This thunderbird was her own design; the thunderbird or great eagle is the symbol of honor, bravery, friendship, love, and spiritual power for Indians. It is our closest link between mortals and the Supreme Being. It is emblematic of the Great Spirit.

Exposure to Shoshone and Hoopa Culture

It was so good to be home again and to find that my relatives were very fond of Bob. Practically everyone on the reservation is related in one way or another, and so there were numerous people to visit. Aunt Eva and Aunt Ida and Grandpa Finn Burnett were still living, and so was Rev. John Roberts, who had officiated at the burial of Sacajawea. During my years away from the reservation, I realized that there were many things I still did not know about the life of my great-great-grandmother. I used this opportunity to learn as much as I could from those who had known her, to gather additional details, and to collect information about their association with her. I visited Sacajawea's grave and put some flowers on it, remembering the day so many years before when I first went to Wind River and saw her final resting place. I always feel connected to her when I visit the cemetery and am happy that she is resting at the foot of the mountains that she loved so well.

It was also at this time that I was given my Indian name. Dewey Washakie was a good friend of our family and knew about my teaching at the Wahpeton Indian School. The name "Ingayah," which means Indian Paintbrush, was bestowed on me by Dewey because of my artistic abilities.

The story that I have always heard is that my great-great-grandmother brought the Sun Dance to Wind River from the Comanche, but this summer was the first time that I attended a Sun Dance. It is the most spiritual activity of our Eastern Shoshone people and one that renews the Wind River community. My participation was as an observer; in a tribal way, I felt spiritually connected to the Sun Dance. Through it I experienced a special reconnection to my family and my tribe.

The first time we observed the Sun Dance, we got to the reservation in time to see the sham battle take place. I had heard that this aspect of the Sun Dance ceremony had not taken place for quite a while, and that it had recently been reintroduced. The tribal members came down out of the mountains on their ponies with the medicine pole for the Sun Dance, and another group pretended to try to take the pole from them.

The lodge itself was round, and the medicine pole was the central support. A buffalo head with sage in its mouth was hung on the center pole, as were offerings of cloth, beadwork, and even some clothing left by people whose health had been restored.

During the three-day and four-night ceremony, the women "shake brush" and sing with the drum group. While I had been away from my reservation for many years, I was able to share in particular aspects of the Sun Dance that close family members were involved in. For example, some of our relatives brought sick family members to the Sun Dance lodge entrance. Those who were in need of healing or special prayers were brought to the lodge so that the prayers of all of the participants and observers could be focused on these individuals. All of the dancers dance for a reason—this can be for the health of their family or of our nation. Their motives can be personal or communal.

The dancers shuffle out to the pole and back numerous times, thanking Our Father and appealing to the Great Spirit to hear their petitions. Our people do not pierce, but like other peoples, we do not eat or drink for the duration of the dance. I remember watching one of my cousins go up to the medicine pole and lick his hands, capturing water unseen to the rest of us. No liquid or food was allowed up close to the lodge, although in those days there were concessions toward the rear of the Sun Dance grounds.

Three of my cousins were dancing, and we camped with a cousin who had a concession near the Sun Dance grounds. We saw the sunrise ceremonies in the morning, and during one of the ceremonies, I did an unpardonable thing. I had secreted a small camera and took it into the entryway of the Sun Dance Lodge. I knew that I should not do this but wanted to be able to remember the events when I was back home. Then, a very interesting thing happened. When the film was returned from developing, those particular shots of the Sun Dancers had nothing on them. That taught me a cultural lesson: that I should heed the advice of my elders. Even as a tribal member who had been away from my reservation for a long time, I should have known better.

I think the Sun Dance for Indians is like a convocation. It is the gathering together of people for a common cause. It is spiritual from beginning to end. It is hard to describe how you feel inside—in your innermost. I don't know anytime I have felt more spiritual. You don't have to be up there dancing to be a part of it. If you are there and using your energies to support the dancers, you contribute to the essence of the ceremony. At other reservation Sun Dances that I have attended and participated in over the years, I have heard the experience described as parallel to the suffering that Jesus Christ endured on the cross. Each individual Sun Dancer was suffering for the Great Spirit by enduring the piercing, fasting, or praying.

As I remember it, our Shoshone Sun Dance had connections to Christian beliefs. Even in the thirties many participants associated the central medicine pole to the cross that Christ died on, and the twelve surrounding poles, which divided and supported the lodge, to the twelve apostles. As an elder, I feel fortunate to be able to take the best of our traditional ways and combine them with the best of Christianity.

It seems as though the beating of the drums resounded in our heads as we wound our way to California. Many of Bob's relatives still lived in Hoopa Valley, California, his home reservation. This is a beautiful little valley northeast of Eureka and Redding. We went to Hoopa while we were in California to visit Bob's favorite Aunt Nettie and other relatives. His Grandma and Grandpa Roberts were still living on the old home place, and so we visited them and stayed with them and his great-grandmother, whom they called Jamma. She was ill and really didn't know anyone, but typical of Indian people and their respect for elders, the family was taking care of her.

At one time Grandma Roberts had been one of the finest basketmakers of the Hoopa people. When Bob's uncle came back from World War I, he sold all of Grandma's baskets, which included some large storage baskets and basket hats; we understood that he had sold them to the Golden Gate Museum. Even then, Grandma was still making baskets and tried to teach me the art, but I didn't have the time or patience to learn.

I also learned during this visit that Grandpa had been one of the outstanding White Deer Dancers and that at one time he had White Deer Dance costumes that he had made. Unfortunately, all that remained of these elaborate costumes were a few remnants, including a bit of beadwork, hand-made shell beads, dentalia shells, and some dried juniper berries. He and Grandma had joined one of the fundamental churches which taught that Indian dancing and related activities were evil and the work of the devil. They gave most of these sacred articles away so that he could be a member in good standing in this church he had joined. They were very involved in this religion, which was a disappointment to both Bob and me. Not only would we have liked to attend a White Deer Dance, but we were also dismayed and saddened because the spirituality of our people continued to be condemned.

Grandma Roberts still made acorn soup. She showed me where she soaked the acorns, under a spring near her house. She soaked them prior to drying and pulverizing the acorn meat, to remove the tannic acid. The end result was a fine acorn flour. When she showed me her cooking basket that was the size of a two-quart kettle, I asked, "How do you cook in that?" She laughed and said, "I'll show you." She built a little fire and selected her special cooking stones to put in it. She soaked the basket to make it water tight, measured out the amount of acorn flour needed for soup, added spring water, and proceeded to drop the hot rocks into the mixture with wooden tongs, removing them as they cooled. This process is ongoing until the cook is satisfied that the soup is done. The acorn flavor was foreign to me; I ate the soup and pretended to like it but was not that fond of it. It was very bland. But I liked and felt very comfortable with all of Bob's family, and the feeling seemed to have been mutual.

THE COLLIER ERA, 1933–45: CHANGING INSTITUTIONAL ATTITUDES
The 1930s was an interesting period, influenced as it was by a renewed interest in Indian people and their culture. This was the time of the Collier administration—a time when it became popular to be Indian again and a time when the policy of the government was to affirm rather than destroy Indian values and culture. It became apparent to the educators in the BIA that if Indian culture was to be retained, it was necessary for American Indians not to lose their Native languages. Bilingual readers were developed and introduced into the curriculum. Not only were these readers written in English and an Indian language like Sioux or Navajo, but the characters in the books portrayed Indian customs and traditions in a positive light.[5]

The BIA tried to encourage economic self-sufficiency on the reservations by promoting community gardens, the raising of chickens and rabbits, and also the production of goat's milk. One of its plans to accomplish this was to buy goats for this purpose. I know that the BIA tried this on the Pine Ridge Reservation in South Dakota. Their reasoning was that when the tribal members left their homes to go to powwows or other Indian ceremonials or gatherings, they left their cows behind with no one to milk them.

The BIA thought that the introduction of goats might alleviate this situation because the Indian people could just pick up the nanny, put it in their wagon or whatever they were traveling in, and take the goat along with them. Then they would have a milk supply handy—a better situation for both human and animal, or so the BIA thought. But goats never caught on, at least not on the reservations around here. Some people liked the milk, but most didn't, and many of the Indian people who received the government

75

goats ate them instead. They used their goats for meat and frequently even ate their breeding stock, especially when it was time for a particular family to supply a meal for a large gathering of folks.

I remember a story that Fr. Harold Jones, the first Sioux Indian Episcopal Bishop, told me of visiting some of his parishioners on the Pine Ridge Reservation. He commented on how delicious the meat was that they were eating for lunch, and the host said, "Our grandfather in Washington provided us with this fine goat." So you see, most people ate their goats and did not breed or milk them.

Of course, we had goats for milking and rabbits for meat supply at the Wahpeton school because the BIA's expectation was that our students would learn to care for these animals and take their skills back home to the reservation. They tried a lot of experiments like this, using the schools to try to get the kids to learn and practice the skills that they wanted the reservations to use. Usually, though, they were unsuccessful. This was around the time of the introduction of the Indian Reorganization Act, and I remember that John Collier came around to the reservations and boarding schools to discuss it with us.

We had an assembly at Wahpeton when Dr. Collier came to visit, and he talked to us about his political and educational philosophies. Collier was a very small man, and some people called him "Rabbit Collier" because he appeared to be a timid individual. Many of us thought, "Lo, the poor Indian" was once again going to be the thrust of the government's message. Once again the government is using us as guinea pigs.

We had mixed reactions to the bill. We thought that the most important components were those that provided money to buy portions of our land back and the low-interest funds available for small business loans. We generally approved of the ideas of self-government for our reservations but questioned the governance charters that were to be imposed *on* us. As it turned out, the bill was good in some respects and not so good in others.

In 1933 we received a directive from Dr. Willard Beatty of the Bureau of Indian Affairs, encouraging teachers in the Indian service to take summer classes at the Milwaukee State Teachers College. The college had one of the best programs in progressive education, and so Miss Dosey, a fifth-grade teacher, and I decided to attend. Progressive education was an integrative method. Rather than separating reading, writing, arithmetic, art, and science into separate disciplines, the unit method worked to integrate the concepts for the children.

A good example would be a farm unit. The children might begin by making and decorating the farm buildings out of cardboard boxes. We then might study the concepts that would be associated with farm life, like keeping records of the sale of produce. The class I took at Milwaukee State taught innovative methods to cover these concepts. I found this method of teaching interesting and challenging but also difficult to use in teaching my students enough of the basics. I felt that sometimes the students were shortchanged by the use of this method alone, and I supplemented it with materials correlated to the state course of study.

While we were in Milwaukee, Miss Dosey couldn't quite understand my great longing for sour pie-cherries, which I consumed by the boxful. Later on, when we were back at Wahpeton and it became apparent that I was expecting a child, she told me that she had had her suspicions due to my peculiar eating habits.

Following summer school in Milwaukee, Bob came to take me back home to North Dakota, but before we left the area we decided to attend the 1933 World's Fair in Chicago. One of the areas we enjoyed most was the Indian village, which is where I first saw Maria Martinez, the famous potter of San Ildefonso. There was a ceramics demonstration in which her traditional coil method was pitted against a potter's wheel. The results were that her ancient technique matched those of the contemporary potter, and in my estimation her pots were much more beautiful. Maria went on to become an internationally known Native potter, whom I was to meet later in my travels to her pueblo. In addition, there were other Native American craftspeople present—Navajo weavers, silversmiths, and others. I learned a lot during my visit to the Chicago World's Fair, not only about our Indian cultures, but also about cultures of other nations.

OUR FIRST CHILD, YVONNE: REEVALUATION OF
"WORKING MOTHERS"

We were overjoyed that I was pregnant but weren't sure what we were going to do, because I wanted to keep on teaching. So, Bob and I went to see Superintendent Carl Stevens and told him that I was expecting a baby and that I intended to continue with my teaching after the birth. He congratulated us but was dubious about whether I would be allowed to continue teaching. This was an unusual request because at this time most women did not continue in their professions, if they even had one, after they became pregnant, or "in the family way" as was the more appropriate term in those days. Superintendent Stevens corresponded with the BIA educational office in Washington DC at length. Finally, the office sent its representative, Miss Rose

Brandt, supervisor of elementary education, all the way out to Wahpeton to confer with us about the pregnancy. It was apparent from the very beginning that she did not believe that this kind of thing could ever work out.

She asked, "Who is going to take care of the baby while you are teaching?" We already had an answer for her. Bob's sister, Jeanette, who was seventeen years old, wanted to come and stay with us and had agreed to take care of the child. Well, Miss Brandt wasn't too sure about that. She said she had known of a couple of other instances where teachers had wanted to continue teaching, and then when the baby came, they had been unable to care for an infant and teach effectively. I assured her that this would not happen in my case. After *much* discussion, to my surprise, she agreed! The Wahpeton administration and the BIA arranged for me to continue to teach; I was granted an unpaid maternity leave for three-and-a-half months (November 1–February 28, 1934). I still have an excerpt from that letter dated October 7, 1933, from Rose K. Brandt. It says: "The objection to a woman with a small child acting as a teacher, as you will understand, is based upon the well-known fact that a child requires a great deal of a mother's energy, as well as considerable time and attention. Unless special care is provided for the child, the result in our Indian schools is likely to be inadequate performance of her function as a teacher. . . . We are recommending leave without pay status until March 1."

A month before our baby was born, my temporary replacement came—she happened to be an Indian teacher and so everything was going according to plan. In fact, after Miss Brandt's visit, the superintendent called me into the office and said, "What are you going to do about nursing your baby?" I said, "I didn't know I could." He said, "Oh, yes, we can arrange that. Put the child on a four-hour schedule, and then you'll be able to nurse her around your teaching schedule. You can simply make up any lost time on the job." So that's what I did.

Before the baby was born, it was exciting for us and for the other employees. We were one of the first couples at the school to have a child. They were anxious to know whether I was going to be able to continue to teach and were so happy when it was arranged that I could. We all were even more surprised when we found that the superintendent said that I could nurse my child. The women on campus had a shower for me, and so this child ended up with five times as much clothing as she needed. Our relatives were excited for us, too, and were happy to know that the baby would have an extended family of Indians on the campus of the school.

It was a difficult birth, but after she was born (January 14, 1934), it was so exciting. Bob was home waiting to hear if he had a son or daughter, those being the days before men came to the hospitals with their wives. We named her Roberta Yvonne after Bob and Yvonne Warrington, the young woman who had been so kind to me when I was a little girl. My husband was adamant about not calling her Roberta because, he said, she would end with the nickname Bobby and he didn't like nicknames. We decided to call her Yvonne because, we thought, there isn't a nickname for that. Almost immediately he began to call her Vonnie, and the name stuck. She was somewhat of a curiosity in the hospital due to her dark complexion and long black hair; she was one of the first Indian babies born in that hospital. Bob and I took her back to our apartment on campus.

I was afraid to bathe her at first—she seemed so tiny; she was seven pounds and four ounces at birth. The campus nurse, a good friend of mine, came over to see how I was doing in caring for the baby. She saw that I was treating her like a china doll, and so she grabbed hold of her and said, "Let me have that kid." She tossed her around and bathed her and got her changed and dressed so fast that I soon got over my fear that she was going to break. Vonnie adapted to a four-hour schedule rather easily, and I returned to work when she was about six weeks old. Jeanette, Bob's sister from Hoopa, had come to live with us and care for the baby. This arrangement worked out well, and I did not have any real problems with my schedule of nursing. We spent a lot of time with little Vonnie. Bob was helpful and loved to play with her and hold her on his lap. When she started taking juice and water and cereal, he had his chance to feed her as well. Since she was the only baby on campus, the employees and students gave her lots of attention when we'd take her out.

My work didn't seem to suffer, but I was so determined not to have any problems that I worked hard to make everything run smoothly. I've always been a survivor, and when I set goals for myself, I work diligently to achieve those goals. Soon I continued to pursue all the duties I had before I became a mother, like assembly programs and a leader of Girl Scouts.

SUMMER SCHOOL AT THE UNIVERSITY OF NEW MEXICO, 1935

The second summer after Vonnie was born, I decided to go to summer school at the University of New Mexico. I wanted to bring Vonnie along with me, even though she was only a year-and-a-half old. So I got in touch with Mr. Blair, the former superintendent of Haskell and current supervisor at the Albuquerque Indian School. He was the man I had gotten to know so well during my years at Haskell. He suggested I bring Vonnie along with me, because there was a new home economics practice cottage on the Albuquerque Indian School campus where we could stay. He set the wheels in motion to find a student from that school who could take care of Vonnie while I was in class at the University of New Mexico.

Train travel in those days with a young child was an experience. Vonnie was very active, and of course, there were no disposable diapers. So I had to rinse out diapers and keep them until we got to the other end of the line. The baby was also nursing on her thumb, which doctors at that time believed was harmful, so I used a thumb guard, which was not at all to this young one's liking.

When we arrived in Albuquerque, there was someone to meet us and take us out to the boarding school campus. The practice cottage was lovely, furnished in the old Southwest style, and the Navajo schoolgirl who cared for Vonnie, Alice, was very dependable and loving. Alice and Vonnie got along famously. The kitchen personnel at the Albuquerque Indian School made sure that Vonnie ate well, and they supervised Alice's performance and routinely spoiled Vonnie as well. Vonnie did have a bout with dysentery that summer; I missed a trip to Carlsbad on account of that but was glad to be with her when she was so ill.

In addition to two anthropology courses that I took at UNM, I also was fortunate to be there at a time when a series of Indian arts courses were being offered at the Albuquerque Indian School in the afternoons. An Acoma woman taught a traditional pottery class; a Navajo woman taught weaving; a Pueblo basketry class was offered; and Allen Houser was scheduled to teach an introductory painting class. I arranged my courses at the university so that I could take advantage of this opportunity. I was able to fit all of these classes into my schedule.

In pottery I learned the coil method and traditional yucca-brush painting techniques. We fired our pottery in sheep dung, and I still have the pieces of pottery that I completed that summer. For weaving, we began with raw wool, which we had to card and comb and wash with yucca suds. We were taught to use a knee spindle to spin our own yarn. I aspired to weave a blanket six feet long and three feet wide, but I ended up with a tightly woven two-foot by one-and-a-half-foot piece.

In the basketry class, we used yucca to weave a basket that was not as difficult and time-consuming as the pottery and weaving. These courses provided me with a profound appreciation of traditional arts and crafts. Understanding the process from its inception and using raw materials to complete the final product not only broadened my horizons but also gave me some experience to share with my students about the complexity of Indian art.

Maggie Bazil Large,
Esther's grandmother

Esther Burnett, ca. 1910, Idaho

Homesteading in Idaho, ca. 1918. From left to right: unknown man, Bernice, Gordon, Millie (mother), June, Esther, Finn (father). In front: Bishop, the dog

Esther Burnett, ca. 1925

Commissioned Officers, Haskell Institute, 1928, from the Haskell Annual.
Esther is in bottom row, second from right

Haskell Institute, 1928, from the
Haskell Annual

Haskell Annual Staff, 1928, from the Haskell Annual. Esther is in second row from bottom, third from right

Esther Burnett, 1929, Eufaula, Oklahoma

Esther Burnett Horne, White Earth Reservation, 1993.
Photo by S. McBeth

Sacajawea Cemetery, Wind River Reservation, Fort Washakie, Wyoming, 1994. Photo by S. McBeth

Esther Horne and Sally McBeth, White Earth Reservation, 1993.
Photo by Doyle D. Turner

Essie at the Circle of Nations Wahpeton Indian School, 1997.
Photo by S. McBeth

Robert and Esther Horne,
North Dakota, 1945

Esther and Nez Perce Delegation, Sesquicentennial of Lewis and Clark
Expedition, 1955

The two courses that I took at UNM were Introduction to Anthropology and Ethnography of the Southwest. In the Introduction to Anthropology course, our Nordic teacher stressed the concept that there were no superior races. I thought, "Hurrah! Finally academics are teaching that no one race or ethnic group, Indians or blacks or Jews, is biologically inferior." I applauded her efforts, because this belief was generally accepted at the time. This was, of course, before the Second World War and Hitler's regime. Ethnology of the Southwest was a very concentrated course, focusing on the Pueblo cultures, including the Hopi, as well as Navajo culture.

Probably one of the most memorable experiences of that summer was a trip to San Ildefonso pueblo. Ruth Muskrat Bronson was traveling in the Southwest that summer in her position as educational specialist at large for the BIA. She was checking on Native American students enrolled in college classes to see how they were getting along. We were delighted to see each other at the Albuquerque Indian School, and she invited me to accompany her to San Ildefonso to visit her friend Maria Martinez.[6] The day we were there, Maria and Julian were decorating and firing pottery. My mind hearkened back to the Chicago World's Fair, and Maria and I discussed her demonstration there. After our visit, Maria asked me to pick out a pot as a gift from her. I chose a black wedding vase that Julian had just finished decorating. That vase, which I received from Maria in 1935, is one of my most prized possessions.

In addition to my visit to San Ildefonso, I visited twenty-one pueblos at one time or another that summer with Elsa Hurlitz, a woman I had taught with at Eufaula. She was in a supervisory position at the Albuquerque Indian school, and one of her duties was to visit the pueblo day schools and work with the housekeepers.

I had an incredibly busy schedule that summer. I did a great deal of studying at night and burned a lot of midnight oil preparing for my classes the next day. I seemed to have gotten along quite well, because Yvonne was well taken care of. Through my classes and travels I became totally immersed in the Native American cultures of the Southwest—I had so much new knowledge to share with my students. I had just about reached the saturation point when it was time to leave. I returned to Wahpeton just in time to prepare for my fall classes.

SECOND DAUGHTER, DIANNE

Soon after, I discovered that I was pregnant again. We were thrilled at the prospect of the arrival of a second child but a bit uneasy because we had to seek the BIA's permission that I might continue to teach; however, it wasn't that difficult to obtain permission the second time. I was given clearance to continue teaching because I had made a supreme effort to excel in all of my academic and volunteer duties. I had succeeded with one child and intended to do the same when I had two. Twenty-two months after Vonnie was born, I had Dianne on November 11, 1935. My pregnancy with Dianne was somewhat more difficult than my first. I had morning sickness more often with Dianne; I could manage to stay in the school building and not be absent from my classroom, but I had to leave for a while every morning.

I was also bigger with Dianne than with Vonnie, and my replacement did not arrive until two weeks before the birth. It was rather difficult for me to teach, as heavy as I was, but I managed. Some of this weight may also have been due to the fact that it was pheasant season just before the birth. Bob would bring in his limit on a regular basis, and other young men would bring in their pheasants to our place to share. I had the reputation of being an outstanding cook when it came to preparing pheasant, which also meant that I had to clean the birds; and I ate my share, perhaps contributing to my weight gain.

It was an easier birth. I didn't have the problems that I'd had with Yvonne, but Dianne was a big baby. She weighed nine pounds and thirteen ounces. Where Vonnie had been very dark with long black hair, Dianne was very fair. She looked so very much like my sister Helen when she was a baby that I thought she must take after the Burnett side of the family.

Jeanette had returned to California to visit her folks before beginning a new job at a health facility in Albuquerque, so we had to find somebody else to take care of the children while we were at work. We had a succession of housekeepers who didn't pan out. I thought I might have to stop teaching and take care of my children; they were more important than my teaching. Finally, we advertised in the paper for a housekeeper. A Swedish woman, Hilma Gebro, from Ledgerwood, North Dakota, applied for the position. As it turned out, she needed us as much as we needed her, and so she spent seven years with us. She had older children of her own and was excellent with our children. She was an extremely fine housekeeper, a good cook, and an excellent seamstress: a real jewel. She was in her late fifties and so was like a grandma to the kids. The kids loved her and called her "G," so that's how she became known to us all.

She also knew when to give us the space and privacy that are so necessary to a family. We paid her twenty dollars a month, which was a high wage during the thirties. Later, we raised her salary to twenty-five dollars a month because we were so impressed with her performance. We became good friends with her family and she with ours. We invited her to accompany us on our trips back home to Wind River and Hoopa Valley because she had never traveled outside of North Dakota, and she could help care for the children.

DEMONSTRATION TEACHING, 1936

Dianne was still in a high chair, maybe around eight or nine months old, when I was detailed to assist in an in-service summer school at the Pine Ridge Boarding School in South Dakota. These in-service summer schools were held at different locations for BIA teachers from all over the continental United States and Alaska. I had been asked to be one of the demonstration teachers for the fourth-grade level, which meant that other BIA teachers would observe my teaching techniques. I agreed to teach this demonstration course at Pine Ridge but didn't want to leave my children in Wahpeton. I've always wanted to have my cake and eat it too.

The BIA agreed to convert a vacant church just off the campus into living quarters for us. So, I took Hilma along with me; she took care of the children and did the cooking for us, and we got along fine. The teaching that I did at Pine Ridge was to "demonstrate" how a fourth-grade teacher could incorporate Native American materials into the subjects that we teach, such as reading, writing, math, and social studies. In addition, we encouraged teachers to invite resource people as aids in teaching this subject matter.

The students whom I had in my classroom for demonstration purposes were fourth- and fifth-graders from the Pine Ridge Reservation. One of the little boys in my class told us that he was related to Red Cloud, and he told us that he had a beaded saddle at home that had come down to his family through Chief Red Cloud. I asked if he could bring the saddle to school to show the rest of us, and that he did. His father also came to talk to the class. I was surprised that his father felt comfortable enough to come to the demonstration classroom and share some of the family's and tribe's oral traditions.

Many of the parents and relatives of the children that I taught during the demonstration session that summer came to visit our classroom and share their native expertise. They brought artifacts from home and sent different kinds of Indian food, including pemmican (dried-meat mixture), corn, wild turnips, wild carrots, peppermint, chokecherries, and wild plums, so that we could see what they looked like and reinforce the fact that a traditional Indian diet was nutritious. We made *wojape*, a wild plum dessert, and frybread for the class and observers, which we all enjoyed.

This innovative type of instruction of the 1930s continues to be used and refined in classrooms of the nineties. These techniques are still considered progressive for today's generation, with the addition of computers and Native American classroom assistants.

In addition to these in-service demonstration classes, there were a variety of other courses in Indian history and other disciplines, offered by experts in the field for college credit right on the site location at Pine Ridge. I took an ethnology of the plains course from Ruth Underhill.[7] I knew she was a well-known anthropologist and author because of the information provided by the bureau in its summer school handbooks. One of the things that I remember quite well was the occasion on which I challenged her on one of her facts concerning Dakota culture. She was offended and a bit indignant that I would question her authority and not just believe everything she said.

I was frankly surprised by her negative reaction, believing that a teacher should welcome questions and differing opinions. I can't remember what the fact was, but I was right! I wasn't rude but simply said that I didn't believe that she was correct. There were some Sioux students in the class who backed me up, which added to her discomfort and angered and embarrassed her even more. I did learn a great deal from her, but I learned a lot more from our Sioux students who were in this ethnology class with me.

I also took an Indian art course from Frederick H. Douglas, curator of the Denver Art Museum. He brought traditional Indian arts and crafts with him to illustrate the concepts and time periods that we studied. This class culminated in an Indian style show. His models were local Indians who dressed in Native American garb and carried artifacts from the tribes that they represented.

THE INDIAN CLUB AT WAHPETON

It was about this time (1936–37) that I began to think about creating an Indian Club at the Wahpeton Indian School. As I thought about how I would begin, I envisioned that the purpose of this club would be to create some carry-over from the reservation to the school and to instill in the children a sense of their worth as individuals as well as members of particular tribal groups. I had been teaching various facets of Indian culture to my students but wanted to reach beyond my own classroom and extend the club membership to all students from the second through eighth grades. In addition, the Indian Club would be a teaching tool for the students, staff, and anyone else with whom we might share our music, dance, philosophy, and way of life. Even in the boarding school, our culture was being maintained and nourished.

Because dance and music are so central to an understanding of Native

American culture, Indian dance became the focus of the club. My students already knew that Indian people "live" their music. What that means is that once we feel the throb of the drum, we become a part of it. I would say that accounts for the vibrancy of the dancing. Dance could be sacred or social, private or public, but always is hallowed with spirituality. The dance is clean, and it is beautiful. The steps are dramatic and interpretive, and truly fine dancers appeal to the imagination of the viewer. My students strove to emulate the movements of animals and birds and to re-create their appearance. We discussed the fact that Indian dancing is the true folk dancing of the Americas and that it is a part of our unique heritage. It was an art form that was ours.

I had neither the expertise nor the experience to teach my students the large variety of tribal dances and the construction of accompanying costumes. Because many of the students had not learned to dance at home, I sought the help of Indian people in the area and that of my students who were knowledgeable. There were men and women on campus and from nearby reservations who came to my rescue and assisted me in constructing bustles and roaches and the other parts of men's costumes.

Although it was unusual for women to teach or aid in the making of these male regalia parts, the men granted me permission not only to teach dancing but also to direct the boys in creating their dance regalia. The reason that people were willing to help me learn these skills is that I was helping to keep our Indian culture alive in this off-reservation boarding school. Many of our cultural beliefs and practices had been repressed when we were confined to reservations and separated from our families in the boarding schools. Some of us who were government employees thought we had the responsibility to foster some of these cultural elements in the boarding school environment.

I learned my beadworking skills from my mother and an old aunt, but I was also able to polish those skills with the help of the mother of a Wahpeton employee from Crow Creek, South Dakota, who was an excellent beadworker. I was therefore able to teach both my boy *and* girl students the rudiments of beading. Girls' dance regalia was much less involved than the boys' because it did not require featherwork. When I did not know how to make something for students' regalia, or couldn't find anyone to help me, we'd look in the library for books by Ben Hunt or Carrie Lyford.[8]

When I say "we," as often as not I am referring to Martha Voigt, a Hidatsa friend from Fort Berthold and a dormitory staff person, and Albert "Chip" Houle, Turtle Mountain Chippewa, another Wahpeton Indian School employee. They were both involved in the Indian Club activities. Martha was active in working with students on costume construction, singing, drumming, and dancing. The school agreed to buy us a drum, and we commissioned one of the best Chippewa drummakers, Leonard McDougall, who lived here on the White Earth Reservation, to make that drum. When Martha retired, we gave her the drum, the history of which was so entwined with the Indian Club and the Wahpeton school. Her knowledge and expertise of the traditions of the three affiliated tribes (Mandan, Hidatsa, and Arikara) added immeasurably to the success of our endeavors. We had quite a few kids from the affiliated tribes at Wahpeton.

Chip acted as our bus driver and supervised the boys when they dressed for performance. His keen sense of humor kept our spirits high, even when we were exhausted. As our dance techniques and regalia were perfected, we were frequently invited to share our cultural traditions with schools, service clubs, churches, and other organizations. They in turn were invited to come to the Indian school to broaden our horizons with some activities or programs in their jurisdiction. This was an effort on my part to educate the public that Indians are people, too. When we performed at a school, the Indian student dancers attended classes with the public school kids.

Those days were so exciting! Finally, we no longer had to hide the fact that we were incorporating our cultural values into the curriculum and student life.

I probably should explain, too, that there were records we used when we practiced our dancing. We didn't have a drum group until much later. A man by the name of Willard Rhodes did a great deal of recording of music on the reservations during the Collier administration. All government school libraries received copies of these records, which were invaluable to us. They were so fine. The traditions and memories that those records captured were so important to the students and to those of us who were teaching these kids the importance of remembering their past. When we heard the beat of the drum, we talked about it being the heartbeat of Mother Earth, who was the mother of us all. The kids, too, began to understand that getting along with one another was not so hard because they were all brothers and sisters. All of those values came together and made us strong. It is hard for me to convey the sense of pride and growth that those students and I felt in those days.

I believe that there's a togetherness in Indian groups that one doesn't always observe in other groups. At least we Indian people feel that. There is a teasing and joking that creates ties and friendships. I was so happy to see that kids were not just thinking of themselves, that they were thinking of the total student body. They learned the importance of the word "we," rather than "I." Their living of Indian values made an impression on people who visited the school. My students took the initiative to welcome visitors to *their* classroom or activity room and to inform them about what we were doing instead of leaving this duty to me. I always believed that if you're going to teach a student to talk and be responsible, then you have to provide the opportunities for that to happen.

This was an exciting period for Indian people during the late 1930s and early 1940s. The young people were meeting with the elders to learn the songs and traditions. The younger tribal members encouraged their parents and grandparents to allow the music to be recorded and the stories to be written down so that they could learn from them. This, of course, followed the period when the BIA frowned on and sometimes actually forbade Indian people to practice the beliefs of their cultures. Many continued to practice their religion and to sing and dance the old way in secret, but much was also lost or forgotten. Drum groups started to come together. Martha Voigt told me about this phenomenon occurring up at Fort Berthold, and cousins and friends from Wind River shared with me the fact that they were doing the same.

WORLD WAR II AND SINGLE PARENTING

Bob was too old to go into the armed forces, so he and his best friend on campus, Louis Brewer, decided to enlist in the Seabees.[9] When he told me that he wanted to enlist (December 26, 1942), I was rather shocked that he would leave me and the girls and told him so. After we talked though, I learned how important it was for him to be "one of the boys" and to serve in the war effort. I remember that my words to him were, "I would rather live without you than with you in your disappointment." Bob did not want me to see him off at the train. He absolutely forbade it, and I agreed. I think that we both knew we would break down, and I guess neither of us wanted to do that. It was around midnight when his train left, and as it left town, I heard the train whistle blow. The night was still, and it was a cold night. The North Dakota air carried the mournful sound so far. I always think of his departure when I hear a train whistle late at night. It was such a sad and lonely time for me.

Contrary to what one might think, given the history of the United States government's treatment of our people, Indian men and women regularly enlist in the armed services. We take great pride in serving our country, and all tribes honor their veterans at powwows or ceremonies. This is true from World War I right up through Desert Storm.

Bob went to boot camp and then began his tour of duty, which took him all the way from New Caledonia to the Philippines. His job was to establish water purification units in the South Pacific for the military and the local populations. We, of course, corresponded frequently during those war years. Sometimes we'd get four or five letters at one time, and then weeks would pass before we'd receive another. The girls really missed their dad, and he missed them, and they wrote letters to each other. Bob saved some of their letters and brought them home. I empathize with the emotional trauma of the families left behind during wartime, and I relive their joy of returned loved ones and think about the adjustments they will face.

During Bob's absence, I had three different housekeepers. Each of these women had husbands who were in the service, and two of them had babies of their own. Their companionship was a source of support, since we were all in the same predicament. As their husbands returned, they moved on. I know that I relied on their friendship so much. I think of this time as the beginning of women's liberation. A lot of women were on their own for the first time, making their own decisions, coping with children and work. Many women joined the military, and others entered the work force in war-related industries. Rosy the Riveter was our model, and women were not only contributing their labor to the war effort but making good wages as well.

I learned to drive after Bob was gone. I did not want to depend on other people to chauffeur me around. In the process of learning, I broke off a part of the door one time and smashed out a couple of headlights getting in and out of the garage. I used to drive clear up to Naytahwaush from Wahpeton, a distance of about a hundred miles, to visit friends. Gas was rationed, but I had some farm friends who were able to give me enough of their extra gas allotment to make the trip. Friends like Howard Le Voy, who owned a little general store, would tell me that if I could get up here to Naytahwaush, he'd see to it that I got home.

Vonnie was my navigator, warning me that I was going too fast or telling me where to turn. It was a time of bonding for the girls and me. Bob was overseas when I bought the cabin up here at Naytahwaush on the White Earth Reservation. We used to come up to visit Howard and Ruby Le Voy, who were White Earth Chippewa tribal members and former employees of the Wahpeton Indian school. Bob and I always thought we would like to have a cabin on one of the lakes if we could afford it.

Bob was the chief petty officer of his battalion, and one of the men in his unit was a very lucky gambler. On a number of occasions, Bob took over his tour of duty in return for half of his winnings. Bob sent this extra money home, and unbeknownst to him, I placed it in a savings account to be used for something special. On my visits to Naytahwaush, I kept my eyes and ears open, hoping to glean information on an affordable lake home. With the help of my friends, I discovered that a little place on South Twin Lake was for sale for $975 in cash. The year was 1943. I had that amount from the gambling proceeds, so I purchased it. It was completely furnished, and the girls and I came up regularly but kept it a secret from Bob. The girls and I never said a word about it. And they say women can't keep secrets!

In addition to gas, many other items were rationed during the war: sugar, cigarettes, meat, and nylon hose, to name a few. We used tokens to buy our allotments of rationed items. I planted big gardens during the war years, and Millie Graff, my housekeeper at that time, and I canned much of the produce. We took a lot of pride in our canning accomplishments, and it was nice to go down in the basement and see those rows and rows of canned beets and string beans, tomatoes, pickles, jellies, and fruits. I missed Bob a lot. I would stay up late at night missing Bob, and the girls missed him very very much, too.

We had been such a close family. The girls were used to spending a lot of time with both of us—reading, playing games, traveling, swimming, just being together. We'd pass the time in the evenings listening to the same radio shows that we had listened to when Bob was home. *Amos and Andy*, a black comedy routine, was a program we all enjoyed. Radio was a wonderful tool for developing the imagination. *The House with a Squeaking Door* was a mystery program that was also a favorite. We regularly listened to these shows when Bob was in the military; they made us feel closer to him, remembering the times that we'd spent together.

I followed newspaper accounts of the war and read the Fargo Forum and listened to the radio for reports of activities in the South Pacific. I followed Ernie Pyle's commentaries on the battles in the South Pacific, to be better informed about where Bob was and what he was doing. We never knew exactly where he was, although occasionally a letter would provide a clue. I later discovered that Bob's Seabees unit, the Eighty-eighth battalion, was in a heavy combat zone. After the war, old buddies of Bob's would relive their war experiences at our kitchen table, and it was from them more than Bob that I learned about some of his war exploits.

Another tragedy of the war years, and a great sadness in my life, was when my brother Finn was reported missing in action. He had become a member of the Kansas National Guard in 1939 while he was at Haskell Indian School. He was still too young to be in the service, but he was an excellent bugler, and his National Guard unit covered up for him and allowed him to join, even though he was only seventeen years old. Perhaps his long tenure as a student at Haskell prepared him for what was to be a long military career. During the Second World War, he made the transition into the air force and was a navigator on a B-17. His plane was shot down on its third bombing mission over Ellis, Germany, on June 22, 1943, his twenty-first birthday.

He never spoke much about the two-and-a-half years that he spent as a German prisoner of war. He and two others survived the crash and were imprisoned. Finn later told us how, one by one, the three of them were repeatedly interrogated and brutally treated while they were in the Stalag prison camp. Two of the boys were shot by their captors. Finn said he was interrogated time and time again and came to believe that the only reason he did not meet the same fate as the other two was because he was Indian.

German people have always had a great respect for and knowledge of American Indian people, and Finn thought that the only reason his life was spared was because the Germans thought Indians had suffered enough. He survived a death march, which is when the prisoners are moved from one camp to another. He said that a lot of the boys died en route because there was little food, and many were weak and sick. Finn and a Navajo boy buddied up together during this march. This young man was very adept at stunning and stealing chickens, and so as they made their way across country, and he happened to see a chicken in someone's yard, he'd kill it and the two of them would hide it under their shirts and eat the meat raw, under cover of darkness.

The girls and I went to Wyoming that summer to be with my mom and support her and the family during this traumatic time. The war department released a list of items that might be useful to send to POWs, and so June and I went to a friend of ours, a pharmacist in Lander, Wyoming, with money contributed by the family. He suggested food supplements, and we also sent dried fruit, cookies, and some books and clothing. Finn said that very little of that ever got through, but when it did, he would share it with others.

POST-WAR ADJUSTMENTS

When the armistice was signed in August of 1945, a friend of mine and I had gone down to the drugstore in Wahpeton, and all of a sudden the whistles began to blow and the church bells all over town began to ring. People were running around me in the streets, crying and hugging and kissing each other shouting, "The war is over! The armistice has been signed!" I was overcome with joy—we would just kiss everyone who came along; it didn't make any difference if we knew them or not. Everyone was so happy!

Bob had to go over to the Great Lakes Naval Station to be examined and given a clean bill of health before he could come home. He had a short seventy-two-hour leave to come home en route to his separation point. When he got off the train, he didn't recognize the girls. He hadn't seen them for two-and-a-half years, and they didn't know him either. They were shy and quiet, although they looked forward to his coming home. Our reunion was joyous, and he was elated to be with us again; the only sadness was that the reunion was short-lived.

During that week, he became reacquainted with the people on campus, and I asked him if he would like to make a trip to Naytahwaush to see the Le Voys. When we got there I said, "I'd like you to meet some of my new friends." When we got to the door of the cabin, I handed him the keys and said, "This is yours." We were all excited, and this event helped to break the ice between him and the girls. They were so anxious to show him around and share this secret with him. He never did let me forget that this was *his* cabin.

Be that as it may, he went to the Great Lakes Naval Station, where he was to be separated from the service. James Cumoford, a World War I vet and dairyman at the boarding school, warned Bob and Louis on their return to take some precautions as they left the service. "Bob and Louie," he said, "you're going to be so glad to be back that you won't think about anything else except getting home; but if you separate yourselves without a thorough ship exam and clean bill of health, you'll waive all your rights to veterans' health benefits." He was speaking from experience. He was a victim of mustard gas poisoning and had made this mistake.

It was lucky for Bob that he heeded Jim's advice because he was diagnosed as having tuberculosis. He believed that he had contracted the disease in the South Pacific during his tour of duty on one of the Pacific Islands, by drinking from a common cup located at the water spigot. He spent about nine months being treated for TB. He was at Great Lakes Naval Hospital for a while, and then he was transferred to the hospital at Niagara Falls, New York. These were hard times for us all. We were so disappointed that after all this time in the service, and with the war being over, he could not even come home.

Bob, too, went through a severe depression. When he was on medical leave, he was very concerned about taking precautions so that we would not be infected with tuberculosis. He would not kiss us or use the same towel, and he became paranoid about sterilizing the dishes. He sometimes expressed the belief that he wouldn't get well. He even suggested a divorce so that he would not be a burden on us. It seemed as though he had been gone for such a long time.

Fortunately for us all, he was discharged from the hospital on June 23, 1946. He came back ready to assume his position at the Indian school, and we settled down to a regular routine. The man who had been taking his place was transferred to Oklahoma. But there was a difficult period of adjustment when Bob came back home after his hospitalization. He was unused to the structure of a family, and I had gotten used to making all the decisions, so it was difficult for me. Bob and the girls needed time to get reacquainted; we were all sort of strangers to one another.

We spent weekends up here at our Naytahwaush cabin. We'd leave on Friday night after work, if we didn't have extracurricular duties, and go back on Sunday evening. We all enjoyed this; it was an important part of our rebecoming a family. I did notice, of course, that Bob spent more and more time away from home in the evenings. He had become a member of the VFW, Veterans of Foreign Wars, and many of his friends were there. We wives used to say that they were fighting the war over again. In truth, that is what I believe that they were doing. Bob had nightmares in which he relived some of his wartime experiences. As he explained what he was experiencing in those nightmares, I got a keener insight into the changes wrought in him by the war.

Finally, by the late 1940s we were beginning to mend as a family. Bob tried very hard to reacquaint himself with our daughters' lives, and we made a supreme effort to make him a part of our family.

FINN AFTER WORLD WAR II

After the war, my brother Finn was finally released, but he was never the same. He received the Purple Heart but talked very little about his experiences during that period. Once when we were swimming, I noticed deep scars near his shoulder blades. It looked to me like he had been hung up on meat hooks, but I didn't ask him about it, and he never discussed it. We were cautioned by the military not to quiz them about their experiences but to be willing listeners. Finn also had flashbacks to his war experiences. For example, once I turned to ask him a question, and he raised his hand to slap me. The look of surprise on my face stopped him, and he said, "Oh sis, I'm so sorry," but he didn't explain. On another occasion while he was spending time with me, we stopped at a cafe on our way to the cabin. We ordered a bowl of vegetable soup, and Finn nearly threw his on the floor when he discovered that there was barley in it. He became livid with anger, and I wondered what was wrong with him. He swore about the soup and told me he never wanted to see that goddamned stuff again. He said he had lived on barley laced with rat turds for twenty-two months. Finally, he calmly reordered, the girls looking on in wide-eyed disbelief.

So, Finn returned from the war a changed person. He had been a very smiley, very happy, very positive young man, and a real delight to be around. We all loved him; everyone seemed to love him. He was the favorite uncle of my two girls. When he came to visit, people on the Indian school campus were always glad to see him, too, because he was so good-natured and so much fun. When he came back from the war, it seemed that his spirit was broken. While he still tried to joke and tease with us all, he spent a lot of time just staring into space. He tried to keep up appearances, but it was clear that he was troubled and traumatized by the war.

He returned to the reservation and worked with a survey crew in the area for a while, but eventually he just went up to the ranch to live with my mother and Vic. He guided friends on sightseeing trips into the mountains on horseback and rode a lot by himself. He sought solace in alcohol, and once when he'd been drinking heavily, he confided in me that he would like to visit the parents of his crew mates to tell them about their last flight. In his anguish he said, "How do you tell their mothers and dads that the last time you saw their sons, their guts were spilling out of their bodies and their brains were splattered all over the place?"

Following the war, our whole nation faced a period of adjustment. Men and women who were returning from the war moved back into their old jobs, displacing those who had replaced them. Many of these were women who had taken over jobs traditionally done by men, and so these women now found themselves out of work. War-related industries also ceased or limited production, and many people were out of work. Price controls were lifted, and inflation was rampant. Battles between unions and management led to many strikes at this time. There was an increase in the price of coal but not in corresponding wages for the miners, great numbers of whom went on strike. There were railroad strikes as well. A number of World War II vets took advantage of their GI Bill in order to advance their education and qualify for available positions, but it was a period of high unemployment.

Those of us who lived through the Second World War still retain ambivalent feelings about the bombings of Hiroshima and Nagasaki. We shared emotions of surprise and sadness that our nation would go to such lengths to end the conflict. It may have been a necessity, but the long-term effects on the people and the environment have been staggering. The people who survived that bombing passed the genetic legacy of that event down to future generations, victims of our inhumanity.

WAHPETON IN THE POST–WORLD WAR II ERA

I was detailed to BIA in-service summer schools throughout the late 1940s and 1950s, and even into the 1960s. I was sent to Chemawa Indian School in Salem, Oregon, in 1947. My function as a staff person was to instruct teachers in effective methods to teach arts and crafts to students in the BIA schools. This class included instruction in beadwork, as well as the construction of decorative articles from odds and ends. While there, I also availed myself of a course on the ethnology of Northwest Coast and Alaskan Natives, which was part of the in-service offerings that summer.

At another in-service summer school at Fort Defiance, Arizona, on the Navajo Reservation (1950), Bob took a class in power plant management and I took classes in the areas of folk dancing and Navajo ethnography. In the summer of 1951 and 1952, I was detailed to teaching duties at the Intermountain Indian School, a nonreservation boarding school for Navajos located in Brigham City, Utah. There I demonstrated teaching by the unit method, which is the integration of materials across traditional subject lines.

I had graduated from the Normal Training Department at Haskell Institute in Lawrence, Kansas, with a teaching certificate, and my ongoing education was through the BIA in-service summer schools. I received college credit for the courses I took and also continued to take extension courses through a number of colleges and universities. North Dakota State University, Moorhead State University, Valley City State Teachers College, Kansas University, the University of Northern Colorado, the University of Minnesota, and the University of New Mexico are examples of colleges from which I have received credit.

During these years, my own children were growing up, and the four of us had very good rapport. I'm glad my daughters grew up in the forties and fifties. I think it was an easier time for young people. It was before the time when drugs were readily available or being used as a wedge between the generations. Adolescence is a difficult period in any era, but we kept the lines of communication open. Vonnie and Dianne were only twenty-two months apart in age, and so they were more like chums than sisters. Due to illnesses resulting from allergies during her early childhood, Vonnie's performance in the classroom was hampered, and so we all decided to have her repeat the fourth grade. So, from that time on, she and Dianne were at the same grade level.

Both Vonnie and Dianne graduated from Wahpeton High School in 1953, and both attended and graduated from the State School of Science (now North Dakota State College of Science) in Wahpeton. Both married men who they met there. This school is a two-year junior college with an outstanding reputation in the technical and health areas. In 1955 Yvonne married Bill Barney. Following their graduation, Bill decided to go into teaching and enrolled at Moorhead State University in Minnesota. Vonnie took some additional business courses so that she could help finance his education. Dianne met Everett Kjelbertson, a full-blooded Norwegian at the college. They both also attended and graduated from Jamestown College in North Dakota and were married in 1957.

THE WELLINGTON ADMINISTRATION AT
THE WAHPETON INDIAN SCHOOL

In 1955, J. W. Wellington came to the Wahpeton Indian School as a superintendent with ambitious plans to change and revamp the whole flavor of the school. One day, after he had been there for a short time, he came to visit me in my classroom and said, "Come here. I want to show you something." We walked down the hall to a window overlooking the empty expanse of land behind the school building, and he told me about his dreams for a new, modern, and efficient school. These dreams included many things that coincided with my own philosophies. He wanted to encourage an Indian pride in and respect for self and heritage. His objectives were to provide a school for formal education, to provide a school with a home atmosphere, and to provide a school with community and social life.

His policy was the development of proper home, school, and community social living that would assure steady advancement of the Indian child toward desirable goals of maturity in the physical, mental, social, spiritual, and moral aspects of human life. The furtherance of understanding and appreciating Indian heritage and culture was also paramount to his plans. He believed this would lead to the ultimate goal of self-sufficiency, acceptance of discharge in full of the duties, obligations, responsibilities, and rights of an American citizen.

I always believed that Wellington knew what he was doing. He had been superintendent at Rocky Boy and at Fort Yates, and he was well acquainted with reservation life and the kind of homes that many of our students came from. You see, by this time, more and more Indian children were attending public schools, and many were adapting fairly well to that integrated type of schooling. Others, however, did not do so well in the public schools, or were from families that were abusive or neglectful, and so were sent to the government boarding schools, both to remove them from bad family situations and to put them in an environment that might be more beneficial to them.

The child and his or her welfare were of prime importance to Wellington, and all of the reconstructions that he began were supposed to better meet the needs of the child. He also expected total dedication from his employees, both in the classroom and in all the other school departments. This was, I believe, to create a better home away from home for the students. His dreams did become a reality. New well-equipped facilities were built, which included classrooms and living quarters. The new buildings were a joy to work in and did create a more pleasant environment for both student and employee.

J. W. Wellington, or "Duke," as we came to call him, also introduced other educational innovations. He worked to create connections between the city of Wahpeton and the school. Wellington encouraged townspeople to take a greater interest in the school by requesting that they take children into their homes for overnight and weekend visits and let them be a part of their family. Now some of us had been doing that with groups of children at the Indian school for a long time, but it wasn't common practice.

It took a lot of work to get the students to understand our expectations of them in relation to these new freedoms that Wellington introduced. Because their behavior would reflect on the school and on Indian people in general, we talked about trustworthiness, having respect for other people's property, and remembering to be careful about how they acted. Sometimes our students took sayings very literally, and so we reminded them that if someone said, "Make yourself at home," it did not mean that they could help themselves to the contents of the house. As always, we taught the children that these were indeed Indian values and that self-control was a value shared by all Indian people.

Some of the relationships that were established as a result of this policy were very strong. Children from the Wahpeton School became very close friends with kids from the town of Wahpeton, and the town's kids would frequently come to stay overnight on campus. After the students returned from their "home" visits, we encouraged them to write thank-you notes to their host families. This, then, became an extension of their English lesson. Doesn't sound like the old boarding school, does it?

I agitated for the non-Indian teachers to learn something about the students' lives—not just from books but from home visitations, styles of parenting, treatment of children, travel to powwows, and the like. So, I talked to Duke about this, and he agreed with me on the need for it. We provided the teachers with orientation sessions on what to expect. It helped so much when teachers became aware of the cultural differences. We talked about our bilingual students "thinking" in two different languages and how challenging and broadening that must be. We also pointed out that students who were weak academically were frequently very knowledgeable in the traditions of their culture and that they therefore had much to offer.

The old school regimen was changing quickly under Wellington's leadership. He also introduced the concept of family-type meals in the dining room, with boys and girls sitting together, and two students acting as host and hostess for each table. This, too, added a touch of home and was a change from the division of sexes to separate sides of the dining area. When the new school was built, he also had a small private dining room set aside, apart from the main dining room, that could seat thirty or so people. This was used by teachers and students to plan small "class/family" meals to which they could invite guests from the community. The children would act as hosts and hostesses, greeting the visitors, talking with them, and frequently formulating a little program for the meal, like a song or a skit. The children would make nut cups or decorate napkins so as to create a real party atmosphere.[10]

Wellington also encouraged taking groups of children out to eat to cafes in Wahpeton, Fargo, or surrounding towns, so that they could have the experience of ordering and paying for their meals, practicing table manners, and tipping their waiter or waitress.

We also went on "mom and dad" trips during the summer. The "moms" and "dads" were consenting married employees who took a small group of students—boys and girls of different ages—on a trip as a family unit. The children helped plan the trip by deciding what they wanted to see and where they wanted to go.

Mr. Wellington did not want our students to be branded as "Indian school kids" because of the clothing that they wore, so he instituted another practice whereby dormitory personnel were instructed to take the children downtown and buy them some clothing that was to their liking. The days of uniformed regimen had come to an end. That certainly added to the kids sense of dignity and pride.

He also allowed me to have a cat in my classroom. A principal was being transferred, and he had a big yellow tomcat that he didn't want to take with him, so he asked me if I might like to have Tommy as a pet for my fourth-grade classroom. I was always looking for ways to enrich the lives of the students, so Tommy became a very important part of our classroom for two years. The kids saved their pennies to buy his food and take him to the vet for his shots. He had his own desk in the room; one little girl made a coverlet for him, and another made a padded comforter for his desk. Most of these kids had left a beloved cat or dog at home, and so Tommy was a great substitute.

Tommy became nationally known when he was written up in the *Indian Education Bulletin*, which was sent out to BIA personnel. Because the kids were inspired to write stories and poems about him and to draw pictures of him, the feature story focused on what a great teaching tool he was. The students even created math problems to determine how much money and time each of them needed to contribute to his welfare. Most importantly, he was their therapist on many occasions. They could hold him or cry on him, share with him their fears and problems, knowing that they would remain secret. I suppose that I am sharing this with you simply to show that all of the stories that you hear about boarding schools do not give the full picture. There were and are some humanitarian people there. We did try to motivate children and to give them love; I loved those children that I taught, and I did what I could to broaden their horizons and give them the love that was a part of the boarding school family.

So, Wellington's goals were realized, and there was a tremendous increase in pride on our campus. His objectives, to provide a home away from home and to provide a school that was a part of the surrounding community, were achieved. He encouraged the teachers and staff at the school, especially those of us who were Indian, to become a part of the community. This really seemed to break down the stereotypes that the town of Wahpeton had, not only about the Indian school, but also about Indian people in general. Sensitivity to and nurturance of our students were the hallmarks of his tenure.

FIFTIETH ANNIVERSARY CELEBRATION OF INDIAN SCHOOL

In 1958, we celebrated the fiftieth anniversary of the Wahpeton Indian School. This was a big event not only for the school but also for the city of Wahpeton. By that time, all of the new buildings that Duke Wellington had agitated for were complete. All of the buildings on campus were named after noted Indian men and women like Sequoia and Curtis and Tinker. The purpose of this was to project to the children a sense of their culture, as well as to honor the unsung heroes and heroines who were, like them, Indian. I was asked to dedicate Sacajawea Hall, the girls dormitory.

As a part of the celebration, we had a big pageant that everyone worked on. The pageant was to show the growth and evolution of the school, and we had a schoolwide contest to name it. An eighth-grade boy came up with the name "Buckskin to Broadcloth," which the committee thought was perfect. I had been named director and narrator for the program because I had grown up in the government boarding school system and was still a part of it. When the superintendent had some real problems with the name, I tried to explain what it meant and why the young man who named it thought it was a good title. It symbolized the changes that Indians had gone through without tolling the death bell for boarding school kids. For better or worse, a whole generation of Indian people were affected in one way or another by these institutions.

But he still wasn't satisfied, and I said, "Well, I thought you gave me the job of directing because you thought I was capable of doing it." He didn't answer me. "Broadcloth," he said. "That's a fancy material that the officers used for their uniforms." I replied, "Do you have a dictionary?" He said, "Yes." So I said, "Please get it." We looked up the word broadcloth, and I showed him that there were two grades of broadcloth, one that was used for uniforms and one that was used for work clothes. I explained that both were a part of the boarding school experience.

Well, he still wasn't satisfied. He said, "You go downtown tomorrow morning and take a poll of men on the street and ask them what 'Buckskin to Broadcloth' means to them. Have them write all their answers down; I want to see them." So I did, and almost without fail, everyone said that it indicated growth in some way to them. There were, of course, two people who didn't have any idea what it meant. One of them was the cashier in the bank, and she said, "It doesn't mean anything to me." I said, "Well, write that down." A man I met on the street said he didn't know, and so I said, "Just write it down."

I took all of these slips of paper and put them on the superintendent's desk on Monday morning before he got in. Later that afternoon, my husband, Bob, came into my classroom and handed me a piece of buckskin from the superintendent. I realized this was a peace offering. He knew that I was not about to back down on an issue so important to the students and staff.

There were a number of scenes in the pageant, giving many students the chance to participate. It was almost like watching a film of my days at Haskell, since it included scenes of Indian dancing, an Indian camp scene, the

Indian agent and police taking the kids away to school, boys' and girls' military drills, farming, and the classroom.

Some of our Holstein cows were noted throughout the nation for the butterfat content of their milk, the most famous of which was Old 21. Her udder was so large that it almost touched the ground, and when she became very old, this cow had the run of the school campus and could eat the grass anywhere she wanted, until she passed away. The kids had heard stories about this famous old cow, and so she became a part of the pageant, too. The students, their parents, and other invited guests were treated to an elk and buffalo dinner held at the Pemmican Lodge, our school dining room. Flandreau sent its band to play, and the event was a great success.[11]

CHAPTER SIX

Events of the 1950s and 1960s

As a well-respected educator and descendant of a noted Native American woman, Essie continued to promote the changing attitudes toward Indians in this country. Her celebration of the 150th anniversary of her great-great-grandmother's expedition with Lewis and Clark is detailed herein. During this period, Essie also took her unique perspective on children and youth to a White House conference in 1960.

The postwar decades brought immense changes in attitudes and actions regarding Native Americans. Essie's recounting of some of her activities during this time highlights the larger events and their impact on Indians in the United States.

LEWIS AND CLARK SESQUICENTENNIAL, 1955

In 1955 I was approached by some historically minded people from the Northwest who called themselves the Greater Clarkston Association. The organizers of this group lived in Clarkston, Washington, and were making plans to follow, as nearly as possible, the original trail of Lewis and Clark—by motorcade—to celebrate the 150th anniversary of the 1805 expedition. They planned to dress up like some of the major players in the expedition and the two organizers were to assume the roles of Meriwether Lewis (Art Rongstad) and William Clark (Harold Cole). They figured that since they were Masons, as were Lewis and Clark, that they were the obvious choices. They also were the organizers of the expedition.

They made preliminary travels along the route for the purpose of planning the trip, and one of their visits took them to the secretary of the Chamber of Commerce at Williston, North Dakota, with whom I had become acquainted during the time he served in Wahpeton, North Dakota. As they were discussing the trip with him, he asked if they had considered including an Indian woman to fill the role of Sacajawea, guide of the historic expedition. This man from the chamber, Mr. Schmidt, said he was well acquainted with Sacajawea's great-great-granddaughter, a Shoshone teacher who lived in Wahpeton. She would, he said, lend authority to their sesquicentennial adventure. They came to interview me, and at first I was reluctant to get involved, thinking that this might be some kind of crack-pot money-making scheme. I talked to these men at length, asking them about every conceivable facet of their proposed trip. My friend Mr. Schmidt assured me that they were honorable in their intentions. I had always wanted to follow in my great-great-grandmother's footsteps, so after much deliberation I said I would go with them.

All of my expenses were to be paid, but there was the matter of my position at the Indian school. The superintendent agreed to "detail" me to accompany the expedition as a part of my teaching duties. He thought it would be good PR for the school, and I believed I would learn a lot and further the cause of Indian history as well.

The expedition left from Fort Mandan, North Dakota, on July 27 and arrived at Fort Clatsop, Oregon, on August 4, 1955. There were thirty-six people who made the entire trip in about ten cars, but other cars would frequently join the motorcade for a day or two at a time. The party was made up of people from all walks of life: a writer, a sculptress, an eagle scout, a real estate executive, and a photographer, among others. Margaret Anderson, a writer from Minneapolis, kept a copious log of the expedition that was deposited in the archives in Washington DC. She kept track of who joined us and for how long, and of our stops and events along the way. I changed cars each day so that I got to know the different people who traveled with us on the expedition.

Much of the route was along regularly maintained highways, but some of it was very rough terrain where only forestry personnel were allowed to travel. They granted us permission and accompanied us along those portions of the trail that were dangerous. Some of them were quite frightening to drive on without a four-wheel-drive vehicle.

We camped some of the time. It was fun sleeping out under the stars and matching wits with bears, raccoons, and other mountain creatures; the forestry personnel stood guard. As I observed the rough terrain that the expedition went through, I thought, "It was no wonder that their moccasins had become shreds." It must certainly have been a very difficult trip for my great-great-grandmother, who was only about fifteen years old and carried her child on her back. Some of the cliffs were almost perpendicular and extremely rough.

It was interesting to see the flora and fauna and to actually be able to dig some camas roots. That was one of the things that I remembered from hearing the stories about Sacajawea. My mother had said that Sacajawea had saved the expedition by contributing to their nutrition with the use of wild foods. Camas roots were one of the things that the original expedition ate in abundance. When we saw the rapids that they had to go through, it became clear to me how the boat might have capsized, and I thought of the papers that Sacajawea saved as she contributed to the expedition.

Every once in a while there was a lonely grave along the trail. These were not related to the expedition but were graves of later pioneers. I remember one was *so* little—a child's grave remaining from some frontier people who made the same trek by wagon train years later. We decided to stop there, and I was asked to say a prayer. My heart ached for the mother who had to leave her child in these lonely recesses.

We also saw many stone carrons, and I wondered if these had been in place when the expedition of 1805 came through. The wagon-wheel trails were still visible along sections of the route, which really made the history come alive. I frequently sat up on the side of a mountain that we had just traversed and dreamed about my great-great-grandmother, who has always been a role model for me. I always wanted to travel the path that she had gone. I never thought that I would have the opportunity to be able to do this.

I wore my buckskin dress on the expedition; it was comfortable in the cool mountain air, but in the lowlands I cooked in it! Various groups from local historical societies, chambers of commerce, service clubs, scout troops, Indian tribes, and women's organizations met us at our stops along the way. Sheriff posses, dressed as mountain men or like members of the expedition, were also a part of these welcoming committees. We were covered by the local press and television stations. In some of the towns along the way, townsfolk even set up grandstands to welcome and observe us as we passed through on our way west.

I made a number of interesting contacts on this expedition. I met two noted historians, namely Russell Reid of Bismarck, North Dakota, and Will Robinson of South Dakota.[1] Both of these men traveled with us for quite a ways, and they were genuinely interested in what I had to say about Sacajawea. You see, they both were of the opinion, as many historians are, that Sacajawea died as a young woman; and so they took exception to what I have always maintained was truth personified. I tried to remember my strong Indian values and to have respect for my brother's vision. I did not quarrel with them about their beliefs and was very gratified that neither of these gentlemen quarreled with what I had to say either.

They knew that I was sincere, that what I said was what I believed, and that I was not just talking to make an impression or to fan my own ego. They had a great deal of respect for what I had to say, and they seemed to be genuinely interested and open-minded about all the different stories that I had heard from my family and from others up at Wind River. Both of these men, at one time or another, admitted that I had almost made believers out of them, but they were unwilling to discount the written evidence that, while incomplete, led them to believe that Sacajawea did not live to be an old woman. What I don't understand is why they think that we Indian people, my family members, and prominent researchers would create such tall tales.

We were also met along the trail by a number of Indian people. A large delegation of Nez Perce in tribal regalia met us, and I remember that there was an old man who had a Jefferson Peace Medal around his neck. I was wearing my replica of the same medal that we believe my great-great-grandmother had been given at the end of the expedition. We shared stories, and I discovered that his medal had been in his family for a long time and had been given to them because of some service rendered for the government. I exchanged gifts with all of the tribal people along the way, since that is our way of honoring them. They admired my buckskin and seemed genuinely happy that this re-creation was taking place. My encounters along the way and the exchange of gifts gave me a warm feeling and an assurance that what I was doing was valuable. It seemed that everyone was receptive, not only to me, but to the whole idea of the expedition.

My sister June and her husband (Bill Walter) met us along the trail, too. They lived in Sunnyside, Washington, and so when we went through Yakima, they came to meet us there. This was particularly emblematic for me because I remember the excitement of Sacajawea meeting her brother, Cameahwait, along the trail. It was a joyful time for me to see Junie after so many years.

I gave many talks along the way about the oral traditions of Sacajawea as my people know them. It seems as if I gave that same talk over and over, many times a day, to many different people; but I also answered many questions about the history of that time period. Of course, there were those who disagreed with me. Again, I tried to have respect for their beliefs. Others were interested in learning more about the oral tradition. I tried to be careful to disagree in an amiable way and not to be too aggressive in my manner of speaking. My grandfather had always told me that this was how my great-great-grandmother was. She was a gentle person.

"Gentle" here is not the same as wishy-washy. There are right and wrong ways to disagree. The right way is not to be quarrelsome and not to insist on having the last word. It helped, too, that I actually knew a number of people who had actually spent time with Sacajawea; for example, my Grandfather Finn Burnett, Rev. John Roberts, and an old cousin of mine, by the name of James McAdams. So, armed with all of this history and being such a devout believer, I swayed a lot of people's beliefs from depending solely on the written word of historians and journalists, to being more accepting of some of the oral traditions of our people.

One thing that I was very careful of on this expedition was to remember my Indian values and to remember that I was a role model for my people. I did not want to do anything that would discredit them or myself or my family. My husband and daughters, of course, did not go with me. Bob and I felt comfortable doing our own things; we trusted each other and had a strong love. Occasionally, some of the men on the expedition thought that they would provide me with the company they were sure I was missing by being away from my husband. I thanked them for their concern and said I would be delighted to have a drink with them if they came to visit in our home. This virtue was as important to me as it was to my great-great-grandmother.

Charbonneau attempted to parcel her body out to members of the expedition, but Clark came to her rescue and threatened to terminate his position. My great-great-grandmother would have fought his abuses as well. Back in an earlier era among our people, if a woman committed adultery, the tip of her nose was cut off so that she always bore that shame. One of our Indian values is sharing; we share food and clothing and that kind of thing, but we also share shame.

I felt her spirit was looking down on me, and I hoped that she was as proud of me as I was of her. I had always tried to do the right thing at the right time in the right place and to be a credit to Sacajawea and my Indian people. It's almost as though I had her permission to do this and that she would be proud of my performance. For, after all, she accomplished so many things on that expedition and became a model for all women.

We made it all the way to the Pacific Ocean and even visited Fort Clatsop, the restored fort where Lewis and Clark and the entire expedition wintered in 1805–6.

The next year, in 1956, we re-created the return expedition. I was the *modern* Bird Woman this time. I flew out to Seaside, Oregon, and took the motorcade back to Wood River, Illinois. We always think of St. Louis as being where the expedition disbanded, but it wasn't; it was Wood River. A bust of Sacajawea that I posed for was unveiled on the return trip at Washburn, North Dakota, which was the original winter campsite of Fort Mandan. Ida Prokop Lee had been commissioned to sculpt a series of ten Indian busts, of which this was one.

For me the trip was a chance to follow the route taken by the Lewis and Clark expedition and to experience vicariously the dangers that Sacajawea had encountered. Another reason for the trip for me was to broaden my historical horizons. I became more and more knowledgeable about the history of the land that had been a part of the Louisiana Purchase. I tried to envision the changes that had occurred in the last 150 years, both to the land and to the people who inhabited the land. It truly broadened my horizons. I shared my new knowledge with a myriad of church groups, school groups, historical societies, and service organizations after I returned home to North Dakota.

The expedition organizers asked me early on in the trip if there was some kind of souvenir of the anniversary expedition that I would like to have, and so I told them that I had always wanted to have a replica of the Jefferson Peace Medal. Sacajawea had been given one at the end of her journey in recognition of the role that she had played in the Lewis and Clark expedition. These two men, Art Rongstad and Harold Cole, honored my request. A coin or medal mold is never destroyed, and so they had one made for me at the Philadelphia mint. I never thought I would receive something so precious. It is one of my most valued treasures.

ANADARKO, OKLAHOMA: SACAJAWEA'S COMANCHE RELATIVES

In 1959, I was invited to go to Anadarko, Oklahoma, to unveil a bust of Sacajawea made by sculptor Leonard McMurry. It was going to be placed in the National Indian Hall of Fame, an outdoor sculpture garden. Sacajawea was the first Indian woman to be voted into the Hall of Fame. Lieutenant-Governor Nigh bestowed on me the title of honorary lieutenant-governor of the great state of Oklahoma.

While I was in Oklahoma for the dedication of this statue of my great-great-grandmother, I decided to look up some of my Comanche relatives. My mother told me that my Uncle Lawrence and Uncle Fred Large (mother's brothers) had made frequent visits to Oklahoma to visit these kinfolk, and that they, in return, had visited Fort Washakie to meet their relatives there. These Oklahoma relations were offspring of Sacajawea and

Jerk Meat, her Comanche husband. Prior to her return to Wind River, she had lived and had a family in Indian Territory, in what is now the state of Oklahoma. Comanches and Shoshones are closely related tribes, both linguistically and culturally.

So, I went to visit this cousin of mine who lived not far from Anadarko. I was not sure whether these folks spoke English or not, so I called on an old Comanche friend, Paul Attockni, whom I had known from Haskell, to act as my interpreter. When we got to their house, they were laughing and looking at me as they conversed in Comanche. I thought they were laughing and talking about me and about Paul being there to do the interpreting, which as it turns out is exactly what they were doing. They had some fun at my expense, but when Paul explained to them that I was the niece of Fred and Lawrence Large, one of the women started speaking in English.

We had a nice visit and exchanged oral traditions about Sacajawea, which were remarkably similar to those I had heard from my own family. She explained that Comanche oral traditions supported our belief that Sacajawea had wandered around for some time after leaving Charbonneau in St. Louis. One of her many names was Wadze Wipe, which means lost woman. She had a few children by her Comanche husband, and these were the people from whom my cousins were descended. After the death of Jerk Meat, she left the Comanches, and it was through the visits between the Wind River Shoshone and Oklahoma Comanche that news of her whereabouts came to light. Granddad Burnett remembered Sacajawea telling him that she had lived with some people to the south who spoke the same language as we did, and she told him of having married and raised a family there.

WHITE HOUSE CONFERENCE ON
CHILDREN AND YOUTH, MARCH 1960

I was appointed by Gov. John Davis of North Dakota to be one of twenty-seven North Dakota delegates to the White House Conference on Children and Youth. I was one of thousands of citizens who were asked to participate in the golden anniversary of a great national tradition that affects the children and youth of this nation. We met first in North Dakota for planning sessions, where we discussed state educational issues. Then we went to Washington DC to talk about these educational concerns. Our concern at that time was for an educational policy that would prepare young people to take their place in the twentieth century. We believed that strengthening such academic areas as the sciences, math, and foreign-language skills would achieve this goal and would encourage an interdependence of nations.

We were greeted by President Eisenhower and spent the week working in groups to create strategies to meet our goals. The exciting thing to me was that there were not only adults but also youth who had a say in the issues discussed, and I was thrilled when the youth in one of our groups selected me as the person they would most like to have as their teacher.

There was a real effort to have all nationalities represented at the conference. There were African Americans, Asian Americans, Native Americans, Chicanos, and others, which made for a very stimulating exchange. There were also international educators, one of whom was a woman sent from Israel to discuss the educational methods of the kibbutz.

In discussions with various groups about our educational philosophy in a nonreservation Indian boarding school, my remarks that we were involved in the total education of the child elicited surprise. I explained that we not only followed the state course of study but that we also incorporated Indian history and values into our curriculum. My explanation of Indian philosophies and values as wonderful rules for living got a lot of support. I don't think I've ever attended an educational conference that I got so much out of and gave so much to.

The organizers impressed on us that we were there for a purpose that was vital to the lifeblood of our nation and the future of our young people. This was not a conference from which we returned and did nothing. We had follow-up meetings, and the material that we came back with was consolidated, refined, and sent out to the field, to educators and others who might learn from and use it. We talked to people, discussed issues, and shared our new knowledge with other educators in the state. While in DC, we also had the opportunity to see Maria Tallchief perform in the Firebird Ballet.[2] She was exquisite.

CHAPTER SEVEN

Retirement and the 1960s through 1990s

Essie was only fifty-five when she retired from teaching, and she has remained an active advocate for Indian people in the years since her retirement. She traveled to Europe as an ambassador of her culture, initiated programs to keep kids in school, worked on Indian arts and dance projects, and has testified on the value of the boarding schools—even for modern-day American Indians.

Again, the personal record of Essie's life is a miniature of the life of the country, as it faces the issues of its Native American populations.

RETIREMENT

In the spring of 1965, in May, Bob and I retired from the Wahpeton Indian School after having served for more than thirty years in the Bureau of Indian Affairs. I will say that it was an ambivalent occasion. We were happy to be retiring and yet saddened to be leaving our friends and our community. Bob was not as unhappy as I because it was *his* idea to retire. We were young as retirees go. Bob was fifty-eight and I fifty-five when we retired. I thought I'd like to teach a few more years, but he said he was going to retire whether I did or not. Like Ruth, I thought, "Where thou goest, I go." I decided I would retire, too. It was a great sadness to be leaving the school.

While Bob's roots were in northern California with the Hoopa and mine in Wyoming with the Shoshones, the employees at the Indian school were our real extended family. This is true for many people in the Indian Service. While we were not going to be moving more than about a hundred miles away to our cabin in Naytahwaush on the White Earth Indian Reservation, it was still hard for me to separate myself from my students at the school. The routine I had grown to love so much, which included my association with the Indian Club, the scouting groups on campus, and so many other activities, was so hard to leave. I was very very close to those children. They spent time in my home and took trips with us; they were a very important part of my life.

Nonetheless, it was an exciting time during the preparations for our retirement. The people at the school went all out, and they had committees working on various duties. They wrote to everyone at the Bureau of Indian Affairs, sending out invitations to people and alerting them about our retirement. They made a huge scrapbook with a list of people who attended the get-together, and they included photos and the letters and telegrams and a list of gifts that we received. Sometimes when I begin to feel depressed, I go get our scrapbook and read some of the things that were said in tribute, and I get excited about my contributions all over again. Especially important are the letters from the students with whom I had interacted over the years. I was very close to these kids, and I think they hated to see me go as much as I hated to leave. It was good to be able to cry together—you know, to be able to put our arms around each other and shed tears. Even now I get emotional thinking about it.

When we decided to retire, we had a family meeting to decide what to do with the Indian artifacts we had acquired as gifts over the years. We decided to donate them to the Richland County Historical Museum in Wahpeton. We had beaded Woodland bandoleers, quillwork, moccasins, war clubs, parfleches, a Hoopa cradleboard, pottery, basketry, and numerous celts and arrowheads donated by local farmers. We gave it all in grateful acknowledgment of our love and appreciation for their acceptance of us as one of them.

Retirement was a great adjustment for me. I guess I would say that I was frightened to be leaving my position at the school. I had been so very busy with my teaching and other related duties, and I was involved in community activities that I knew I would miss. I missed my best friend and best teacher Martha Voigt; we were kindred spirits, she and I. We could lean on each other in times of need. Our house has always been a place where a lot of kids congregate. That did not change much even after we moved out to Naytahwaush. Our kids and grandkids became regular visitors as did old friends from the BIA, former students, and a variety of other people. For Bob, there was fishing and hunting, snowmobiling, and ice fishing. Local Chippewa friends invited him to go ricing with them in the autumn, and he had a lot of work to do on the cabin to turn it into a year-round home.

I continued to make frequent trips back to North Dakota to the boarding school, sometimes just to visit the kids and sometimes on more official business. I was invited by the superintendent to hold orientation sessions for new BIA teachers throughout the state, sessions in which I discussed the development of identity and pride in the Indian child. Part of this orientation entailed providing teachers with examples of how one might incorporate Indian materials and values into the curriculum. At the same time, I was becoming involved in educational and church-related activities in Naytahwaush, Minnesota, and was happy to be included in the goings-on of my new Chippewa community.

I used to drive all the time when Bob was overseas in the service, but when he returned, he sold my favorite little car and bought a big one. He always wanted to be in the driver's seat, and I didn't care, so for the most part I stopped driving. North Dakota was one of the last states to require a driver's license, but after retirement I needed a license so that I could be more independent. A lot of us women on the reservation had been driving for years with no licenses, so we all decided to get ours together. I was nervous about taking driver's training but took some lessons from a high school teacher in Mahnomen, Minnesota.

I studied real hard and did well on the written part of the test but had a difficult time passing the driving portion. I have a phobia about police anyway. Every time I'd go to take the driving test, I failed because the sight of a police uniform unnerved me and I made stupid mistakes. The first time, I remember, I got into the car and was in the middle of an intersection when I realized that I had forgotten to put on my seat belt. So I stopped right there and said, "Oops, forgot to put my seat belt on!" Of course I got scrubbed that time. I tried again and failed again.

All of the other women with whom I had started had all passed, with high scores, and here I was unable to pass the driving test. Finally, an old friend told the local officer that maybe I wouldn't be so nervous if he didn't wear his uniform. So, I went to give it one more try, and the officer wasn't wearing his uniform. I did better—just wasn't as scared, I guess. I remember toward the end of my test that I was asked to parallel park, which was definitely not my forte. The officer politely asked, "Mrs. Horne, would you like to try that again?" I don't remember how far away I was from the curb, but I must not have been too close. I asked, "Did I pass?" He said, "Yes, you passed." So I replied, "Then, no way! I *don't* want to try again." I've never encountered anything that threw me like getting my driver's license. We all had a big party after I finally passed that test.

In the pages that follow, I have highlighted some of the activities that brought me the most joy during my retirement. These all relate to working with our young people and the community. They include a trip to Europe, work with the 4-H, work with students at risk through Circle 68, the creation of Chippewa decor for the Episcopal village mission, a monograph on Sacajawea, and the senate hearings to keep the Wahpeton Indian School open.

THE GOODWILL TRIP TO EUROPE, 1965

Just after our retirement, in the summer of 1965, I was chosen to travel to Europe as a goodwill ambassador. At first there were three of us who were scheduled to go, but in the end I went alone due to the cost of such a trip. The way that the idea for this trip came about was that Gov. William Guy and his friend Robert Dean were discussing ways to promote travel to and interest in North Dakota and the United States, and they came up with the idea of sending a Native American ambassador to Europe. The result of their planning was that the United States Travel Service and North Dakota Travel Department also thought it would be a good idea and so funded this month-long goodwill tour. It was called "Visit USA, Visit North Dakota." Besides encouraging people to travel to the United States and North Dakota, another of the goals of this trip was to encourage Europeans to buy our authentic Indian arts and crafts rather than cheap Japanese or Taiwanese imitations. This machine-made beadwork had become more readily available in souvenir shops, and we thought it cheapened the beauty of our hand-beaded belts, medallions, and other items.

The timing of this tour in 1965 coincided with a growing interest, both here and abroad, in Indian history and culture. So, with my knowledge of Indian arts and crafts, as well as culture and education, I was chosen as an ambassador to travel to nine European countries: West Germany, Belgium, the Netherlands, Denmark, Norway, Sweden, Italy, France, and Austria.

I was schooled in Bismarck, North Dakota, for a week prior to departure, schooled on my itinerary and what my duties as goodwill ambassador were to be. Mr. Floren Zapp of the United States Travel Service, with offices in Frankfurt, Germany, accompanied me for the first week of my travels. He wanted me to be comfortable on foreign soil and so taught me a few words of German and schooled me in the socially acceptable graces that I needed to know in the various countries that I visited. He advised me to converse with the young in the countries that I was scheduled to visit, since they were required to take English in their schools.

Miss Von Schnakenburg, a public relations person with Lufthansa German Airlines, was in charge of my itinerary. She knew where I was supposed to be, what day I was supposed to be there, and who I was supposed to meet. She and Mr. Schultz, from the United States Travel Service, were at my disposal to answer any questions that I might have or to inform me of any changes that might occur in my schedule. Our embassies, too, had been alerted, and so I could call on the embassy attaché if I were in need of assistance.

When I landed in Frankfurt, however, nobody was there to meet me at the airport. I found my way to my hotel via taxi, a bit worried that I had been forgotten in a country where I could not speak or read the language. On the way to my hotel I exchanged some of my currency for German marks, and I remember seeing a smiling tiger ESSO gas station sign that read: "Put dem tiger in der tank." That familiar sign made me feel more at home. As it turned out, Floren had left a message for me at the hotel, and so everything worked out fine.

The promotional work was done via trade fairs, radio and newspaper interviews, photo sessions, and television spots. I do not speak a foreign language; my only knowledge of any language other than English was the smattering of Shoshone that I had learned at home and some Latin that I remembered from my schooling at Haskell. It was interesting to see myself speaking a foreign language on European television. They would dub my message in the language of the country that I was visiting at the time, and so I felt quite the sophisticated world traveler.

I took a number of beautiful pieces of Indian beadwork, quillwork, and pipestone, donated by our reservations in North and South Dakota, to present to foreign dignitaries like President Charles de Gaulle of France; Willy Brandt, then Mayor of West Berlin and later Chancellor of West Germany; Lord Mayor Bull of Oslo, Norway; and Urban Hensen, the Lord Mayor of Copenhagen. I was amused when the Lord Mayor of Copenhagen called me a "synthetic" Indian because I was not dressed in buckskin and didn't wear my hair in braids. I did have on contemporary Indian clothing made by Kiowa and Comanche artisans from the Southern Plains Indian Museum in Anadarko, Oklahoma, but that was not what he expected to see an Indian woman wearing. When I responded, "I see, Mr. Lord Mayor, that you are not wearing a horned headdress, the traditional garb of a leader of your people. Does that make you any less Danish?" he just smiled, but the exchange was recorded by his press secretary.

An even stranger experience occurred when I was to meet President de Gaulle to present him with his ceremonial pipe. I was accompanied by an official photographer from one of the major Paris newspapers, someone who had come along to photograph me presenting the pipe to de Gaulle. Before we went into the palace, the photographer said he thought it would be interesting for me to have my picture taken with one of the palace guards. I did not know that these guards were not to leave their post under any circumstances. Just about the time that the photographer's flash went off, the other guards surrounded us and immediately confiscated the pictures. The guard with whom I was to be photographed had accidentally moved out of his cubicle, which alerted all of the other guards to attention.

We were kept there for some time until all of us got clearance to leave. Members of the palace personnel told us that they had considered arresting us for this incident, but they didn't. As it turned out, I never did get to see de Gaulle, and so I presented the pipe to one of his aides. We were all really scared by the gravity of this now-funny situation and laughed nervously as we got back into the limo, relieved to be on our way.

On another occasion, when I was traveling from Hamburg to Copenhagen by train, our train was put on a ferry. The captain announced that we could leave our train and go up on deck to have lunch and enjoy the view. I had no idea that there was more than one train on the ferry, and so when it came time to board, I got on the wrong train. I walked up and down every car, and finally went to the conductor and said, "There is nothing familiar about this train." He said, "Madam is on the wrong train. Your train is over there." By that time the trains were preparing to depart. I ran as fast as I could across the tracks, but they had already taken up the steps to the train. I swung back up onto the train like a monkey onto a tree, feeling young and independent though very undignified. At least I had not been stranded on the wrong train. That would have been a real catastrophe!

I regularly visited with what are called "Indian Clubs" while I was in Germany. These Indian Clubs showed a great deal of respect for Indian culture, more than one finds in this country. Each club would select a specific state or tribe to study. They thoroughly researched their tribe by reading early historical accounts and becoming familiar with Bureau of American Ethnology publications. Many of them even visited reservations to learn about the techniques and materials necessary to create their artifacts and to learn about the culture and history of their specific group. They did not sell what they made, nor did they "play" at being Indian. For the most part they were adults who were doing a great deal of in-depth study.

Being objective, I couldn't find a great deal of fault with what they were doing. I was, in fact, ready to criticize the German Indian Clubs until I became acquainted with the people who belonged to these groups. For example, the Wyoming Club studied the Shoshone and Arapaho tribes. They knew about our culture and history, and made beautiful reproductions of our arts and crafts. They had such a deep appreciation for what they were doing. When I met with this group in Stuttgart, they brought out foot-lockers full of dresses, shirts, breechcloths, moccasins, leggings, gauntlets, and all matter of beautiful Indian paraphernalia that were equal in quality to those made by our finest Native American artists. Their quillwork, bead-work, and dressing of hides were comparable to the finest museum pieces.

The Wyoming Indian Club members were very excited about the Linden Museum in Stuttgart and demanded that I see it. It houses one of the finest collections of northern plains Indian artifacts in the world, most of which were collected by the Prince Maximilian-Karl Bodmer expedition of the Upper Missouri River in 1833–34. The president of this club was quick to let me see how knowledgeable he was about what the museum housed. I mistakenly identified a war bonnet case as a quiver and was immediately corrected by my guides. At their request, I taught them some men's and women's traditional dance steps.

I took a number of side trips while I was in Europe. The images of my trip to East Germany have remained vivid after all these years. I was staying at the Berlin Hilton, and I took a sightseeing bus over into East Berlin. That experience had an impact on my views of life behind the iron curtain, and I certainly appreciated being an American more after going through Check Point Charlie. They searched my luggage and my handbag, and I was not al-lowed to take a camera; they even changed drivers at the border. To me it was so disheartening to observe those people basically interned behind the Berlin Wall. They had guards on top of buildings and on the ground, and there were a lot of police dogs; every so often we would see a wreath of flowers that had been placed along the base of the wall where someone had tried to escape and been shot.

There were no smiling faces on the street. I saw school-age children in uniforms near the War Memorial, but even when we talked to them and smiled, they didn't smile back. Their faces were like granite. We saw the large nurseries where the preschool children went during the day while their parents were working. I still have a mental picture of the elderly sitting on benches. They looked dejected and silent. I was told that the elderly can walk over into West Berlin for a visit. I don't know if that's true or not, but it did appear to me that the state did not care much about folks who were not productive anymore. Even in the beer gardens, people seemed to be somber and reflective. It was such a relief to get back to West Berlin. Another re-minder of that division was that every day at six o'clock in the evening, the bells all over West Berlin tolled for about five minutes to remind the East Germans that those west of the wall had not forgotten them. I was so relieved and surprised when the wall finally came down a few years ago. I never thought I would live to see the day, and my heart leapt with joy.

When I was in Italy, I met a young man who said his last name was Sacajawea. After talking to him for quite some time and doing some reflective thinking about his age and appearance, I wondered if we might not be related. I had a number of relatives who were in the European theater during the war, and I thought it just might be possible that he had been fathered by one of my cousins, or maybe even my youngest brother Finn.

Sarain Sacajawea told me that he was going to send me something when I returned home, and when I got back from Europe, I received a carving that looks like an Iroquois mask. On the back of this he drew a snake. I had mentioned that the Shoshones were sometimes referred to as the Snake Indians. He sent my mother a little stone that he wanted thrown in Bull Lake, located on the Wind River Reservation. He sent it to her in a little medicine bag. Mother threw that stone in for him and said a prayer. The Lander, Wyoming, newspaper photographed the event, and my mom sent the clipping back to him in Italy. My mother gave me the little bag, and I keep medicine in it and carry it with me all the time. Sarain was going to come and visit me a number of years ago. He got as far as Canada, but then I never heard from him again.

I wrote home to Bob fairly often and regularly wrote to my grandchildren, of which I had two by this time. I called back to Bismarck once a week to report on what I was doing. The radio station taped my reports and broadcast them over the radio on Saturday mornings. I had to stay up quite late every Friday night because of the time difference.

I had enjoyed the challenge of being on my own in Europe, but even so I was very happy to be home again. I had enjoyed my travels and believed that I had gained some stature as a person as I met the press and helped to give people in Europe a better understanding of Native American culture. I tried to answer their questions about our culture truthfully and honestly. I thought that my trip had been a success: I had learned of some outlets for our Indian arts and crafts overseas. In fact, later we did send a number of shipments over to Europe. No doubt we would have been able to sell more Indian arts and crafts on the European market had their economy not been at such a low ebb.

Upon my return to the states, I was met by Sen. Quentin Burdick and his aide. Burdick acted as my liaison with Vice President Hubert Humphrey; Phileo Nash, commissioner of Indian Affairs; and press agents from the *Washington Post*, the Associated Press, and a Washington DC television station. The first relative that I saw on my return was my cousin Sen. Milward Simpson of Wyoming and his wife, Lorna. When I finally landed back in North Dakota, I was met by Bob and the girls and my son-in-law Bill Barney. Later, Gov. and Mrs. William Guy held a reception for me at the governor's mansion. I also was expected, in the months to come, to discuss what I had learned with Rotary Clubs, City Business Clubs, Women's groups, service clubs, and so forth.

A number of people that I met in Europe visited us in Minnesota after my return. A young brother and sister from Amsterdam, who were entertainers, had given a performance in Detroit Lakes. I received a phone call one evening from a friend in White Earth who said that these young folks wanted to come and see me. They came, and we sang folk songs through most of the night. Another time a couple of Norwegian nurses came by. One of them brought me a carved troll, knowing that I liked trolls so much. We were also visited by a couple from Zurich, Switzerland, who had an "Indianer Museum." They were traveling in the United States to purchase Indian artifacts for their museum. We gave them some rice knockers, a large Ojibway willow basket, a piece of Shoshone beadwork, and some wild rice. For a while after that, we exchanged our wild rice for their Swiss chocolate at Christmastime.

INDIAN CIRCLE, 1968

Circle 68 was a summer program designed to help Indian high school students at risk. It was an attempt to keep juniors and seniors from dropping out of school by engaging them in classes and activities about Indian culture and history taught by our Native people. It was believed that by immersing these students in their own Indian culture and encouraging an exchange with members of other tribes, they would develop a pride in who they were and increase their feelings of self-worth. It was also the intent of the program, funded by the Bureau of Indian Affairs, that these students would have the confidence in themselves to continue their education at the college level.

It was in the early summer of 1968 that a committee from the program requested my assistance in pulling its efforts together. The program had already begun but had become fragmented and was not accomplishing as much as they hoped it would. For the most part the counselors in the program were young Indian college students, and they were not exactly sure how to go about pulling the kids together. The program was in need of some direction and discipline. In addition, the instructors were more intent on skiing, fishing, and boating than on teaching.

I said that I would be glad to help them out but that I would need the assistance of my good friend Martha Voigt. She is a Hidatsa woman and old friend from Fort Berthold. She and I had spent a lot of time together at Wahpeton and had worked with the Indian Club there, and so we knew how to work as a team to accomplish the objectives. Our roles were to teach regalia making and Indian dance. I was a consultant who assisted in all facets of the program.

I tried to challenge the students and Circle personnel to share what they knew and to be willing to learn from others. I wanted to instill in them the excitement to know and to learn, and to understand more about who they were. I resorted to my use of Indian values to accomplish this and talked about bravery, generosity, and respect for elders and for others. The kids were interested in learning those values and were surprised that these were integral to their culture. They responded so positively—they became more self-disciplined and more self-confident.

Other teachers had been hired to teach about the culture areas of Indian people as well as about various tribal histories. After I was hired as a consultant, Ed McGaa, Ms. Lyons, Gerald Vizenor, and others assisted in the instruction. Fritz Scholder even sent an exhibit to be viewed by the participants.[1] We all worked together to give focus to the classes and the Circle really began to come together. Students were sharing; they were ambitious, and they began to think of the group as more of a "we" than an "I." I used the old story of the quail hunter and the quail to explain the idea of group cohesion and accomplishment. You see, there were these quail, and they were really smart. They could talk together and make plans together. They knew that if they all worked together, they could outwit the hunter and fly away with his net. This was their plan: One group would distract him and another confiscate his net so that he would no longer be able to hunt them. The problem was they took to arguing among themselves as to who would do what; so the hunter threw his net on the birds as they argued and had a fine quail meal that evening.

Students began to work more diligently, perfecting their regalia and dancing skills. They began to appreciate the depth of their Indian heritage and the expanse of its spirituality. Collectively, we all agreed that only those who completed their regalia would be allowed to take them home at the end of the summer. There was only one student who failed to complete her project.

Circle 68 was held at the Chippewa Ranch located between Naytahwaush and Mahnomen, Minnesota. It was a facility formerly used by the Job Corps, which contained dormitories, a dining room, a gym, and other meeting areas. The students were from all over the United States and represented a number of different tribes including Chippewa, Hopi, Tewa, Santo Domingo, Zuni, Apache, Navajo, Ute, Shoshone, Lummi, Winnebago, Mandan, Sioux, Cheyenne, Kiowa, Comanche, Pawnee, Otoe, Ponca, Cherokee, Creek, and Seminole. There were about 125 students, who were willing learners and anxious to share the knowledge of their cultures. A great many of them were familiar with their tribal cultures but needed some direction and discipline. Many were drummers and singers, and so we had a lot of expertise. We formed our own drum group, and Martha sang with them, having been honored by an Hidatsa drum group to take her place at the drum.

One young man, who was Apache, wanted to learn to fancy dance plains style, and so a Sioux student from Fort Yates and he exchanged information. The student from Fort Yates helped the Apache boy to make a traditional Sioux regalia, and he also taught him the dance steps. The Apache boy taught the Sioux how to construct Mountain Spirit Dance regalia and schooled him in the dance and its meaning.

I remember one young Ute boy in particular who had not learned to dance at home, and he wanted so badly to learn to Indian dance. He just couldn't seem to get it—the rhythm, I mean. He was one of the older boys and just had the hardest time hearing the drum. I said, "Well, take hold of my hand and we'll dance together." He took my hand and we tried. It took days, but finally, all of a sudden, he closed his eyes, listened to the drum, and began to dance. He was so excited about it. One of the staff members from Pine Ridge, a fellow who was an excellent dancer himself, was observing this lesson and our intensity. From the corner of the room he caught my attention and held up his fingers in an "O," to let me know that he really approved of this method of interactive dance and of letting the drum direct the dancer.

At the culminating program, there was such a variety of tribal presentations that it reminded me of the Gallup Ceremonial.[2] Students performed the Buffalo Dance, Intertribals, the Mountain Spirit Dance, the Deer Dance, and many others. It was publicized through radio, television, and other advertising media, and people came from miles around to see the performance.

Our attempts to instill pride in these students were successful, as demonstrated in the beautiful program that they presented. Over that summer, they developed into proud, responsible, and mature young adults. As for me, the experience strengthened my belief in the potential of our people. If you believe strongly enough in the capabilities of individuals, they will meet and even exceed your expectations. People of all ages need tender loving care; they need to feel that someone believes in them and is concerned about them. I knew that those kids would do well, and they did. I wouldn't let them believe anything else.

CHURCH WINDOW, 1969–1972

I'm Episcopalian, and when I first came up here to Naytahwaush and started going to church at the old Samuel Memorial Mission, which was founded in 1892, I noticed that it had a very lovely old stained-glass window, but the frame around it was plain plywood. I thought we needed to have a frame that would complement the beautiful window. I would sit in church before the service began and daydream about what I could do to beautify it for the church communicants. About two-thirds of our communicants are Chippewa, so I decided that maybe I could utilize some of their lovely floral designs on the frame. I had done quite a lot of mosaic work in jeweling bottles and Easter eggs, and I had cans of old jewels donated by the merchants of Wahpeton to use either as decoration on Indian fancy dance regalia or for different kinds of arts and crafts. I shared my thoughts with Fr. George Schulenberg, our vicar, and the parishioners were enthusiastic about my ideas.

The plan was to beautify the interior of the church by creating a jeweled and beaded frame for the nine-foot stained glass window, using Chippewa floral designs and motifs.

The church furnished the seed beads, which they had recently started selling to our local beadworkers. The church could purchase them in larger quantities and so sell them at a much-reduced cost to people who did beadwork. Beadwork was beginning to flourish, and the church both provided beads and marketed the completed pieces, thus supplementing incomes and creating a healthier reservation economy. When the bishop made his annual visit, he informed us that Joston's Jewelry Manufacturing Company of Owatonna, Minnesota, had an abundance of defective jewels that they would be happy to donate to our church if we could find a use for them.

The whole community participated in the church project. Some brought old pieces of beadwork—family heirlooms from which we copied traditional floral designs—and others sorted the jewels by color. Mrs. George (Etsuko) Schulenberg and I completed the final gluing of the jewels and beads onto the plywood frame. As Etsuko and I were placing the beads and jewels into a mosaic-type design, both of us kept trying to think of some biblical passage that would convey the meaning of the design on the frame. We felt that it needed a spiritual meaning as well. I was reading *Time* magazine and came across an article about the astronaut Buzz Aldren. His favorite Bible passage was, "I am the Vine, you are the branches," from John 15:5. I thought, "That's it." Our floral designs were connected by a vine, with small branches attached, the perfect symbol of the religious meaning we wanted to convey.

We began the project in 1969 and did not finish it until 1972. It took us nearly four years. We both made a small panel for ourselves as well so that we would have it as a remembrance should we move away from Naytahwaush. I still look at the window frame, which has been moved into the new church, and think, "What an amazing accomplishment for two novices to complete!"

After we finished the frame, we sewed some antique Woodland beadwork pieces on white buckskin and used them to decorate the altar, the pulpit, and the credence tables. The pieces of beadwork were in very bad repair, and many of the beads were missing. So some of our Episcopal women from the area refurbished them, and they became a part of the church decor. My niece, Mrs. Gary (Donna) Twitchell, a very fine beadworker, beaded an Indian style cross, a sheaf of wheat, and a cluster of grapes. These three beaded sacramental emblems were also sewn onto the buckskin on the front of the altar. So that's the story of the interior of the church; it has served to give our people a sense of pride in and respect for their Chippewa Indian culture.

NAYTAHWAUSH 4-H, 1970

The little school here in Naytahwaush had a 4-H Club. There were twenty-seven kids in the club, about half girls and half boys, ranging from nine to thirteen years of age. The county extension agent, Mae Kersting, a friend of mine, asked if I would be willing to help these kids to present something "Indian" for the annual "Share the Fun" night, which was held at the County Seat in Mahnomen every year. They were competitive presentations, with each local 4-H group vying for first place. I said, "I'll help you if you want to do something that's traditional, but I won't help you play Indian." All of the kids in the group were Indian, but none of them knew how to do the Native dances nor did they have Indian dance regalia. The principal of the school, Harold Searles, became involved and informed me that there was a fund in the school treasury for teaching Indian culture. He made this fund available to us, and so we set about learning some Indian dances and making our costumes.

We began by scrounging materials from the rummage boxes of the Episcopal and Catholic churches in the village, and soon the mothers and grandmothers became involved. We cut an old velvet purple stage curtain into breechcloths, and decorated the breechcloths with ribbon work.

Jingle dresses are a traditional Chippewa dance dress, having been given to the Chippewa of Mille Lacs Lake through a woman's dream. I did not know how to make these dresses in the traditional style, so I went to some of the Chippewa grandmas and asked them how to make the dresses and jingles. Some chose not to help, thinking, "Let this Shoshone woman find out for herself." I'm a very positive thinking person, and eventually there were more than enough people willing to help me make the jingle dresses. One of the women in the village supplied us with her jingle dress to use as a pattern, and a family who had moved here from Grand Portage offered to make all of the jingles for the girls' dresses.

The jingles are made from snuff box lids, which local volunteers collected from the nursing homes in Mahnomen and the surrounding areas. We even had collection boxes at some of the local stores. Bob made beading looms for each of the kids so that they could contribute to the beading of their own costume accessories, and some of the men from the area assisted the boys in making roaches.

Martha Voigt came for a while to assist in costume design and construction and to give instruction in sequin embroidery. Former students from Circle 68 (Theresa Bunker Olson, Susan Olson Coleman, and others) helped with sequin embroidery, and mothers became involved as seamstresses. It really became a community project. So many people were involved and supported our efforts to teach these young Indian kids about their heritage and culture.

The children became more and more involved; they wanted to work all day and all night, practicing and making their costumes. We had begun preparing for the festivities in the early spring while the kids were still in school, and we continued into the early summer. The kids would always say, "We're not going to win," to which I would reply, "Well, you know you're good, and I know you're good. Just do your dances the best you can, and if you don't win, it will be because the judges don't understand Native American culture. They may not even know how to judge you." Believe it or not, when it came to the performance, our kids did win! They were excellent.

The judges were drawn by the intensity of the children's performance and their knowledge of what they were doing.

Our dancers almost brought the house down with the applause that they received. It goes back again to my philosophy that if you believe enough in kids and give them enough pride in themselves, they're going to surprise you with what they'll do. There was no mistaking the pride and the joy that these children experienced in what they were doing. In fact, they were so good that they went on to compete at the regionals where they also took first place. This entitled them to an all-expense-paid trip to perform at the Minnesota State Fair in St. Paul.

Our Indian kids were the darlings of the media at the state fair. Television, newspaper, and radio covered their performances. They were only scheduled to perform once but danced numerous times to accommodate the hordes of people attending the state fair who wanted to see their program. The Naytahwaush community council provided each kid with enough spending money for the trip.

This is one of the most exciting experiences that I've had in teaching Indian youth. I was *so* proud of those children; they transformed themselves from shy and quiet kids to knowledgeable and exuberant individuals. As for me, I continued to teach Indian dance at the school as a part of the physical education program until my age caught up with me and my energy was at low ebb.

SACAJAWEA MONOGRAPH, 1979–80

An angry phone call from my sister Bernice disturbed my tranquillity at my lake cottage in Naytahwaush. "Essie," she said. "You need to come home immediately." Bernice lives at Fort Washakie on the Wind River Reservation, and she was upset by a series of articles in the Lander paper, *The Wyoming Journal*. "That old liar Blanche Schroer is at it again! She's trying to make all of us look like fools and liars." Blanche Schroer, a self-styled woman historian, had written an article in *Wyoming Magazine* about Sacajawea; it was picked up by the Lander paper and reprinted.

Schroer explained that the stories and oral traditions of our people concerning Sacajawea's return to our reservation were fabrications and myths. She reasoned that they were false since everyone knew that Sacajawea had died in 1812. She took it upon herself to end our stories once and for all, and she did so with a vengeance. She believed that written history was true and oral history was not. Some of the people in our tribe petitioned my sister Bernice Twitchell to respond to the attacks of this old white woman. They were so angry! Some of those old Shoshones said, "We should hang that son of a bitch." I flew out to Wyoming and stayed for about six weeks. Bernice and I wrote rebuttal articles, and the Lander paper published them.[3]

I had heard countless people remark that Schroer's writing denied the very integrity of Finn Burnett and Rev. John Roberts. Everyone said that if those two gentlemen said that they knew Sacajawea, had done things with her, and were present at her burial ceremony, then it must be so. They were honorable men, men of impeachable integrity; they had no reason to distort history. Schroer claims that our oral traditions were attempts to romanticize our history and for our reservation to lay claim to Sacajawea's burial spot. She suggests that Reverend Roberts was intentionally vague about his identification of the old woman he buried, Porivo, as Sacajawea. She also says that old Shoshones whom she has questioned told her that Porivo was never called Sacajawea until so dubbed by Hebard. If this is true, it is either a case of these elders not understanding what Schroer was asking them or of telling them what she wanted to hear so as not to appear to be impolite. There are many stories of Indian people creating answers to the questions of anthropologists and historians either as jokes or to comply with requests.

We had a great deal of support from the media. They said they were glad that some Shoshone people had spoken up on this issue. So, we haven't heard from her anymore; maybe she's lying low until we both pass on. I do not deny her and others their right to believe what they understand as the truth; it baffles me that she is so intent on trying to discredit our beliefs. I find solace in this quote by George Washington Carver that I've made a part of my philosophy, "I will let no man belittle my soul by making me hate him."

When I returned to Naytahwaush, I decided it would be much easier to honor people's requests for information on Sacajawea by putting all of the materials that I had collected over the years together under one cover. I had done a lot of speaking on my ancestor, beginning way back in the 1920s when I was at Haskell, and people had always said I should write a book about Sacajawea to help answer people's questions about her—and share it with the public.

I had begun writing down the oral traditions and stories about Sacajawea when I was about eighteen or nineteen years old. Every summer when I went home, I'd make a point to spend some time at Fort Washakie with Granddad Burnett. He would tell the same stories over and over again; he never tired of retelling them, and I never tired of listening. As I talked to my grandfather, I knew that I was listening to history—a local history of my family and tribe. Listening to and telling stories were how we taught our children. They were our method of committing to memory the history of our people to pass on to our children, and they to their children.

In 1932 I asked Granddad Burnett if he would write down some of the information he had gleaned from his personal association with Sacajawea; I wanted to keep a record in his own handwriting. I was desirous of any information he remembered about her talking about the Lewis and Clark expedition, her return to the Wind River Reservation, and her later life. So in response to my specific questions, he sent me two rather lengthy letters that are reprinted in appendix C.

Rev. John Roberts, the Episcopal minister who officiated at her burial, also told me stories and eventually wrote them down for me. He said that Sacajawea was given a Christian burial. The church made a rough box for her and wrapped her in skins, and she was buried that way on the Wind River Reservation. His letter is included in appendix C as well.

I also used data from Grace Raymond Hebard and Charles Eastman to support the oral traditions of my Shoshone people, and I put them together into a self-published monograph in 1980 (Horne 1980). The first time I did a printing, I had 150 copies made. To date I have printed 350 copies that I share with people when they request information of me (see appendix C).

SENATE HEARINGS, 1982

In February of 1982 I took part in some hearings in Washington DC. The BIA was proposing to close three off-reservation boarding schools, one of which was Wahpeton. In the fall of 1981, I received a call from the president of the Federal Employees Union at the Indian school, Mitchell Gripentrog, who appealed to me to come back and help us save our school. I became part of a group of concerned people who represented the school and community. North Dakota senators and representatives, and other elected officials, were also involved, and a group of us went to DC to testify before the Senate Select Committee on Indian Affairs, chaired by Sen. Mark Andrews of North Dakota. I had never been a part of anything quite like this before. There was standing room only in the hearing room, and there was an abundance of media present.

In the hearings, a number of us testified that the school should not be closed. Most of the children who attended boarding schools in the 1980s were from dysfunctional families. Abuse and neglect resulting from increased alcohol and drug use have had a negative effect on the people of many reservations. There were four of us who testified that the Wahpeton Indian School should remain open. Administrators and teachers were prohibited from testifying, and so Walsh County Judge Ted Weisenburger, Wahpeton Chamber of Commerce Executive Vice President Lynn Bueling, and myself went to speak on behalf of the school. Sen. Mark Andrews subpoenaed Leroy Chief, superintendent of the Wahpeton Indian School, and so he was allowed to participate in the hearings.

Judge Weisenburger, who served as the tribal council judge in Devils Lake, North Dakota, had sent many kids, by court order, to Wahpeton. This was in lieu of sending them to correctional facilities, and he spoke of the healthy attitudes that were present at the school and the positive effects that the school had on each child. He said that the government is indirectly responsible for poverty on reservations that results in alcoholism and neglect, and so he holds that it is the government's responsibility to provide these kids with a healthy home away from home.

Lynn Bueling of the Chamber of Commerce provided testimony from a community standpoint. He explained what fine things the school was doing for the children from the perspective of the town, and how it had become integral to the community.

I spoke about the educational and cultural advantages of boarding schools. As a former teacher, I testified about the curriculum and about the positive things that a school like Wahpeton can provide for Indian children when the staff, teachers, and administrators are sensitive to the needs of the kids. I noted that for some students, the school had provided the first real contact that they had with their ethnic heritage.[4] I took photos of the "old" school to contrast with pictures of how it looks now. Those drew a lot of attention, because they were proof positive that the buildings at the schools were not run down and dilapidated as Ken Smith, assistant secretary for Indian Affairs, had claimed.

I explained that he had been misinformed about the conditions of the school and invited him to view the photos that refuted his testimony. He sat there really nonplussed. Later, he did come out, at our invitation, to see the school. He said he was very impressed and thought the school's chances of remaining open or being closed were fifty-fifty.

He still voiced the objection to the off-reservation boarding schools that Indian children should be educated as close to home as possible, and in their own communities. We agreed but pointed out that rarely are these facilities available and that frequently it is in the best interest of children to remove them from unstable homes to schools that provide them with a stable environment. Here, they also have the opportunity to interact with other Indian students until such time as their families are better able to care for them. We argued that the BIA should not be blind to the social needs of Indian people.

We knew we had won a big battle when word came from Secretary of the Interior James Watt that the Wahpeton Indian School would remain open. It was the kids whose lives this decision would impact the most. This was the beginning of another school year (1982), and the kids were elated as they returned to their familiar and happy environment on the Indian school campus.

The school has had its ups and downs since then. A few years ago, in 1993, Wahpeton was changed from a Bureau school to a Grant school. It is chartered by the Sisseton-Wahpeton tribe (Sioux), and the governing board is made up of Native American people basically representing the students enrolled at the school. Five of the six members of the governing board represent the tribes with the largest student enrollment, and representatives are limited to one per state. The sixth member represents the charter organization.

In 1995, the Circle of Nations Wahpeton Indian School was named as a Therapeutic School. It now serves at-risk Indian youth. Interestingly, two of my former fourth-grade students from the Wahpeton Indian School—Joyce Melk Burr (Turtle Mountain Chippewa/Oglala) and Karen Starr Gillis (Arikara)—are serving as superintendent and assistant superintendent, respectively.

CHAPTER EIGHT

Retrospective

Now in her eighties, the great-great-granddaughter of Sacajawea looks back on a life that has mirrored the social and cultural changes that have filled the years since 1909. Philosophies of life are rooted in the lives of those doing the philosophizing. In the case of Essie Burnett Horne, that life has generated deep-seated conclusions about activism, education, feminism, grandmothering, who is Indian? spirituality, and death.

The thoughts of a wise but unassuming woman concerning these central issues of life comprise the culmination of this life history.

I have traveled around the United States, to Canada, Mexico, Hawaii, the Caribbean, and through Europe. I wrote a book on Indian education that was not published. I was blessed with a loving and understanding husband, and I have wonderful children, grandchildren, and great-grandchildren. I feel very fortunate that the Great Spirit has blessed me with many honors and a full, happy, and rewarding life.

I continue to be involved in education and to act as a consultant for individuals, schools, and colleges across the United States and abroad. Interviews that I've granted have been taped and used for reference material. Over the years I have had numerous students who have contacted me to come to their classes or schools to deliver presentations on Indian values and the contributions of American Indians to American society. I still regularly visit the Naytahwaush school on the White Earth Reservation in Minnesota to talk to the children about the Lewis and Clark expedition, and I am an adopted grandma of the children of the Wahpeton Indian School in North Dakota, now known as the Circle of Nations Wahpeton Indian School. I am grateful that I've retained my physical and mental health. The following sections include stories and thoughts about my philosophies of life.

ACTIVISM

I believe that Native American activism really began soon after Europeans landed on the shores of the Americas. To me, activism simply means not being passive. That Europeans were never able to enslave us is proof of the fact that we are not a passive people. We have endured confinement on reservations, the Trail of Tears, the breaking of treaties, and endless attempts to wipe us out.

I followed with interest the growth of the American Indian Movement (AIM) and other organizations whose intent was to draw attention to the plight of American Indians, in the hope that our lot could be improved. They said that they espoused a return to tradition, but most of their events were organized so as to garner front-page headlines. I never quite understood the connection between the two, especially when their rhetoric began to include the belief that an armed revolution was an answer to the problems faced by Indian people. Be that as it may, it was in Minneapolis in 1969, at a convention of the Minnesota Indian Education Association, that I first witnessed the infiltration and demands being made by the Black Panthers and AIM.

I was greatly surprised and a bit shocked when Dennis Banks and George Mitchell, two of my former students from the Wahpeton Indian School, came up and put their arms around me and walked beside me.[1] They were laughing and teasing me, and Dennis said, "Mrs. Horne, you know, you might well have been called the mother of AIM." And I said. "And how is that?" And they said, "Well, you used to tell us, 'Keep your heads up. Don't smell your knees. And don't be a puppet on somebody else's string.'" And I said, "Well, those are my very words, and I still believe in those things. I'm not always in sympathy with the way that you do things, but I am happy that you are drawing attention to the problems faced by our people. I am proud that you remember those things I was trying to teach you when you were my students." I chuckle when I think of their labeling me the "mother of AIM," but I am proud of their recognition of the small part I may have played in their activism and self-esteem.

Another time at a National Council of Churches meeting (1969), Dennis [Banks] was up on the stage demanding that their concerns be taken seriously. AIM was intent on bettering the education, housing, and health of Indian people. They were also distressed by police brutality, poor conditions in prisons, and the large percentage of Indian people and other minorities who were incarcerated. I was sitting up front near the stage, next to Dr. and Mrs. Norman Vincent Peale, and along crawled George [Mitchell] on hands and knees to my side and tugged on my skirt and said, "Well, how are we doing?" So as not to draw attention to myself, I whispered, "Well, you seem to be doing very well." All of us sitting at the table had a laugh over those antics.

I don't remember that either Dennis or George were particularly good or outstandingly poor students. I guess I would describe them as run-of-the-mill, as far as academic performance goes. I do remember that they were both very interested in Indian history and Indian culture. I also remember that as a little boy, Dennis was particularly interested in the contributions of Indians to the American way of life. I remember telling this to Jerry Roy, another member of AIM and a good friend of mine from up here at Naytahwaush, and he said, "Oh, so that's where Dennis gets his speech about the contributions of the Native American to the white man's way of life." I have always taught my students that what is American is basically Native American—from the Declaration of Independence to popcorn and potato chips.

Leonard Peltier was also one of my fourth-graders.[2] I remember him as a mild-mannered, happy kid who was very interested in his Indian heritage. In a recent interview that Janice and Leroy Chief sent me, interestingly he recalled my influence. He said, "Mrs. Horne taught us the different meaning of war paint designs and how great Pocahontas was."[3]

EDUCATION

Many of my younger friends help keep me up-to-date on educational issues. The old becomes new, I think, if you wait long enough in education. That's what I believe. The three D's—discipline, dependability, and desire—are really central to education.

I attempted to incorporate Indian values into every sphere of instruction—classroom, scouting, Indian Club, sports, everything! The five values that I focused on in particular were bravery, generosity and sharing, respect for elders, individual freedom, and respect for the environment. These had been impressed on me by both my mom and dad, and by Ella and Ruth, when I was young, and so I wanted the kids who were far away from home and family in the boarding school setting to be aware of their Indian identity and their Indian culture. This was critical during much of the time that I was teaching, because in the 1920s–40s, many Americans were intent on losing their unique cultural heritage and becoming part of the melting pot.

More and more Indians were moving to the city or were no longer aware of their special history or spiritual philosophies. Here at Wahpeton, we had kids from all over the northern plains who needed to be reminded of their cultural background. The government had been so intent on erasing our Indianness, and the boarding schools in particular tried to teach us to be like the non-Indian.

When I talked about *bravery*, I taught that bravery is much much more than being physically strong and that the highest form of bravery is having the strength to discipline oneself. In a classroom or in after-school activities, the students were encouraged to be strong enough and brave enough to be responsible for their own behavior. In traveling off-campus for Indian Club presentations, athletics, scouting activities in the community, and so forth, the students took charge of themselves and thus alleviated the necessity of our disciplining them. The students learned to be responsible for their own behavior so as not to bring down shame on everyone in the group.

Generosity includes the sharing of material goods as well as the sharing of praise and shame. The Indians of long ago regarded the goods of the world as belonging to everyone. People shared food and shelter with the knowledge that when they were in need, the favor would be returned. This was the Golden Rule personified. I also taught that when someone receives an honor, the group shares in that honor and so the individual should not be put down for succeeding. And when a shameful act is committed by a tribal member, our whole group suffers. For example, the students in my classes at Wahpeton believed that one unruly member reflected poorly on all of us but that we also shared in the glory of students who achieved success.

Respect for elders is another primary Indian value. In the olden days, the Indian people had no written language, and they carried all that they had learned in their heads. Since wisdom was passed down from one generation to the next, they acquired knowledge by listening to those older than themselves. The example set by the Indian Club at Wahpeton in showing respect for teachers, advisers, and dormitory personnel, as well as for the traditions of their tribal elders, was noted by other students. It wasn't long until this value became evident in the behavioral patterns of the students throughout the school. Teachers and staff complimented them on incorporating this Indian value into their lives.

Individual freedom means making responsible decisions and choices for oneself, as well as respecting your brother's or sister's vision. This must come from within but can be developed by listening to the advice of others. In this way the group can maintain its strength through the dependability of individuals.

I also stressed the importance of concern for the *natural environment*. To the traditional American Indian, nature includes all things. There is, we believe, an interconnectedness among all parts of the natural world, including humans, animals, birds, insects, plants, and the elements, as well as a connection between the natural and supernatural. All were believed to be part of the circle of life. Students understood this environmental concern as not breaking limbs off trees, not littering, and not abusing animals; because really, they are our brothers and sisters. And it seemed that children really caught on to those things easily. Remembering that the wind is the breath of the Great Spirit, and that the Great Spirit, God, and the Supreme Being are all one and the same, was almost second nature to them.

Lastly, my advice to all teachers of Indian students is to get to know as much as you can about the richness of the students' various cultures. I do not mean generic information on "Indian" culture but specifics on Navajo or Lakota or Chippewa beliefs. If there are powwows, attend one. Be sensitive to Native American perspectives on death and on extended families; do not assume that your students feel the same way about things that you do. For example, in a number of Plains Indian tribes, it is customary to honor the deceased with a memorial one year after they have passed away. This may be as important as the funeral itself, and children are expected to attend. Children may also have more than two sets of grandparents, because this kinship term is frequently extended to many individuals of that generation. Do not patronize your students. Respect them and they will respect you.

FEMINISM

I have always thought of Sacajawea as a forerunner of the women's movement. Maybe my relationship to her is why I've always been a forward sort of woman. In some Indian tribal prophecies, this is the time of the woman— of female leadership. There seems to be a renewed focus on the importance of women in all of our varied roles.

For example, Sacajawea is associated with the beginning of the women's movement in this country. I believe that the suffragettes used her as a symbol for their cause due to her position in Chief Washakie's council and her eloquence in speaking on behalf of maintaining the peace between Indians and whites. They may have exaggerated her role as pilot of the Lewis and Clark expedition, but they resurrected her memory and brought her to the attention of the public.

I think, though, that she's been a symbol for Indian women for a long time. She represents different things to different women, depending on their perspective. There is, of course, the view expressed by some of our radical Indian women who think, "Hmmm. Big Deal. She guided these white men through our territory. She was a traitor to her people." This really begs the question of why she was there and what she did. She was not hired as a guide but accompanied her husband, Toussaint Charbonneau. She acted as translator and probably anticipated a reunion with her Shoshone people. She had been captured by the Hidatsa when she was ten or eleven years old and had not seen her family since then. Charbonneau, a French-Canadian trapper and trader, bought or won her from the Hidatsa, and she became his wife.

When Charbonneau, who was passing through Fort Mandan in what is today North Dakota, told Lewis and Clark that he spoke Minnetaree and some other Missouri River tribal language, and that he had a Shoshone wife, they hired him almost immediately, requesting that he bring his Shoshone wife with him. Lewis and Clark knew that they would be traversing through Shoshone country and that a female Indian translator would be invaluable. To Charbonneau, Sacajawea may have been little more than a piece of property—his justly deserved winnings in a game where he made the rules. She was young; she was Indian; she had a newborn infant to care for and protect; and he was a typically abusive "squaw man." Sacajawea, then, can also be viewed by Indian women as a victim—a female captive, a woman abused by her white husband.

If she is a victim, however, she is also a survivor. She left an abusive relationship and began an independent journey to discover who she was and what her roots were. *This* expedition, her second, brought her into contact with other tribes and eventually brought her back home to her people. My great-great-grandmother was a legend but also a real woman with human frailties and real problems.

I think many women look to her as a source of strength. Her practical knowledge of the land, her endurance and tenacity, and her leadership as an elder have all endeared her to Native American women.

Later in my life, I was active in Ohoyo. Ohoyo was a group founded in the 1970s by Indian women; its purpose was to create a forum to explore the many issues affecting us Indian women. I found it very exciting and stimulating to listen to these bright and wonderfully keen-minded women discussing what they were doing in their different fields. We were a group whose focus was to discuss women's changing roles in today's society. Their words challenged me to rethink some of the issues that we face as Indian women. One of the things of which we were advocates was that we push our men harder without it being evident that that's what we are doing. We need not deprive them of their dignity, but neither should we allow ourselves to be pushed around. I was surprised that so many of these women were passive in their roles as women and were afraid to upset the position of their men.

We discussed how some of our Indian men get to the top of the corporate ladder and then become caught up in their own importance; they become self-righteous and arrogant, and lose track of their Indian values. This is not to say that women don't do this as well. Just look at AIM and tribal politics. We discussed how men and women need each other. We need to nurture each other, to share our strengths. That's how it was in traditional societies. That's how we create strong families and strong communities—by working together and respecting each other.

Throughout my lifetime I have always relied on the support of women friends. They sustain me when I am down, listen to me when I am in need, and I value these special relationships as I have grown older. I have always valued close relationships, like those with my mother, my father's sisters, with my teachers Ruth Muskrat Bronson and Ella Deloria, with other women such as Louise Peake and Martha Voigt, and with my daughters Vonnie and Dianne, and even my granddaughters, Debra, Jennifer, and Sarah.

In addition, through my involvement with my Episcopal church family in Naytahwaush and Wahpeton and on the state and national levels, I have established a core of relationships with a myriad of kind, understanding, and talented women. Women whose traditional knowledge of Indian culture was far greater than mine shared what they knew with me.

All of my close relationships with women, including female students, have molded me into the person that I am today. Each of us shared our special visions, instilling a broad sense of who we are as women with each other.

GRANDMOTHERING

I think of the grandmother's role as the epitome of Indian education. She is the dispenser of culture to the children. My mental picture of an Indian grandma is of an old woman sitting on the ground with children sitting around her listening with rapt attention. It was her responsibility to recount to them the myths, the legends, the tales, the history—all of the tribe's oral traditions. Through these, the children learned what it meant to be a member of their tribe. Grandmothers helped care for children, attended to the sick, and gathered and prepared food; their duties were essential to the continuation of Indian culture. The values that the children were expected to live by, the spiritual traditions, and the skills necessary for survival were passed down through the elders.

In Native societies, the term "grandmother" refers to any older woman in the community. She doesn't have to be biologically related to you for you to call her "Grandma." An Indian grandma, like any good teacher, combines friendship with discipline. Sometimes her love is a tough love; other times it is tender. Today, older Indian women are frequently the glue that holds a family together. Their special relationship with their grandchildren provides the opportunity to keep the tribal beliefs alive.

I think a lot of non-Indians have lost respect for their elders. They just aren't as important to them anymore. While some of our people may not revere the grandmas and grandpas as much as they used to, many still retain a great respect for the wisdom that comes with age. Fortunately, there has been a resurgence of interest in oral tradition. The younger tribal members understand that their elders are the source of that tradition, and they are making haste to take advantage of this knowledgeable resource.

I like living here on the White Earth Reservation. I like being in this community because of my relationship with the Chippewa people. It took some time to establish a rapport, but over the years I've become a member of this community. When I was selected as Senior Citizen of the Year in 1985 by the community, the presenter of the award posed an interesting question. He asked, "Essie, did we adopt you, or did you adopt us?" My reply was, "We've adopted each other. This is one of the greatest honors that has ever been bestowed on me, and I will treasure it for the rest of my life." And this really sums up the depth of my feelings for my community, the Anishanabe people of White Earth.

One story of grandmothering that holds a great deal of meaning for me goes back to my old Haskell friend, Louise Breuninger Peake. She and I attended a Sun Dance at Crow Dog's Paradise on the Rose Bud Reservation in South Dakota. Louise's youngest daughter's husband's son, Scott Raymond, was going to be one of the dancers in the Sun Dance, and he invited Louise and me to be his grandmothers for this ceremony. I was familiar with the Sun Dance, because our people Sun Dance, but we don't pierce. Louise, who is Cherokee, had never attended a Sun Dance. It was a very spiritual and sacred time for us; we prayed that our "grandson" would have the strength to pull the thongs out by himself. While attending this sacred ceremony, I had this feeling in my innermost of total spirituality, total commitment, and a closeness to the Great Spirit. I don't differentiate between

God and the Great Spirit. To me they are one and the same; my Christianity and my Indianness balance each other.

I am very family oriented. I treasure all of my relations, both biological and nonbiological. In particular, however, my blood relatives are a central part of my life. My children, grandchildren and great-grandchildren, and all my relations hold a special place in my heart.[4] It is sad to grow old but nice to ripen.

WHO IS INDIAN?

The questions of Who is Indian? or How Indian are you? are ones that I am becoming more and more aware of and more and more perturbed by. As Indian people have intermarried with non-Indians, or members of other tribes, and as we have accommodated ourselves to the twentieth century, these questions are regularly directed at us by both Indian and non-Indian interrogators.

To me, an Indian is anyone who chooses to be identified as an Indian, regardless of blood quantum. Nobody asks other individuals what their blood quantum is—not the Vietnamese, nor the Kurds, nor the Bosnians or Serbs. It seems to me that if you choose to identify yourself as an Indian, and you are a direct descendent of someone who is recognized by their tribe or the government as an Indian, then regardless of blood quantum, you are an Indian! Just because I don't live on the reservation does not mean that I don't have a very close tie with my tribe. I simply chose to help my people—the children from many tribal groups—to promote a pride in self and a pride in their tribe.

I also quite often visit my allotment of 160 acres when I am home. My allotment is grazing land with a few trees and a creek running across it, for which I'm grateful. The Bureau Realty Office at Wind River has contacted me numerous times to see if I would sell. This has been an ongoing request from the late 1920s when I was a student at Haskell until 1997. I have no intention of selling my land. I treasure it and am proud to have title to a piece of my reservation. It is a part of my home, of my heritage. My children may sell it to the tribe or to whomever when I die. Until then, it is a symbol of my Shoshone blood.

Those children, a whole generation of Indian kids including me, who for one reason or another were sent to boarding schools were separated from their tribal group. That doesn't make us any less Indian. That doesn't mean that we don't know who we are.

One's complexion, unfortunately, will always be an issue of acceptance by the community. I know of many mixed-blood families where the lighter-skinned children are not readily accepted by their Indian community and the darker-skinned children are labeled as "Indian" by the white community. What kind of nonsense is this that we can't accept our own?

A definition of "who" is Indian may be of some importance, but it has been argued about and tossed around by individuals, tribes, and the BIA until no one is really sure what is important and what is not, or, why we argue about the issue. Our Indian blood gets thinner and thinner, and the acculturation becomes greater and greater. It may be that a hundred years from now we're going to be a lot less Indian, a lot less traditional than we are now. Alcohol and drugs are destroying us; our families are breaking down.

Nevertheless, we're trying very hard to hold on to our culture. So many things were beaten out of us, made illegal, or denounced as savage and heathen. We're making an effort to hold on to our oral traditions—because they really contain who and what we are as Indian people. I think it's going to be a long time before our oral traditions are destroyed or lost, if ever. The Europeans who came here and took away our land—they destroyed their own culture; they forgot their mother tongues in the quest to be American. We are the original Americans, and we have survived as Native Americans.

SPIRITUALITY

As we, as human beings, move into the twenty-first century, we are going to have to slow down, or at least learn to take things one step at a time. We need to focus on the positive in our lives and not always complain about the negative. As an elderly person, I am very aware of this. The most prominent topic of conversation among many of the older people that I live with in my apartment building in Wahpeton is their ill health or their most recent operation. One woman reburies her husband, who died in 1980, nearly every time that we sit down to visit. So, I try to counsel her to think of the positive things about their life together and what a joy it was to have him when he was alive. I have a great deal of faith in the power of positive thinking.

I do get depressed occasionally, but when I feel myself allowing the pain in my joints or the sadnesses in my life to overwhelm me, I get busy—call a friend, write letters, read a book, or get out of the house. I regularly go to the senior center here in Naytahwaush for lunch. That interaction helps me to keep my finger on the pulse of the community. We need to exercise our minds as well as our bodies. "Use it or lose it." As a result, I look back over my life and see all of the happiness and don't dwell on my advancing years.

I have had a number of bouts with illnesses over the past several years. In 1983 I had a third recurrence of pneumonia. I was hospitalized and through x-rays they discovered that I had a large mass in my lungs that was the consistency of fiberglass. Exploratory surgery was performed to determine if the mass was cancerous. The doctors discovered that it was a healed-over area of tuberculosis; but in the surgical process my right vocal chord was injured, and I was unable to speak out loud for six months. I discovered a lot of things about myself during that time.

One thing was that I became more sympathetic with people with disabilities, and the other was that once my voice was recovered, I vowed never to complain about my aging body again. Some people who did not know how to cope with my inability to talk above a stage whisper avoided me, while other people yelled so that I could hear them. There was no guarantee that I was ever going to get my voice back, but there again, with prayers, positive thinking, and an anointing with oil by Fr. George Schulenberg, I did regain my voice after six months time.

I also had uterine cancer in 1989. I felt lucky that the tumor broke and that it was discovered in time that I could take radiation treatment. During the thirty radiation treatments, I made many friends with other people who were being treated for cancer at St. Luke's Treatment Center in Fargo. I discovered that there were many people who were worse off than I was. We became a support group for each other, confiding our fears and talking about our lives. I took the med van from Wahpeton to Fargo; the drivers of the van were retired professional men who volunteered their time to care for those of us who could not make that drive. I visited with them as well as the other cancer patients who were going to Fargo. I still see a lot of those people today, and the volunteer drivers always ask how I am doing.

Some, but not all, Indian people have accepted Christianity. This does not mean we have abandoned our culture; it is but another expression of our spirituality. Conversion to Christianity does not mean discarding the older, traditional ways, nor does it require replacing one belief system with another. It is, rather, a mixing of the two. There is one Creator, and we bring the powers of our tribal and Christian ways together.

We have to thank Mother Earth for her blessings. And we all do it in our own way. Indian people don't necessarily distinguish between the natural and the supernatural. Everything is a part of the universe. When you are in need, the natural and the supernatural worlds will communicate with you, advise you, and help you to find a way to solve your problem.

DEATH

In 1973, Bob wanted to take what we called a sentimental journey. We went back to the Hoopa Reservation in California, and Bob visited all of his old childhood haunts. We visited with his family, and it was on our return home that I could tell that Bob was not feeling too well. We thought perhaps that it was due to his back, which had been bothering him since he had helped his Aunt Marie Roberts till her garden in California. He continued to feel worse and worse all summer. He just lay around, which was quite unusual for him, because he was always so active. One morning in September, he woke me up saying that he had a 104-degree temperature. We took him back to Fargo to the Dakota Hospital where he was diagnosed as having prostate cancer. He died on January 7, 1974.

I stayed with Dianne and Ev for the rest of that winter but then returned to our home in Naytahwaush at the end of May. It was this time, while I was staying here by myself, that was the most difficult period of adjustment, because it was then that I had to face the fact that Bob was not coming back. I do believe that Bob's spirit maintains a presence around our lake home. I've have a recurring dream; this dream is that Bob is not dead. The people in the dream change, but always I say the same thing to them: "See? I told you he wasn't dead." The feeling in the dream is so joyful—because he is still alive. Perhaps he is . . . in some way that manifests itself in my sleeping state. It was then, too, that I began to think about the inevitability of my own death.

Death doesn't hold a trauma for me. I can think about it easily. I don't believe that this life is all that we have; I do believe in the hereafter. This is a combination of my Episcopal beliefs and Indian spirituality, which substantiate life after death. There are many things that we do as Indian people, like feeding the spirits, that confirm our understanding of the hereafter.

I receive solace from the Psalms. One of my favorite passages is, "We are like a puff of wind; our days are like a passing shadow." I think of death as a transition rather than a termination. I picture the transitional process as being like walking down a tunnel toward a brightly lit area that is the abode of God. How can one describe the epitome of beauty? As I have experienced the deaths of loved ones, including Bob, my mother, Finn, June, Helen, my son-in-law Bill, my great-grandson Jordan, and lastly my daughter Vonnie, I am happy in the knowledge that I will be seeing them all again.

In my discussions of death with Fr. Doyle Turner and my daughter Vonnie, who was battling cancer, it all goes back to the Psalm about our lives as a passing shadow. As I ponder these insights, I've had a desire to make preparations for my own demise. I asked my friend and spiritual mentor, Doyle, to help me make these arrangements. I knew he would advise me on how to blend the Native and Christian elements, both of which are so important to me. Doyle said, "Essie, I am happy to help you with this. This is a gift from you to your children."

THE WHY? OF RECORDING THIS STORY

I have often heard the quote attributed to Gen. Philip Sheridan, "The only good Indian is a dead Indian," and I wonder if he would have included me in his generalization. When I am dead, and those relatives of my generation who remember hearing about the life of Sacajawea are dead, who will care about a history now two hundred years old?

For me, the question of whether Sacajawea died when she was twenty-four or nearly one hundred is not an academic question. It is family history; it is the oral tradition of my ancestors that was passed down to me, and it is therefore a part of who I am. This is why I record this story.

It has often been said that the boarding school created a generation of confused and lonely children. While this may be true for some, it does not ring true for many of us boarding school students. This is why I record this story.

I want to pass down some of my educational methods of working with Indian students. Instilling a sense of pride and dignity in our young tribal members is critical to our survival as Indian people. We must convince indigenous people that there *is* a place for them in the twenty-first century and that the richness of their heritage need not be abandoned. This is why I record this story.

I have led a rewarding and interesting life that reflects a history of the twentieth century. As a Shoshone woman who has weathered a life spent away from my people, but who has been enriched by her contacts with so many other tribes and cultures, my experiences may provide a prototype for future generations of Indian people. And this is why I record this story.

Epilogue

Sacajawea is a pivotal figure in Esther Horne's life. The name Sacajawea evokes the image of a young Indian woman—her infant strapped to a cradleboard—pressing westward, pointing out the way to the Pacific for the famed Lewis and Clark expedition of the early 1800s.

Knowledge of her role in the expedition and the controversies surrounding her later life are critical to an understanding of much of Horne's own life. Esther Burnett Horne considers herself to be a great-great-granddaughter of Sacajawea. She is related to Sacajawea through Maggie Bazil, Essie's grandmother. Maggie's father, Bazil (also known as Pa:si), is believed by some to be the adopted son and probable nephew of Sacajawea (see the Family Tree). Horne remembers many of the stories that she heard about Sacajawea and recounts those traditions in her life history. Throughout her life she has worked to keep the memory of her great-great-grandmother alive.

WHAT'S IN A NAME?

A note on the spelling and meaning of Sacajawea's name is in order. I use the spelling "Sacajawea" throughout the book, since it is preferred by the life history's coauthor, Essie Horne, and by the Shoshone tribe. I am aware that "disciplined" scholars (Lange 1986, 32–33) are expected to use the spelling "Sacagawea," since it is the most common approximation of the spelling of her name in the journals of Lewis and Clark, who wrote her name phonetically (Anderson 1978).

Over the years, writers have employed numerous spellings and pronunciations, including Sacajawea, Sacagawea, Sakakawea, Tsakakawea, Sacajowa, and Saykijawee. There is a great deal of controversy surrounding this woman's name, and two major theories relate to the proper spelling, pronunciation, and meaning of the name (see Anderson 1978; Hebard 1933,

285–93; Liljeblad 1958; Rees 1958; D. Robinson 1924a, 1924b; W. Robinson 1956, 44n. 60; Saindon 1988; Schroer 1978, 1980; Shaul 1972).

One theory is that the name is of Hidatsa origin and means "Bird Woman" from *tsakaka* (bird) and *wiis* (woman). Since the Hidatsa language does not contain the hard "j" sound, the name should be spelled and pronounced Sacagawea (or Sakakawea). Lewis's journal entry of May 20, 1805, appears to support the Hidatsa derivation. He writes: "[A] handsome river of about fifty yards in width discharged itself into the shell river . . . this stream we called Sah-ca-ger we-ah or Bird Woman's River, after our interpreter the Snake woman" (Thwaites 1904, 2:52).

The Sacagawea preference is associated with those who maintain that this woman died in 1812. Their reasoning is that Sacajawea is not a Shoshone name, and indeed some linguists do not believe it has a comprehensible Shoshone meaning.

The other theory, most often associated with those who believe Sacajawea died in 1884, says that the name *is* Shoshone and means "Boat Launcher" from *sac* (boat or canoe) and *jaw-e* (to throw, cast, or launch). The first publication of the Lewis and Clark journals in 1814 by Biddle and Allen ([1814] 1902) used the spelling Sacajawea and likely influenced future generations to retain that spelling. Historians are not sure why they chose this configuration, rather than Sacagawea, which is more common in the journals. Irving Anderson, who insists that Sacagawea (with a "g") died in 1812, suggests that Clark sometimes formed his handwritten "g's" like "j's." His careless penmanship may have created the confusion (1978).

This writer questions whether it will ever be determined how her name was actually pronounced (or spelled) since professional linguists of the Hidatsa and Shoshone languages differ considerably in their conclusions about the meaning and spelling of her name (Ronda 1984, 257). It is also unclear how a resolution of the controversy over the "correct" spelling of the name would directly relate to conclusive evidence that would verify where or when Sacajawea was buried.

EXPEDITION MEMBER, 1805–1806

Sacajawea was the only woman who accompanied Lewis and Clark in their expedition across the newly acquired Louisiana Purchase. I begin with what is known of Sacajawea's life as described in the journals of Lewis and Clark and then move into the lesser-known period of her life. Sacajawea joined the expedition on April 7, 1805, and left it on August 17, 1806.

Thomas Jefferson (1743–1826), third president of the United States from

1801 to 1809, as well as armchair explorer, was responsible for initiating and supporting the Corps of Discovery, which has become known as the Lewis and Clark expedition of 1804–6. This expedition through the American West, led by Meriwether Lewis and William Clark, was one of the most successful explorations in American history. Lewis and Clark left from St. Louis, Missouri, followed the Missouri River to its source in the Rocky Mountains of eastern Montana by boat, found a way across the Rockies with Indian assistance, ascended the Columbia River to its mouth at the Pacific Ocean, and eventually returned to St. Louis (Ambrose 1996; Moulton 1983, vii–ix).

In addition to charting the territory and recording new plant and animal species, Lewis and Clark also wrote about many of the American Indians whom they encountered on their journey. For the most part, these were peaceful and amiable encounters, due in part to the presence in their party of a young Shoshone woman variously known as Sacagawea, Sacajawea, Sakakawea, and nicknamed Janey by William Clark.

This first Anglo exploration across the northern plains and the northwest United States set the stage for further investigations and intrusions by trappers, traders, prospectors, soldiers, and eventually miners, ranchers, farmers, and business people. Without a doubt, it was the beginning of the end of aboriginal lifeways and freedoms.

Little is known of Sacajawea's childhood. The only sources of this limited information are two entries in Captain Lewis's journal of July 28 and August 19, 1805 (Thwaites 1904, 2:282–83, 370–72), historical reconstruction, and Shoshone oral traditions. Sacajawea was probably born around 1788 (the Shoshone believe it was 1784) in a Shoshone village in the Lemhi River Valley in what is today Idaho. It is likely that she was a member of the Agaiduka or Salmon Eater band of the Shoshone tribe (Anderson 1980, 7–8). When Sacajawea was twelve to fourteen years old, she was captured and taken prisoner near what is today Three Forks, Montana. Most historians believe that the Hidatsa Indians from the Knife River village of Metaharta (in present-day North Dakota) were her captors. Sometime between 1800 and 1804, she and another Shoshone girl were purchased by Toussaint Charbonneau, a French-Canadian fur trapper and trader. Charbonneau was eventually hired as interpreter by Lewis and Clark.

Most of what is known about Sacajawea's life is recorded in the journals of Lewis and Clark. This is admittedly only a seventeen-month period, but these records provide insights into Sacajawea's personality and describe her role in the expedition.

I have identified four roles that Sacajawea assumed with the expedition. These are interpreter, guide, emissary, and counselor. The following brief analysis is my interpretation of Sacajawea's impact on the success of the expedition. It is drawn from my reading of the original journals of Lewis and Clark, and on the writings of Lewis and Clark scholars.

Interpreter

Sacajawea's most important role was likely that of interpreter. On November 4, 1804, soon after the arrival of the expedition at Fort Mandan where its members wintered in 1804–5, Clark's field notes reveal that Charbonneau, interpreter for the Gros Ventre nation, wished to hire on as an interpreter. He writes that "a french man by Name Chabonah, who Speaks the Big Belley [Gros Ventre] language visit us, he wished to hire & informed us his 2 Squars were Snake [Shoshone] Indians, we enga[ge] him to go on with us and take one of his wives to interpet the Snake language" (Osgood 1964, 174).

Sacajawea was chosen, although no mention is made at this time that this teen would be carrying a young child across the Rocky Mountains and westward. Sacajawea had given birth to a son, Jean Baptiste Charbonneau, on February 11, 1805, at Fort Mandan. The infant became the youngest member of the expedition, which left the Fort in April of 1805.

On April 7 of that same year, Clark listed the entire membership of the party, including "Shabonah and his Indian Squar to act as Interpreter and interpretess for the snake Indians—one Mandan & Shabonos infant. Sah-kah-gar wea" (Thwaites 1904, 1:287).

Interestingly, the journals of both Louis and Clark suggest that the captains recognized Sacajawea as having potential value as an interpreter. Early in the expeditions travels (May 20, 1805), they named a river "Sah-ca-ger we-ah or bird woman's River, after our interpreter the Snake Woman" (Thwaites 1904, 2:52). Sacajawea's presence offered Lewis and Clark the assurance that they would be able to converse with, and perhaps obtain horses from, the Shoshones. As the expedition continued westward, both Sacajawea and Charbonneau became vital links in the long and cumbersome translation process. Clark explains this complicated process, which was especially necessary west of the Continental Divide. "I spoke to Labieche in English—he translated to Charbonneau in French—he to his wife [Sacajawea] in Minnetaree [Hidatsa]—she in Shoshone to the boy [Shoshone]—the boy in Tushepan [Flathead] to that nation" (Jackson 1962, 519). This quote provides substantive proof of Sacajawea's importance as interpreter, even after the expedition moved west out of Shoshone territory.

Guide

A much-debated second role is that of Sacajawea as expedition guide. Sacajawea has been described by many as the guide and pilot of the Lewis and Clark expedition, but there is little information in the journals of Lewis and Clark to support this contention. She was unfamiliar with most of the terrain through which the expedition traveled and so could not have directed the expedition to the Pacific Ocean. Sacajawea's geographical knowledge was limited to the region near her homeland in the Three Forks area of the Upper Missouri River. Here she recognized landmarks and provided some direction to Lewis and Clark but otherwise did not routinely point out the trail.

On two recorded occasions, in late July–early August 1805, and on the return trip in 1806, Sacajawea did act as a guide. In the summer of 1805 she recognized landmarks in the area of her homelands and reassured Lewis and Clark that they were on the right path. On July 22, 1805, Lewis noted Sacajawea's familiarity with the territory through which they traveled, and she recognized the summer area of her people. "The Indian woman recognizes the country and assures us that this is the river on which her relations live, and that the three forks are at no great distance. this peice of information has cheered the sperits of the party who now begin to console themselves with the anticipation of shortly seeing the head of the missouri yet unknown to the civilized world" (Thwaites 1904, 2:260).

On the homeward journey, Sacajawea recommended passage through the Bozeman Pass. Clark writes on July 13, 1806, that "[t]he indian woman, who has been of great service to me as a pilot through this country, recommends a gap in the mountain more south which I shall cross" (Thwaites 1904, 2:260). Many refute Sacajawea's role as guide (Anderson 1973; Chuinard 1976; Clark and Edmonds 1979, 87–102; Frazier 1967; Jackson 1962, 639; Kingston 1944; Poole 1964; Rees 1958; Ronda 1984, 256–59; Schroer 1978, 1980; Snyder 1974; Taber 1967). One's position in this particular debate depends on how the term is defined. Lewis and Clark both acknowledged that Sacajawea acted as guide on occasion; Clark refers to her as "pilot," supporting her role as guide.

Emissary

Meriwether Lewis knew that if he did not find Sacajawea's tribe of Shoshone people as he descended the western slopes of the Rockies that the Corps of

Discovery might not survive the winter. He writes, on August 8, 1805, that "as it is now all important with us to meet with these people as soon as possible I determined to proceed tomorrow with a small party to the source of the principal stream of this river and pass the mountains to the Columbia; and down that river untill I found the Indians; in short it is my resolusion to find them or some others, who have horses if it should cause me a trip of one month. for without horses, we shall be obliged to leave a great part of our stores, of which, it appears to me that we have a stock already sufficiently small for the length of the voyage before us" (Thwaites 1904, 2:321–22).

Finally, on August 13, 1805, Lewis (and Clark) did come into contact with some Shoshone people with whom they were able to communicate through sign language. On August 17, Charbonneau and Sacajawea, who had not been with Lewis and Clark at the time of initial contact with the Shoshone, met the party that was indeed Sacajawea's own Shoshone band. She was overjoyed at seeing her people again, but it was the unexpected reunion with her brother that is one of the most touching and emotional entries of the expedition journal. She had, of course, not seen her sibling since her abduction years earlier. As she sat and stared at Cameahwait, recognizing him as her brother, "she jumped up, & embraced him, & threw her blanket over him and cried profusely" (Jackson 1962, 519).

During her absence, Cameahwait had become a chief of the Shoshone Indians. Sacajawea, both sister and emissary, was instrumental in convincing her brother to provide horses and guides for the westward journey across the Bitterroot Mountains and through the Salmon River country to the navigable waters of the Clearwater and Columbia Rivers. She also had to convince her tribe to live up to their commitment to provide horses for the journey, since it is recorded that due to hunger in the village, they nearly went buffalo hunting with the promised horses. The guns and food that Lewis and Clark traded for the horses finally convinced Cameahwait and his band not to renege on their promise. Her negotiations with and relationship to Cameahwait were certainly central to the success of the expedition.

Equally significant in terms of her role as diplomat was her presence as an Indian woman with child. Clark noted the reactions of Indian groups upon seeing Sacajawea and her son. On October 13, 1805, Clark records that "[t]he wife of Shabono our interpreter we find reconsiles all the Indians, as to our friendly intentions as a woman with a party of men is a token of peace" (Thwaites 1904, 3:111).

Again, on October 19, 1805, he writes that "as Soon as they [Native people of the Columbia River region] Saw the Squar wife of the interperter they pointed to her and informed those who continued yet in the Same position I first found them, they imediately all came out and appeared to assume new life, the sight of This Indian woman, wife to one of our interpr. confirmed those people of our friendly intentions, as no woman ever accompanies a war party of Indians in this quarter" (Thwaites 1904, 3:136).

While some disparage this "role" as due only to the "accident" of her female sex it was nonetheless a wise diplomatic decision for Lewis and Clark to have included Sacajawea and Jean Baptiste in their expedition, whether they knew the full implications at the time they made their decision (Lavender 1958, 67). Her presence and her connections made her role as expedition emissary a natural one.

Unconventional Counselor

A fourth role relates to Sacajawea's resourceful nature, pleasant personality, and courage as a young mother. Technically, Sacajawea may not have been a true counselor, but it is nonetheless true that the joy that she and her young child brought to the expedition is referred to many many times in the journals.

Clark was particularly impressed by Sacajawea's service and strength, and he nicknamed her "Janey" in his expedition journals. The explorers had a lot of affection for her son, Jean Baptiste. William Clark nicknamed him "Pomp" or "Pompy," called him his "little dancing boy," and offered to educate him and raise him as his own child.

On August 16, 1806, Clark wrote in his journal: "This man [Charbonneau] has been very serviceable to us, and his wife particularly useful among the Shoshones. Indeed she has borne with a patience truly admirable the fatigue of so long a route incumbered with the charge of an infant, who is even now only nineteen months old" (as quoted in Anderson 1980, 59).

A picture of Sacajawea's warmth and patience emerges from the pages of the expedition journals on numerous occasions. Another example occurs after the expedition when Clark wrote a letter to Charbonneau dated August 20, 1806 (only six days after he and Sacajawea left the expedition). "Your woman who accompanied you that long dangerous and fatiguing rout to the Pacific Ocian and back, diserved a greater reward for her attention and Services on that rout than we had in our power to give her at the Mandans" (Thwaites 1904, 7:329).

Sacajawea collected wild foods to supplement the expedition's rations. She boosted morale when the members were cold and weary. She even saved valuable instruments and records from being lost overboard in a storm when the expedition was traveling on the Missouri River. Captain Lewis writes in his journal entry of May 16, 1805, of this near-catastrophe that "the Indian woman to whom I ascribe equal fortitude and resolution, with any person onboard at the time of the accident, caught and preserved most of the light articles which were washed overboard" (Thwaites 1904, 2:39).

Sacajawea's services as interpreter, guide, emissary, and counselor certainly seem to have contributed to the success of the expedition.

The final journal entry in which Sacajawea was mentioned was on August 17, 1806; this is the last detailed written information about this young woman's life. The entry is brief and does not even use Sacajawea's name. Clark says, "[W]e also took our leave of T. Chaboono, his Snake Indian wife and their child who had accompanied us on our rout to the pacific oceean in the capacity of interpreter and interpretes" (Thwaites 1904, 5:344). She and Charbonneau and their one-and-one-half-year-old baby left the expedition at Fort Mandan, where they had joined it seventeen months earlier.

THE DEBATE

Little is known of Sacajawea's life after the expedition. This fact has been the basis for speculation by Natives and non-Natives alike. The interest of historians, novelists, poets, feminists, and the American public in this nineteenth-century teenage Shoshone girl is still very much alive. The amount of secondary literature available is dizzying in scope. Because the controversies surrounding the death of Sacajawea are complex, disentangling fact from legendary fiction is a formidable task. There are two opposing camps, each with culturally entrenched beliefs about what happened to Sacajawea after she and Charbonneau left the expedition.

One view is based on historical documents: pieces of information, which, because they were written down and preserved, are held to be accurate and reliable. The other version is less precise. It is woven from bits and pieces of memories, stories, and the oral histories of Western Indian tribes as well as non-Indians who are believed to have had contact with Sacajawea.

After the Expedition, 1806–1812: The South Dakota Version

Most non-Indian academic historians writing today believe that Sacajawea died at Fort Manuel Lisa in South Dakota on December 20, 1812. Historical records suggest that Charbonneau, Sacajawea, and Jean Baptiste went east to St. Louis, Missouri, around 1810 to accept Clark's offer of 320 acres of land and additional pay and the money to finance the education of their son. City life, however, did not agree with Toussaint Charbonneau, and he and

Sacajawea left St. Louis to return to the Upper Missouri to work for Manuel Lisa, a famous Missouri Fur Company trader. Jean Baptiste Charbonneau probably remained in St. Louis to begin his education under the patronage of William Clark. Sacajawea is believed to have been ill and to have died of a fever shortly after returning to the Missouri River country. According to this position, she could not have been a contemporary of Chief Washakie (who died in 1900), as many Eastern Shoshone assert. In this view, she was reunited with her Shoshone people only once after her abduction from them—and this was en route to the Pacific Ocean with Lewis and Clark in 1805.

Evidence for this account can be found in numerous documents that record the presence (and death) of a wife of Toussaint Charbonneau in the vicinity of Fort Manuel Lisa in 1811–12. The negative evidence that her name is not recorded (written) anywhere after this date is also cited as proof of her death in 1812.

Three of the most important documents that support this position will be cited and discussed. The first of these comes from the journal of Henry Brackenridge (author, statesman, and lawyer) of Pittsburgh, who was on board a trading boat in the vicinity of Fort Manuel in 1811. His journal entry of April 2, 1811, records that a wife of Charbonneau was on the Missouri River in 1811 and that her health was poor. He says, "We had on board a Frenchman named Charboneau, with his wife, an Indian woman of the Snake nation, both of whom had accompanied Lewis and Clark to the Pacific, and were of great service. The woman, a good creature of a mild and gentle disposition, greatly attached to the whites, whose manners and dress she tries to imitate, but she had become sickly, and longed to visit her native country; her husband, also, who had spent many years among the Indians, had become weary of civilized life" (Brackenridge 1816, 10).

The second piece of evidence comes from the journal of John Luttig, who was the head clerk of Fort Manuel Lisa. He wrote the following journal entry on December 20, 1812, one year and eight months after Brackenridge's document. "[T]his Evening the Wife of Charbonneau a Snake Squaw, died of a putrid fever she was a good and the best Woman in the fort, aged about 25 years she left a fine infant girl" (Luttig 1920, 138).

Not published until 1920, the above is believed by most historians to provide conclusive evidence of Sacajawea's death in 1812. Sacajawea's age would have been around twenty-four to twenty-six years old. There are records that make reference to an infant girl, Lisette, but her whereabouts after 1812 are unknown. It is likely that she was taken to St. Louis, Missouri, where she and her brother, Jean Baptiste, were eventually officially adopted by William Clark (Anderson 1973, 1980; Luttig 1920, 106 and 134).

A third piece of evidence came to light in published form in 1962. Donald Jackson (1962, 638) had heard of an account book belonging to William Clark that listed on the cover the whereabouts of the expedition members. This account book is currently in the Graff collections of the Newberry Library in Chicago. On the cover Clark wrote, "Se car ja we au Dead [Sacajawea Dead]." This cash book is dated 1825–28; it is not known exactly when Clark wrote his infamous note on the cover. Historians thus rest their case with what they believe is fairly conclusive evidence that Sacajawea died in 1812.

After the Expedition, 1806–1884: The Wyoming Version

An alternate version of Sacajawea's later life, however, persists. Oral traditions of the Shoshone, Comanche, Mandan, Hidatsa, Gros Ventres, Yakima, and others maintain that Sacajawea lived to be an old woman (ninety-six to one hundred years old) and died on April 9, 1884 (Eastman 1925; Hebard 1933; Howard 1971, 175–92). According to these oral traditions, Sacajawea left Charbonneau in the St. Louis area and headed west, perhaps around 1810.

She wandered from tribe to tribe in what are now the states of Kansas and Oklahoma, finally settling with the Comanche. There she married a man called Jerk Meat and had children with him. Upon the death of her husband, she traveled up the Missouri River in search of her own people. Reunited with her son, Jean Baptiste (now Baptiste) and an adopted nephew Bazil, she settled in the Fort Washakie area of Wyoming. She was now called Porivo and arrived back in time to be present at the negotiations for the treaty of 1868, which ceded Shoshone lands to the government and created the Wind River Reservation (Hebard 1933, 153–201).

Some say she helped her Wind River Shoshone people in their transition to life on their newly created reservation and that she was venerated by her tribe and buried on the Wyoming Reservation in 1884. Others maintain that the assistance she provided to Lewis and Clark (and the subsequent opening of the Louisiana Purchase) left her only marginally accepted by her Wind River people. She lived her later life out on the reservation but not as a central historical figure.

The most important non-Indian figure in the controversy concerning Sacajawea's later life was Grace Raymond Hebard (1861–1936). In her 1907 article, "Pilot of First White Men to Cross the American Continent," followed by her 1933 book, *Sacajawea: Guide of the Lewis and Clark Expedition*, Hebard wove stories collected from informants at Wind River with other pieces of evidence which suggest that Sacajawea lived to be an old woman of about one hundred years and was buried on the Wind River Reservation in 1884. Hebard's research and convictions influenced the writings of many subsequent scholars and popular writers.

The debate over when and where Sacajawea died and was buried became so heated in the early part of this century that the commissioner of Indian affairs requested that Charles Eastman, a noted Sioux physician and graduate of Dartmouth College and Boston University, make an official investigation to end the speculation once and for all. His task was to resolve the squabbles between the states of South Dakota and Wyoming over the final resting place of the now-famous "guide" of the Lewis and Clark Expedition.

He arrived at his conclusions eight years before Hebard's book was published. It is, however, not clear if Eastman's investigations were independent of Hebard's. Eastman's 1925 report was based on the oral traditions of the Shoshone of Wyoming, the Comanche of Oklahoma, and the Gros Ventres of North Dakota. It contends that Sacajawea died in 1884 and was buried at the Sacajawea Cemetery in Fort Washakie, Wyoming. His report, completed 40 years after one "Sacajawea" died and 112 years after the death of the other, only added fuel to the fire. Historians argue that as an Indian person, Eastman may have had an agenda of his own and that his historical scholarship is questionable. Many American Indians, of course, disagree with this derogatory assessment.

Unanswered Questions

There are numerous unanswered questions surrounding this debate. Historical investigations have revealed numerous inconsistencies; a few examples are discussed in this section.

Jean Baptiste Charbonneau, for example, was originally declared to have been buried next to his mother at Fort Washakie in 1885. Actually, he died and was buried at Inskip's Ranche in Oregon near present-day Danner in 1866 (Anderson 1970, 1978). Who, then, was the "Baptiste" who, according to Hebard, acknowledged but paid little attention to his mother Sacajawea (Hebard 1933, 70–173)?

If Sacajawea was so well known, why did Rev. John Roberts not identify her by name at the time of her death? Roberts explains that Sacajawea never boasted of her service to Lewis and Clark because some tribal members may have been scornful of her role in the expedition (Bell and Cofts 1987, 25).

Will G. Robinson (1956, 6), Russell Reid (1950), and Stella Drumm (Luttig 1920, 134) counter with the argument that if oral history says she was important enough to counsel with the whites as representative of her tribe, why did the tribe not proclaim her as Sacajawea at her death?

If Sacajawea was so well known, why did neither Luttig nor Brackenridge (the two journalists whose writings are cited to substantiate her death in 1812) identify her by name? Tribal historians argue that Charbonneau had at least three Shoshone wives and that Brackenridge and Luttig do not name which of Charbonneau's wives died; they may have misidentified the correct wife. Tribal historians also contend that Clark's information about Sacajawea's whereabouts as recorded on the cover of his account book might also be in error. On that same cash book Clark noted that Patrick Gass, another member of the expedition, was dead, when in fact he was not.

There are other inconsistencies in the written record. For example, Clark recorded (on the same cash book cover) that Toussaint Charbonneau was in Würtemberg, Germany. Historians insist that he meant to write Jean Baptiste Charbonneau (Toussaint and Sacajawea's son, who was in Germany). Was there possibly another son of Charbonneau (by one of his other wives) to whom Clark refers? In the adoption records, the age (and name) of Jean Baptiste Charbonneau is incorrectly recorded. The records (Luttig 1920, 106, 134) record that the age of the boy "Tousant Charbono" is about ten years of age—a mistake that Clark, who knew when the boy Jean Baptiste was born, would not have made. Was this then Luttig's error, or was there another child (Toussaint Jr.) who claimed Charbonneau as a father but not Sacajawea as a mother? A number of entries in this cash book would also indicate that two of Charbonneau's sons were being educated by Clark. Perhaps Clark refers to only one son, but he does use two names: Jean Baptiste Charbonneau and Toussaint Charbonneau.

Clark also clearly spelled Sacajawea's name on the cover of this cash book with a "j" (not a "g")—an error that is inconceivable according to many historians who insist that her name is Hidatsa, not Shoshone.

Historians (Anderson 1973, 1976; Jackson 1962, 640n. 2; Robinson 1956; Schroer 1980) insist that these objections are superficial and that the strength of the written record should stand. This claim notwithstanding, the inconsistencies in the written record remain unexplained, and Sacajawea's grave has never been located (Anderson 1976, 149).

Other published sources, however, also raise important questions. Many reputable ethnographies of the Eastern Shoshone make reference to Bazil and an aged Sacajawea. Äke Hultkrantz, for example, says, "There is no doubt that the woman who died this year [1884] on the Wind River Reservation and who was called 'Bazil's mother' was Sacajawea" (1971, 294n. 6). Milford Chandler (1969), Frederick Hodge (1910, 2:401), Robert Lowie (1924, 223), Demitri Shimkin (1947, 316), Judith Vander (1988, 206n. 3), and Peter Wright (1980, 140) all refer to Sacajawea's presence on the Wind River Reservation in the 1880s.

Historians might argue that these ethnographers were misled by Hebard, her informants, and revisionist histories. Still, perhaps these references should not be dismissed in their entirety, and each should be examined on an individual basis.

MOTIVES

The written records contain convincing but inconclusive evidence that Sacajawea died in 1812. If historians are correct, two unanswered questions persist: Who fabricated this elaborate story, and why?

The Suffragette Connection

The evolution of the interest in Sacajawea and the subsequent debate concerning the year of her death may have begun with the woman's suffrage movement. In 1902, Eva Emery Dye, Clackamas County chairman for the Oregon Equal Suffrage Association, wrote a historical novel, *The Conquest; The True Story of Lewis and Clark*. In this book Dye portrays Sacajawea as the guide of the Lewis and Clark expedition. In Book II, Chapter 27—"The Home Stretch"—Dye writes that

> Sacajawea, modest princess of the Shoshones, heroine of the great expedition, stood with her babe in her arms and smiled upon them [the members of the departing expedition] from the shore. So had she stood in the Rocky Mountains pointing out the gates. So had she followed the great rivers, navigating the continent.
>
> Sacajawea's hair was neatly braided, her nose was fine and straight, and her skin pure copper like the statue in some old Florentine gallery. Madonna of her race, she had led the way to a new time. To the hands of this girl, not yet eighteen, had been intrusted the key that unlocked the road to Asia. (Dye [1902] 1936, 290)

Some suggest that she and others created this heroine for their cause. Eva Emery Dye, in fact, admits that she was in search of a strong women of the past with whom suffragettes could identify. She writes:

> My thoughts were turned to that memorable Lewis and Clark expedition and I was persuaded by my publishers to weave a story about that. . . . I struggled along as best I could with the information I could

get, trying to find a heroine. . . . I traced down every old book and scrap of paper, but still was without a real heroine. Finally, I came upon the name of Sacajawea and I screamed, "I have found my heroine."

I then hunted up every fact I could about Sacajawea. Out of a few dry bones I found in the old tales of the trip I created Sacajawea and made her a real living entity. For months I dug and scraped for accurate information about this wonderful Indian maid.

The world snatched at my heroine, Sacajawea. . . . The beauty of that faithful Indian woman with her baby on her back, leading those stalwart mountaineers and explorers through the strange land, appealed to the world. (Powers 1935, 410)

It is clear that some aspects of Sacajawea's life have been embellished and that many of the creative legendary components of Sacajawea's life emerge from Dye's early writings. For example, Sacajawea's role as singular expedition guide and the hint of a romantic relationship with Clark have become a part of the legend that surrounds this heroine's life. As far as designating Sacajawea as guide, however, Dye was following the lead of an earlier historian, Elliott Coues (1893), who also designated Sacajawea as the guide of the expedition. She also may have relied on Clark's own words from his journal entry of July 13, 1806: "The indian woman who has been of great service to me as a pilot through this country recommends a gap in the mountain more south which I shall cross" (Thwaites 1904, 5:260).

Nonetheless, Dye did create an image of Sacajawea at odds with more recent scholarship. As mentioned previously, few contemporary historians accept that Sacajawea acted as chief guide and pilot to the expedition.

Dye was one of the first to mythologize Sacajawea. She did so to create a heroine for the Portland Centennial Lewis and Clark Exposition and for the annual meeting of the National American Woman's Suffrage Association, both held in the summer of 1905 in Portland, Oregon (Laut 1905; Sanford 1905). Suffragettes used stories of Indian women to serve their cause because these women seemed to offer an alternative to American patriarchy. Women like Sacajawea and Pocahontas also were suitable candidates because they mediated between white and Indian cultures. They are perceived as having assisted America in "civilizing" the land and the occupying indigenous populations. The citizens of this country may also have been more accepting of these historical Indian figures because they could be seen as exonerating the notion of manifest destiny (cf. Landsman 1992 and Remley 1982).

Grace Raymond Hebard took a consequent step in keeping Dye's legends alive. Many historians have documented that some of the oral testimonies presented as fact in Hebard's book are suspect (cf. Anderson 1973, 1976, 1980; Crawford 1927; De Voto 1954; H. A. Howard 1967; H. P. Howard 1971; Jackson 1962, 638; Miller 1981; Reid 1950; Ronda 1984, 256–59; and Schroer 1978, 1980). But what were Hebard's motives for creating a Sacajawea who lived to be nearly one hundred years old? Her detractors cite a three-fold explanation. The first (following Dye) was to enliven the strong image of Sacajawea for the woman's suffrage movement. The notion that Hebard was misguided and confused because of her dedication to the woman's movement emerges frequently in the historical writings about Sacajawea. The second was to glorify her home state of Wyoming by locating Sacajawea's final resting place in that state rather than South Dakota. The third was to make a name for herself. If these above-cited writers' assessments of Hebard are correct, the story of Sacajawea's life from 1812 to 1884 did not begin with the Indians themselves but was the result of Hebard's amateur scholarship and tall tales.

Certainly, however, not all of Hebard's research can be discounted (Anderson 1973; Clark and Edmonds 1979; Gilbert 1972). The question is, Which sections are valid and reflect the testimony of her Indian informants and which have been elaborated to serve her agenda? The answers to these questions are unlikely to ever be answered.

The Fort Washakie Connection

One also wonders what motives could be attributed to the Shoshone people of the Fort Washakie area of the Wind River Reservation, as well as other tribes, to go along with a lie created by a self-aggrandizing white woman. These Indian people maintain that their oral traditions support the post-1812 life of Sacajawea.

The choices are limited. The first possibility is that they knowingly created a "false" Sacajawea to humor Hebard. Or perhaps they allowed Hebard to convince them that the old woman, Bazil's Mother—Porivo—buried by Reverend Roberts in 1884, must have been Sacajawea. Perhaps Hebard planted in their minds the seeds of a growing story that they eventually came to believe in order to bring glory to their tribe (Schroer 1980). Or finally, perhaps they allowed Porivo (a false Sacajawea) and Battez (a false Jean Baptiste) to convince them that they had been a part of the expedition when in fact they were not (Porter 1961).

Central to all of these alternatives is not only the claim that the Indian people of Fort Washakie knowingly lied but also that Rev. John Roberts,

Finn Burnett, Dr. James Irwin, Sarah Irwin, James Patten, Edmo Le Clair and numerous other non-Indians whose remembrances support Hebard's position (cf. Bell 1989, 6; Bell and Cofts 1987, 25–26; David 1937, 307–16; Hebard 1933; Horne 1980; Patten 1926; Spring 1941) participated in the lie as they sought publicity and notoriety.

The issues are problematical, and the historical Sacajawea may always remain an enigma, since both sides of the debate invite speculation. Nonetheless, the controversy surrounding Sacajawea has served to highlight the Native American voice that questions the hegemony of the written word over oral tradition. Many Native Americans question why oral histories are discounted as subjective, while what is written is not, although it is filtered through personal, historical, and cultural lenses.

Esther Horne has something to say about this. She suggests that the crux of the issue is the legitimization accorded to the written record, whereas oral tradition (the very basis of much Indian history) is frequently not accorded as much validity. Noted Lewis and Clark historian Irving Anderson, for example, writes that "one scratch of the pen at the time of an event is worth tenfold the testimony of many witnesses relying upon memory subsequent to the event" (1973, 8). Acoma author Simon Ortiz counters Anderson's assessment. He says that "Indian people must value their history. Recognition of this oral history is the truest affirmation of the moral values of our lives. This history contains within it all the struggles that our people have gone through. Therefore its continuance means the continuance of our current struggles and our lives" (1977, 14).

The complexity of this dilemma is clear. The historical documentation is based on recorded written testimony, corroborated by yet other written sources. The strength of the Native American view is based on its reliance on moral convictions. What this means, in part, is that American Indians believe that people who pass knowledge down to others orally develop the skills of remembering and telling accurately. To question the validity of oral history is to question the integrity of American Indians. Their perspectives are important, not only to an understanding of their history, but also to an understanding of their perspectives on the present and future. Oral traditions retain the past for future tribal members.

An examination of how people use oral tradition to talk about the past (and themselves) and to understand the human experience is beyond the scope of this epilogue. It is important to note, however, that historians, cultural anthropologists, archaeologists, and Native American scholars are beginning to address these very issues (eg., Ambler 1995; Basso 1984;

Cruikshank 1990b; DeMallie 1993; Dongoske, Jenkins, and Ferguson 1993; Ortiz 1974; Rosaldo 1980a, 1980b; Simonelli 1995; Trouillot 1995; Vansina 1965). At the very least Native Americans want the scholars who study them to recognize that the information embedded in oral traditions may contain some valuable "truths" (Zimmerman 1995). Native American oral traditions and narratives are important expressions of culture, and they may constitute a very different understanding of the past.

In an insightful essay on history and narrative, historian William Cronon says, "[W]e cannot escape confronting the challenge of multiple competing narratives in our efforts to understand the human past" (1992, 1367). Cronon further reflects that this vision of history, which includes narratives that may be at odds with one another, is not very reassuring to historians; we must nonetheless listen to and consider what is being expressed in alternative interpretations.

I believe that the dispute over when Sacajawea died will never be resolved to the satisfaction of all. Therefore, I seek metaphorical significance in the roles attributed to Sacajawea as preserved in Shoshone oral tradition. She is traitor and heroine; she is an Indian woman abused by her white spouse and a fiercely independent woman who assisted her Wind River people in their accommodation to reservation life. She is a wanderer, a mother, a captive, an elder. All of these speak to the question of how people use oral tradition and stories to talk about their past, to understand their present, and to survive into the future.

Sacajawea has become an appealing figure in the history of the American West, and she continues to capture the romantic imagination of both the Indian and non-Indian Americans. As Essie points out in her life history, it is said that there are more monuments, memorials, rivers, lakes, and mountain areas named after Sacajawea than any other American woman. Novelists, poets, historians, anthropologists, and feminists have created, resurrected, and immortalized the mystique of Sacajawea. Legend, mixed with fact, has shrouded this extraordinary woman's life in myth and mystery. Differing accounts of her role in the Lewis and Clark expedition, as well as the date of her death, remain contested and may never be resolved. Controversies aside, Sacajawea emerges as a courageous, determined, and admirable Indian woman. The ongoing disputes have served to keep the memory of this woman alive, a woman whose accomplishments might otherwise have been noted and forgotten.

The Editing Process: Examples of the Transition from Spoken Word to Written Text by Sally McBeth

Many of the things that were discussed in tape-recorded interviews (in Wahpeton, North Dakota, and in Naytahwaush, Minnesota) did not make the final cut for this book. Essie and I would lapse into discussions (and we intentionally left the tape recorder running) about a variety of topics, many of which we chose not to include in this final manuscript. Some of these are detailed in the introduction to this volume; others were simply discussions between friends.

We have had a lot of time over the past ten years to work on refining what would be included in the final draft. By 1989–90 we had produced an incomplete version of the manuscript, which I labeled, "Version I—Incomplete." A second draft was completed in 1991; it was called "Version II—Semi-Complete." "Version III—Complete" was finished in 1992, but of course it wasn't complete. It was followed by partial rewrites in 1993, 1995, and 1997. Remember, too, that every line of every sentence of every page was coedited by Essie and me. All sections were read back to her at least twice.

Some of the editing was easy and straightforward. An example from chapter 2 illustrates this process:

Well, I was born in 1909, on November 9, and the earliest thing I can remember is being set on top of a . . . it seemed to me to be a very tall dapple gray horse, and I don't know whether this is something that I made up or whether this is truth personified. I know that sitting on the horse is truth, but it seems to me I still had a diaper, and I never checked that out with my mother to see whether that was true, you know, that I was that young. I suppose I probably was only about a year or two old, or something like that. And that would have been somewhere in Idaho since my mother and father had had to run away to get married.

This portion of the transcribed tape became:

I was born in 1909, on November 9, and the earliest thing I can remember is being on top of a very tall dappled gray horse. It seems to me I still had on a diaper. I don't know whether this memory is something that I made up, images remembered from what I've been told, or simply the truth. Could I remember being that young? I would have been a year or two old and that would have been somewhere in Idaho since my mother and father had to run away to get married.

An example from chapter 3 is included to demonstrate how my questions were incorporated into the text as well as to show how Essie's reflections were incorporated into the final draft.

MCBETH: Were you missing your mom a lot during those years that you didn't get home [from Haskell]?

HORNE: Yes I missed my mother, and my mother was not a person who wrote a great deal of letters; she didn't write very often. So, when I did receive a letter from her, I really treasured it, and Bernice and Gordon and I read it over and over. Of course, I remember Gordon was on the opposite side of the campus. That was hard to get used to not to be able to talk to our brother whenever we wanted to talk to him, but Bernice and I, it was good to be together.

But Bernice did not stay in Haskell, more than, she was there for a couple of years. She couldn't adjust to the school. She was so homesick that she was sick so much of the time that they finally sent her home.

This interview piece became:

We didn't hear from home very often; sometimes it would be months at a time. My mother had not gone to a government boarding school, so she didn't seem to realize how important letters and packages were. I used to write home rather often, asking for money, talking about what we were doing at school, and wishing that I could come home. I missed my mom so much, but she was not a person who wrote many letters. So when I did receive a letter from her, I really treasured it. Bernice and Gordon and I would read it over and over. Of course Gordon was on the opposite side of the campus, and it was hard to get used to not being able to talk to your brother whenever you wanted. So it was good for Bernice and me to be together. Bernice did not stay at Haskell more than a couple of years. She couldn't adjust to the school; she was so homesick that she was physically ill much of the time, and they finally sent her home.

The beginning of the paragraph was condensed from at least four other times in recorded interviews and numerous "off-the-record" reminders that

Essie's mother's lack of writing (while her children were off at boarding school) did not indicate that she did not care about her children. Rather, Essie attributes her not writing letters to the fact that her mother had not attended a boarding school and so did not understand the importance of receiving letters.

Other sections required a great deal more cutting to get to what we both agreed was the most important material. This final example from the introduction reveals the mutually heavy-handed editing that was done quite regularly:

When I think of the years that I've lived, so much of what I learned about, and this is a little bit bating the question, but a lot of what I learned about Indian cultures, about the other cultures aside from my own tribe, was what I learned from Haskell. I think we haven't touched on this particular part of the boarding school, but it seems someplace I read a statement by you, or maybe it was something that you said to me, and I said to you that one of the things that the boarding school fostered was the understanding of different tribes of each other as we got a bird's-eye view of many tribes by being a boarding school student. At Haskell, for instance there, I can hardly hazard a guess, I suppose that there were a hundred or more tribes represented at Haskell.

Although we were not allowed to speak our own language and dance our own dances, and that kind of thing, we certainly, just because of the fact that we were thrown together—all these various tribes were associating with one another—naturally we would talk to each other about our beliefs and the things we did at home and differences between your tribe and the differences between my tribe—and our *lives*! And we really, it's kind of a cultural and historical feast, as I think about it, because we were sharing so many things that were foreign to each other and just really being saturated with all these things. I say other cultures because each tribe is so, you know, has a culture unto itself. And speaking for myself I know I learned a great deal about other tribes and was so interested in them, and so interested in how different they were from, you know, from my tribe, the difference, you know, differences in their arts and crafts and all of those things the schools that were really trying to take the Indianness out of the Indian putting a lot of Indianness into the Indian, into, as I said, Indianness *into* the Indian just by throwing us all together in a group.

This conversation was transformed into the following paragraphs as we elaborated on the meaning of Horne's boarding school experiences for a portion of McBeth's introduction:

When I think back on the many years that I have lived, so much of what I have learned about Indian cultures, aside from what I know about my own tribe, I learned at Haskell. For me, one of the things that the boarding school fostered was an understanding of different tribes. We were not allowed to speak our own languages or dance our own dances, but by the very virtue of our being thrown together, we associated with one another and would talk to one another. We discussed our beliefs, our homes, our food, our arts and crafts . . . our lives! I think of the boarding school as a kind of cultural and historical feast. I was tremendously enriched by my association with people from other tribes.

The schools were trying to take the Indianness out of us, but they never succeeded. Not completely, anyway. They actually ended up putting a lot of Indianness into the Indian just by throwing us all together in a group. The boarding school may have contributed to the breakdown of the family and may have increased the rate of alcohol abuse. I have read that this may be so. They also unwittingly created a resistance to assimilation, which might take shape in very subtle or quite rebellious forms. The experience of us boarding school students, both good and bad, strengthened our resolve to retain our identity as American Indians and to take our place in today's world.

There are wordings in the above examples that are not evident in the transcription as quoted. For example, the admission that Essie realized that some Native Americans believe that the boarding school may have contributed to the breakdown of the family was something she wanted to include in this section. She wanted her reader to know that she was aware of, although not in total agreement with, this belief. The quotes "tremendously enriched," "But they also unwittingly created a resistance, which might take shape in very subtle or quite rebellious forms," and "strengthened our resolve as American Indians to take our place in today's world" were extracted from other interviews and interwoven by us both into this explanation of Essie's boarding school experiences.

In March 1997, we spent a week together in Wahpeton, North Dakota, going over those sections that I wanted to be absolutely sure were not only accurate, but also reflected Essie's sense of the past and of herself. As late as March 1998, as I was getting the final manuscript ready for publication by the University of Nebraska Press, we were on the phone daily, finalizing all last-minute changes and additions.

Awards, Honors, and Publications of Esther Burnett Horne

AWARDS AND HONORS

1929–65   Bureau of Indian Affairs Demonstration Teacher in Elementary Education and Indian Lore

1933   Organized First All-Indian Girl Scout Troop in the United States in Wahpeton, North Dakota

1935–85   Fiftieth Year Honoree: Member of Fort Nightly Literary Study Club of Wahpeton, North Dakota

1952–53   Member of National Bureau of Indian Affairs (K–6) Curriculum Committee for BIA Schools; Minimum Essential Goals

1955   "Guide" to Sesquicentennial Re-creation of Lewis and Clark Expedition

1955–65   Included in *Who's Who in North Dakota*

1956–63   Indian Affairs Chair of North Dakota Federated Women's Club

1959   Honorary Lieutenant Governor of State of Oklahoma

1960   Member of Governor's Committee at White House Conference on Children and Youth in Washington DC

1963   Named as First Master Teacher of the Bureau of Indian Affairs

1963–68   Member of Episcopal Church National Indian Worker Committee

1964–69   Delegate to General Assembly of National Council of Churches

1965   Distinguished Service Citation Bureau of Indian Affairs: "Her career has been one of singular leadership and noteworthy contributions. She exemplified the highest type of teaching, both in the classroom and in associated areas of education. With rare ability, enthusiasm and initiative she has enriched the academic, social and cultural needs of hundreds of Indian children. Seldom has one had so much to offer so many." [Excerpt from Citation signed by Stuart Udall, Secretary of the Interior, 1965]

1965	North Dakota and United States Travel Bureau's Goodwill Ambassador to Europe
1965–74	Member of Minnesota Indian Education Committee
1966	Woman of the Year: Bismarck Lasertoma Club
1974	Included in American Indian Women (Gridley 1974)
1982	Expert Witness for Senate Select Hearings (U.S. Senate Select Committee on Indian Affairs 1982)
1982	Testified at Public Hearing on Closure of Wahpeton Indian School at BIA Area Office, Aberdeen, South Dakota
1982	Included in *Ohoyo Ikhana: A Bibliography of American Indian-Alaska Native Curriculum Materials: Curriculum Resource Personnel* (Nelson and Walton 1982, 254)
1983	Certificate of Appreciation from State of Minnesota Committee on Indian Work
1989	Certificate of Recognition from North Dakota Centennial Commission
1991	Honored by Wahpeton Rotary for Contributions to History of Native Americans
1985	Coauthored (with Lena Robertson, Sioux), *Native American Spiritual Service*. Used at Triennial Meeting of Episcopal Churchwomen in Anaheim, California. Also used at Episcopal Church of Valley City, North Dakota (1986), Indian Episcopal Convocation in St. Paul, Minnesota (1987), Episcopal Church of Fairbolt, Minnesota (1987). Episcopal Bishop gave special commendation for service
1985	Included in Episcopal Church, Province VI, Women of History Project Monograph
1985	Senior Citizen of the Year. Naytahwaush, Minnesota
1989	Outstanding American Indian Elder of the Minnesota Indian Education Association
1991	Recognized by Wahpeton Rotary for donation of Native American artifacts to Richland County Historical Museum
1996	Recognized by Richland County Historical Society (North Dakota) for contributions to the preservation of Richland County's History
1996	Honored by North Dakota Council on Indian Ministries

PUBLICATIONS

1939   "Using Indian Symbolism in a Modern Manner," *School Arts* 38 (9): 313

1949   "Cotton Light Bulb and Glass Jar Decorations," *School Arts* 49 (2): 65

1951   "Glove and Potato Puppets," *Child Life*, September 1951, pp. 30–31

1980   *Oral Traditions of Sacajawea*, self-published monograph

1996   "Hearing the Wind Songs: Reflections of a Shoshone Indian Elder," *Journal of Women's Ministries* 12 (1): 6–7. Excerpted in *Bismarck Tribune*, *Sheaf* (North Dakota Episcopal Church Newsletter), *IKHANA* (Newsletter of American Indian/Alaska Native Ministry of the Episcopal Church), and *Minwaajimo* (Newsletter of the Episcopal Churches of Northwestern Minnesota)

Memories of Sacajawea
by Esther Burnett Horne

This information (excerpted from Horne 1980) has been compiled and preserved by my sister Bernice Twitchell, Gladys Roberts Graham (Rev. John Roberts's daughter), and myself.

MAGGIE (BAZIL) LARGE

Our grandmother, Maggie (Bazil) Large, who was the daughter of Sacajawea's son, Bazil, told this story to her children and it has been handed down from generation to generation.

William Clark, of the Lewis and Clark expedition, had grown fond of Baptiste while on their journey and had asked Charbonneau and Sacajawea to bring the boy to St. Louis to be educated. They promised they would. After the expedition returned from their journey to the Pacific Ocean and arrived back to the Mandan Village, Charbonneau, Sacajawea, and Baptiste left the party and traveled over the territory, working at different jobs with the fur traders. When Baptiste became of school age, Sacajawea took him to St. Louis to be educated under the supervision of William Clark. While Sacajawea was in St. Louis, her older sister, Otter Woman, died at Mandan with a fever, leaving two children, Toussaint Jr., and a daughter, Lizette. A fellow by the name of John Luttig became their legal guardian, and as he was unable to take care of the children, he turned them over to Clark. At this time, Sacajawea adopted Toussaint Jr. for a companion for Baptiste and named him Bazil. Clark kept the girl Lizette. He supervised their education along with Baptiste. Sacajawea stayed with Bazil and Baptiste in St. Louis for a few years. Charbonneau came to visit them and wanted Sacajawea to return with him to work for the fur traders. She refused and he was abusive to her and whipped her. She left and traveled for a time, finally coming to the Comanche village. The tribe named her Porivo "Chief" as she carried a small bag with papers in it to show who she was and what she had done. She also wore a medal around her neck with President Thomas Jefferson's head engraved on it. The medal had a gold rim around the outside. White people looked up to her.

Sacajawea married a Comanche warrior by the name of Jerk-Meat and raised a family. One son's name was Tincannaf, who had a daughter by the name of Tabcutine, who visited Andrew Bazil here on the reservation and Andrew went to Oklahoma to visit the family. After her husband, Jerk-Meat, was killed in battle, Sacajawea left the Comanche. [I also have visited some of our Comanche relatives in Oklahoma—EBH.] On her arrival at Fort Bridger, she was happy to see her sons, Bazil and Baptiste. Bazil recognized her first. Sacajawea spoke at the signing of the treaty, and the treaty was signed by Bazil. Indians called her Wad-ze-wipa (Lost Woman).

Sacajawea gave the first Sun Dance for the Shoshone Indians at Fort Bridger. Bazil was the leader of this dance. Indians always believed very strongly in Sacajawea and what was said about her in regard to the voyage she had taken and what she said about her trip with the expedition. She was called Sacajawea, Porivo, Wad-ze-wipa, and other names by different members of her tribe.

Maggie (Bazil) Large said her dad, Bazil, always told the children to respect their grandmother, Sacajawea, because all the white people respect her and honor her everywhere. Maggie said the children in the family had seen the bag the papers were in. They were papers about the expedition, two written by Clark and one written by Lewis, together with a certificate of good character given to her by Brigham Young, president of the L.D.S. Church. There were only a few people who knew about these papers outside of Sacajawea's close relatives. On her arrival at the reservation she was accompanied by her son Bazil, his wife, and their children, Maggie, Nancy, Ellen, Andrew, and Edrocke. All of them were given a comfortable house near the agency, located about one hundred feet southeast of where John Burn's store was later erected. There they lived until 1884 when Sacajawea died.

FINN G. BURNETT

As told to Esther (Burnett) Horne and Bernice (Burnett) Twitchell
by their paternal grandfather, Finn G. Burnett

On May 1, 1871, Finn accepted the position of boss farmer on the Shoshone Wind River Reservation, Wyoming. His job was to teach the Shoshones agriculture. It was here in Wind River Valley that he met and became closely associated with Sacajawea and Bazil. He became extremely knowledgeable about the Lewis and Clark expedition by listening to Sacajawea tell of her experiences during the expedition. Sacajawea showed Finn, Dr. Irwin, and his wife the bronze Jefferson medal she wore around her neck and the papers she carried in a bag that were signed by Lewis and Clark. Finn held the medal in his hands several times. According to the old Indians grandfather talked to, Sacajawea's name was given to her by her people when she was a child. Her name means Boat Woman. She was known by Sacajawea while on the expedition. There was never any doubt in their minds! They also said she was a sister of Chief Cameahwait. It has been historically recorded that the sister of this great chief was indeed the guide for the Lewis and Clark expedition. Granddad told us to always be proud of our Indian heritage because we were great-great-granddaughters of Sacajawea, the Indian girl guide of the Lewis and Clark expedition. (Our father was Fincelious G. Burnett Jr., and our mother was Millie Ethel Large, granddaughter of Bazil.) Our grandfather was fond of telling us over and over again about what Sacajawea had told him regarding the trip up the Missouri River, the expedition's need of horses, and their meeting with her people, and her joy at seeing her brother, Chief Cameahwait. She spoke of the rough terrain on the western slopes and said because of the shortage of game, the expedition members were reduced to eating dog. She said she would have starved before eating dog and instead had dug and eaten roots. She told of obtaining canoes to travel down the Snake River. When she would tell the story of the whale she saw on the beach, the other Shoshones would not believe her. She told them it was as big as a house. Their reply was "ishump" (it's a lie). She told them of the expedition's winter quarters and on their return how she had gone across country to the beginning of the Yellowstone where the expedition was united. He said her many stories led him to believe she had lived with the Comanches for many years following the expedition and then had returned to her people.

It was during these travels that she had seen the vast Comanche and Mormon fields of grain. This probably led to her great interest in helping to teach the Shoshones agriculture. Sacajawea had a great respect for the white people and was influential in keeping her tribe at peace with them. Much of this was due to her command of the English language. She could communicate her tribe's wants to the government and the government's wishes to the Shoshones. Grandfather Burnett said her best likeness was the statue by the sculptor Henry Altman. It can be seen in Dr. Grace Raymond Hebard's book. Some of the friends of our granddad (Finn G. Burnett) whom he mentioned as knowing Sacajawea, Bazil, and Baptiste personally were Chief Washakie, Hebe-chee-chee, Barbara Meyer (Baptiste's daughter), Quintan Quay, Weech, Wesaw, Moon-Ha-Ve, To-saby, Edmo LeClair, John Enos, Dick Washakie, James and John McAdams, Rev. John Roberts, Dr. Irwin and wife, Mr. Lane, Joseph Slade, Charlie Oldham, William McCabe, Ed St. John, Charles Harrison, and Bill Roger.

Letter from Finn G. Burnett to Esther Horne (January 10, 1933)

Dear Granddaughter:

Your great-great-grandmother Sacajawea came to the Shoshone Agency with your great-grandfather Bazil in the fall of 1871. Sacajawea, Bazil, and your grandmother were given a house near the agent's office. Both Sacajawea and Bazil spoke good English and proved very useful as interpreters and advisers to Dr. James Irwin who was agent at the time.

Mrs. Irwin, Charles Oldham, and I spent many happy and interesting evenings at their home listening to Sacajawea's stories of her eventful life, her capture by the Missouri River Indians, which the Shoshones call "Saguan-oga," meaning muddy river. Her history of the Lewis and Clark expedition was very interesting, and Mrs. Irwin, who was the agent's wife, wrote all of the stories, and as I remember it was written on legal cap paper in pencil and there were about fifty or maybe seventy-five pages of history. Unfortunately, this manuscript with other valuable documents was destroyed when the office, which was a log building, was entirely destroyed by fire.

Your great-great-grandma and your great-granddad taught me the Shoshone language. Sacajawea and Bazil generally conversed in French. Chief Washakie, Weech, Moon Habbie, Wesaw, ToSiah, and Saruagon—who, except Washakie, were French half-breeds—all conversed in French when together. Sacajawea was an expert sign-talker. In fact, the Shoshones believed that she talked all languages. They often said that she appeared to be able to converse with anyone she met, of whatever tribe or nationality.

Sacajawea was remarkably spry and well preserved for a woman of her age. We estimated her age at eighty-odd. She was more spry and appeared to be younger than her daughter-in-law, who was your great-grandma. Sacajawea was of a happy disposition and loved to talk and tell of her adventures. She became sick, decrepit, and was scarcely able to walk eighteen months or a year before she passed away, which occurred in 1884.

The Reverend John Roberts, whose address is Wind River and who since 1883 has been in charge of the Shoshone Episcopal Mission, has a record of her death and burial. Sacajawea was a remarkably intelligent woman and was of incalculable value to Dr. Irwin, who was agent for the Shoshones. None of us understood a word of the Shoshone language and very rarely was one of the Shoshones able to speak English.

The next spring, 1872, we started [to teach] the Indians to farm, and without Sacajawea and Bazil's influence, aid, and advice, we would have had poor success. There was not one of them that had ever harnest [sic] a horse or had held a plow. None of the horses had ever been harnest [sic], but with Sacajawea's and Bazil's aid and advice, we succeeded unusually well and raised a fine crop on 320 acres of land, which was plowed the previous fall with six yoke of oxen to the team. You should have seen those Indians after we got them started. All of them wore blankets. Can you imagine an Indian driving a green team, holding onto a plow and trying to keep track of his blanket at the same time? Well, we succeeded in raising a fine crop of wheat, oats, barley, and potatoes that first year.

Frank Trumball and I ran the mill and ground that wheat into flour—this being the first flour ever manufactured in the State of Wyoming. Quite an honor, don't you think? The small mill had one set of stone burs and old-fashioned batting cloths. I think that the capacity of the mill was eight or ten 100-lb. sacks per eight-hour day. Frank was the miller, and I ran the engine. Sacajawea and Bazil took a great interest in the mill and of course spent a lot of time with us trying to understand the process of making To-so-te-cup [bread]. They rendered great help in our successful beginning in farming that year of 1872.

General Armstrong, who spent a long life in the Indian service, contended that the Shoshone tribe had produced two of the greatest Indians ever known, Sacajawea and Chief Washakie.

Yours sincerely,

Your Granddad, Finn G. Burnett

Letter from Finn G. Burnett to Esther Horne (June 27, 1933)

Dear Esther:

Your letter of the 16 of May overtook me on the 25th. In answer to your questions in regard to Bazil, your great-grandfather, and your great-great-grandmother, Sacajawea.

Bazil was a large fine-looking half-breed, five feet ten or eleven inches in height. Weight two hundred and ten or twenty lbs., he was no darker than a dark-complected white man. Sacajawea in speaking of him called him her son. They came to this agency in the fall of 1871 and lived together in a house set apart for them near the agent's office until she passed away in 1884.

Baptiste, who was dark as a full-blood Shoshone, came to this reservation in 1873. Sacajawea never lived with him; in fact, Baptiste never remained on this reservation but a few months at one time. He would generally visit in the fall and go with the village on the fall and winter hunt, and in the following spring he would leave the reservation, and now and then it would be two or three years between his visits.

Sacajawea and Bazil resided continually on the reservation in the house that was allotted to them; they were well provided for, and it was not necessary for them to accompany the village on the fall and winter hunt.

Sacajawea and Bazil were of great value to the agent, Dr. James Irwin, as interpreter and adviser. Both of them talked good English and French. Sacajawea is the only woman that I ever knew to be allowed to speak in council. Bazil was a chief and an eloquent speaker in council; he frequently called on his mother, Sacajawea, to verify some of his statements, as they both had traveled great distances and had associated with white people and visited their cities and saw many wonderful things which were unbelievable by the Indians.

Sacajawea had a remarkable memory, a faculty of description so vivid in describing a journey, incident, or place; her description was so vivid and impressive that you never forgot it. For instance, when I was first requested to write what she had told me of the Lewis and Clark expedition, I was accused of copying Lewis and Clark's history of the expedition. I had never seen the history!

God bless you and your dear ones, is the prayer of your
GRANDDAD (Finn Burnett)

ROBERT AND LUCINDA HEREFORD

**This story was told to Bernice Twitchell (Mrs. Horne's sister)
by Hereford relatives**

Robert Lewis Hereford and his wife, Lucinda, were partners with Jack Robinson in ranching on Henry's Fork. A few years later Robert bought a ranch of his own on Birch Creek. He raised a large family, and several of his daughters married ranchers on Henry's Fork. In the year 1896, Robert and family moved to Fort Washakie Agency where he was superintendent of Indian farms. His children who married on the reservation were Ellen, Viola, Virginia (Jennie), and John. After Jennie's husband, Neil Driskell, passed away, she married Edward Martinez. We were well acquainted with these relatives, as Robert Lewis Hereford and his wife, Lucinda Robinson, were my husband's (George Twitchell) great-grandparents. We have visited with Jennie, Ellen, Viola, John, and George (my husband's grandfather). It was very interesting to hear their story about Sacajawea, which their mother, Lucinda, had told them. Lucinda said, "I was a young woman when my mother, Marook, and I first saw Sacajawea at the signing of the treaty in the Bridger Country and heard her speak. Her son, Bazil, was there too, and signed the treaty." (This is the treaty of 1868.) Lucinda further stated, "Sacajawea stayed at Fort Bridger two or three years after the treaty was signed and became well acquainted with my mother (Marook). She said Shoshone Indians called Sacajawea "Porivo" after she told them what the Comanches had called her while she was in the Comanche country and of her hardships while guiding the Lewis and Clark expedition westward to the Pacific ocean." We were shown the papers she carried in a bag and the medal she wore with a picture of President Jefferson engraved on it. Sacajawea could speak several languages and talk sign language. The Indians knew she was a great woman.

The old-timers and their families living in the Bridger Valley who knew Sacajawea was Porivo of the Bridger Country and Wind River Reservation were Jack Robinson, Henry Perry, Robert Hamilton, Eugene Hickey, Bill Williams, Jim Baker, Henry Frap, Joseph Parrot, Joe Walker, and Jim Bridger. These men knew the facts; they were there.

REV. JOHN ROBERTS

Letter from Rev. John Roberts to Esther Horne (May 3, 1933)
[This letter and the three that follow were written by Rev. John Roberts to Esther Horne in response to letters from her requesting information about Sacajawea. Horne worked for many years to collect memories of Sacajawea before those who knew her (or claimed to know her) were still alive.]

My dear Mrs. Horne:
Your letter reached me yesterday on my return from Casper, Wyoming. Dr. Grace Raymond Hebard, the eminent historian, whose address is Laramie, Wyoming, has published a noble history of your great-great-grandmother Sacajawea, the heroine guide of the Lewis and Clark expedition. In it is given a full record of life of your famous ancestor; the facts recorded were given Dr. Hebard by your grandfather, Mr. F. G. Burnett and others who were well acquainted with Sacajawea or "Bazil's Mother."

Her grave in the Shoshone Indian Cemetery, Wind River, Wyoming, is marked with a concrete column in which is embedded a bronze tablet with the inscription prepared by Dr. Hebard, Ph.D.: "Sacajawea. a guide with the Lewis and Clark expedition, 1805–6. Died April 9, 1884. Aged 100 years. Identified by Reverend John Roberts who officiated at her burial." Close by her grave is that of Bazil; it is marked by a handsome and massive granite headstone with the inscription prepared by Dr. Eastman, M.D., Sioux-Indian: "Bazil, son of Sacajawea, age 86 years, Died 1886. He was re-buried here January 2, 1925." Bazil's headstone was erected to his memory and paid for by Dr. Hebard, as was another like it on the grave of Barbara Meyers, granddaughter of Sacajawea.

Dr. Hebard has also ordered two other headstones, one for Andrew Bazil, son of Bazil, and one in memory of Baptiste, the baby son of Sacajawea whom she carried on her back on the expedition.

Your grandfather, my old and true friend Mr. F. G. Burnett, has done more to elevate the Indians on this reservation and to make them self-sup-porting, self-respecting and good people than anyone else. My sight is dim; I am eighty. Mr. F. G. Burnett must be about ninety.

With kindest respects,

Sincerely yours,

John Roberts

Missionary Clergyman to the

Indians, 1883–1933

Letter from Rev. John Roberts to Esther Horne (ca. 1930)

This is an accurate report regarding my knowledge of Sacajawea.

The Right Reverend John F. Spalding, Bishop of the Missionary jurisdic-tion of Colorado and Wyoming, sent me here in 1883 to establish the Sho-shone and Arapahoe Indian Mission of the Protestant Episcopal Church.

I arrived at the Shoshone Agency on February 10 after a hard journey over the main range of the Rockies from Green River, the nearest railroad sta-tion, a distance of 150 miles, which took up eight days traveling in a sleigh, most of the way over the snow-covered mountains.

The next day after I arrived, I went to the U.S. Indian office where a few aged Indians were assembled, the bulk of the tribes being absent on their annual winter buffalo hunt. Among those present was Bazil, one of the head men, an aged and fine specimen of an Indian. I was introduced to Bazil by James Irwin, M.D., U.S. agent in charge of the Shoshone Reservation. Ba-zil was able to talk English brokenly. I was also told that he could speak French. The agent then took me to Bazil's camp to see an aged woman who was called by him Bazil's Mother. She was seated on the ground in a tepee; her hair was gray and she had the appearance of being very old. Dr. Irwin alluded to her connection with the Lewis and Clark expedition, and he seemed to be keenly interested in the fact I was interested in the old woman because of her great age, for at the time I knew very little of the Lewis and Clark expedition.

Bazil was a great friend of Dr. Irwin, U.S. agent on the reservation in the early seventies. At one time Dr. Irwin told me that Bazil demanded permission from him to bring his mother's tent and pitch it close to his house, for, said Bazil, "I am going away on a buffalo hunt, and I want you to take special care of her, for she has been a great friend of the white people in the early days."

Bazil proved to be a very dutiful son to his mother. He was in reality only an adopted son and nephew. He cared for her tenderly and had his daughters and other women of the camp see to her every need. She was well provided for. The U.S. agent issued her plenty of beef, flour, groceries, and even tobacco, which she liked to smoke.

Sacajawea's son, Baptiste, alluded to by name by Captain Clark of the expedition, lived about three miles above the agency at the foot of the mountains. I came to know Baptiste and Bazil very well later on.

After the death of Charbonneau, Sacajawea's French and Indian husband, Sacajawea was lost to the whites and Shoshones for many years while she was visiting kindred tribes of her people. She spent several years with the Comanches, who are the same as Shoshones and speak the same language, but the homing instinct in her led her during her latter days to seek her own people in the mountains of Wyoming.

Sacajawea used to amuse members of her family by relating to them some of her experiences during the expedition. One time she told them that she had seen at the Great Waters toward the setting sun, a fish as big as a log cabin. Captain Clark mentions the fact that they had found a dead whale washed ashore when they reached the Pacific. Sacajawea and her two sons were unable to read or write. Bazil and Baptiste could not possibly have known the things which they did regarding the long journey unless their mother had told them.

During the latter years of Sacajawea's life here she was known to the whites and Indians as Bazil's Mother. On my Parish Register of Burials, I recorded her burial under the date of April 9, 1884, Bazil's Mother, Shoshone, age 100, Residence, Shoshone Agency, Cause of death—Old age. Place of Burial—Burial Ground Shoshone Agency. Signature of Clergyman— J. Roberts.

Letter from Rev. John Roberts to Esther Horne (ca. 1930)

Sacajawea was also known to the Indians by other names, according to the

Shoshone custom, as Wadze-Wipe, the Lost Woman, Booe-Nive, Grass Maiden, Barribo, Water White Man.

On the morning of April 9, the following year, I was told that Bazil's Mother had passed suddenly away during the night in the log cabin that was in the camp on her shakedown of quilts, blankets, and pelts. The agent had a coffin made for her, and he sent employees to dig her grave on the eastern slope of one of the foothills, a mile and one-half west of the agency where there were four graves of white people who were killed by hostile raiding Indians. This burial ground has subsequently been set apart by the Indian Office as a Shoshone Indian Cemetery, but it still remains a part of the Reservation.

Bazil died a few years after his mother. He was buried at Mill Creek about four miles from the agency but was subsequently laid to rest beside the grave of Sacajawea, his adopted mother. When she died, he had requested a Christian burial for her.

Baptiste was buried, according to the ancient custom of the Shoshones, in the rocks in a canyon west of the mission at the head of Dry Creek. Not many years ago, government officials, with some of the Shoshone Indians, tried to recover his body and place it in the Shoshone cemetery, but they were unable to do so as his grave had been washed away. The headstone in his memory was placed at the grave of Maggie Meyers, daughter of Baptiste.

The Hon. James I. Patten, who was appointed U.S. Agent of the Shoshones in the early seventies and for many years previously had known them and spoken their language, was himself convinced that the claim of the old Shoshone woman, Bazil's Mother, was genuine. Mr. F. G. Burnett, U.S. government farmer, resident on the reservation for more than a quarter of a century, was well acquainted with Sacajawea and spoke to her many times concerning her connection with the expedition. Richard Morse, for many years a government employee at this agency, also knew Sacajawea personally. These three reputable, worthy pioneer men, as well as Dr. Irwin, the agent, were convinced that the claim of Sacajawea, buried here, was true; that she was connected with the Lewis and Clark expedition.

I firmly believe that the old Shoshone Indian woman whom I buried in the Shoshone Agency Cemetery in Wyoming is the true Sacajawea, guide of the Lewis and Clark expedition—J. Roberts.

Letter from Rev. John Roberts to Esther Horne (April 12, 1948)

I arrived at the Shoshone Indian Agency February 10, 1883, after a hard ride by stagecoach from the Union Pacific Railroad at Green River, Wyoming.

We encountered a heavy snowstorm and were eight days and nights on the trip across the main range of the Rocky Mountains, between Green River and the Shoshone Indian Agency. During this time the government thermometer in the weather bureau office at Fort Washakie, near the Indian agency, registered fifty-seven, fifty-eight, and fifty-nine degrees below zero for three consecutive nights.

The morning after my arrival, I paid my respects to the United States Indian agent, Dr. James Irwin, M.D. He took me to a camp near the Indian agency to see an aged Shoshone woman living close by in her adopted son Bazil's camp. Dr. Irwin told me she was connected with the Lewis and Clark expedition. Bazil, her nephew and adopted son, said she had reached a great age and that she had helped the "first Washington" to cross the Rocky Mountains and reach the "great water toward the setting sun."

Sacajawea's own son, Baptiste, I knew well. He lived a few miles from the Shoshone Indian Mission. His son, George Bazil, or Witogan, a member of the Indian police, told me his father, Baptiste, told him many times that his mother carried him (Baptiste) as a baby on her back while she guided the "first Washington" across the mountains to the "great water towards the setting sun."

Sacajawea died on April 9, 1884. Her grave is in the Shoshone Indian burial ground close to the Shoshone Indian mission, Wind River, Wyoming. The grave is marked by a cement column on the face of which is embedded a bronze tablet on which is inscribed the epitaph prepared by Dr. Grace Raymond Hebard, historian of the University of Wyoming, Laramie, Wyoming. The inscription on the tablet read:

Sacajawea
Died April 9, 1884
A Guide With The
Lewis and Clark Expedition
1805–1806
Identified 1907 by Rev. J. Roberts
Who Officiated at her burial.

Letter from Major General H. L. Scott to Rev. John Roberts (July 26, 1932)
My dear Mr. Roberts,

I am putting in writing what I told you verbally about the old woman you buried.

I was investigating the matter of the controversy as to Sacajawea's burial place and went with Mr. Moses of the *Great Falls (Montana) Tribune* to visit an old woman in Browning, half French and half Blackfoot, who claimed to be over one hundred years old. I asked her about all the noted people on the Missouri in early days, and she answered me promptly and accurately as to things I knew about. She had been married long before to Armell, and her name was, when talking to me, "Mrs. Reavis," if I remember my notes correctly. I asked if she knew Charbonneau and his snake wife. She replied that she knew them when she lived at Fort Clark on the Missouri near Fort Berthold, North Dakota. I asked where Sacajawea was buried. She answered, "I do not know. She left the river."

With very high regard I am

Sincerely yours

H. L. Scott

Major General

U.S. Army Rtd.

Notes

INTRODUCTION: COLLECTING AND COAUTHORING A LIFE HISTORY

1. Life histories have long been regarded in anthropology as legitimate, if not perfect, approaches to understanding other cultures, because they emphasize the experiences of individuals and provide an insider's view of their life and culture. The amount of published material on life history and autobiography has grown immensely since the pioneering works of Thomas and Znaniecki (1918), Dollard (1935), Allport (1942), Kluckhohn (1945), and Misch (1951). The history and theoretical background of the biographical approach to anthropological fieldwork have been well documented; helpful discussions and useful bibliographies of a general nature can be found in Bertaux 1981; Blackman ed. 1992; Haviland 1991; Langness 1965; Langness and Frank 1981; Mandelbaum 1973; Mintz 1989; Olney 1988; Rosenwald and Ochberg 1992; Shaw 1980; Watson 1976; Watson and Watson-Franke 1985; and Weintraub 1978.

American Indians have been and continue to be popular subject material for life histories. References to this phenomenon as well as complete bibliographies can be found in Bataille and Sands 1984; Brumble 1981; Krupat 1985; Ruoff 1990; and Wong 1987.

Of course, many Native American autobiographies and life histories have been criticized owing to their western (non-Native) literary form and inaccurate interpretations by their non-Indian collectors. Cook-Lynn (1996) is particularly critical of "collaborative" life histories; her perspectives are central to an understanding of the problems associated with this genre. Sarris (1993, 79–114) provides a provocative assessment of the benefits and drawbacks of the narrated approach to American Indian lives. In addition Brumble 1987; Clifford 1978; Krupat 1985, 1992; Murray 1991; and Vizenor 1989 examine these criticisms.

Historically, the life history has moved from a method in which the aim was to salvage the last vestiges of a vanishing people to one that records the lives of Natives as adaptive players, resistors, actors, and collaborators in the preservation of their own pasts and presents. See, for example, Bruner 1986; Clifford 1983; Haviland 1991; McBeth 1989, 1993; McBeth and Horne 1996.

Autobiographies, life histories, and oral traditions by and about women have also en-joyed a renewed interest as evidenced by numerous books and essays on the topic pub-lished within the last ten years or so. Brodzki and Schenck 1988; Geiger 1986; Gluck 1977; Gluck and Patai 1991; Hoffman and Culley 1985; Jelinek 1986; Lawless 1991; Patai 1988; Personal Narratives Group 1989; Smith 1987; Smith and Watson 1992 provide a few exam-ples of this interest.

Essays on narrative, life history, autobiography, and so forth, can be found in journals of anthropology, ethnic studies, folklore, literature, medicine, psychology, sociology, women's studies, as well as other journals. *The Journal of Narrative and Life History*, an indicator of the acceptance of these genres, began publication in 1991.

2. My understanding of issues of cultural representation and narrative self-expression have been influenced by Abu-Lughod 1993; Appadurai 1992; Atkinson 1990; Bohannan 1995; Bruner 1986; Clifford 1983; Clifford and Marcus 1986; Fabian 1983; Foucault 1972; Geertz 1986, 1988; Krupat 1996; Marcus and Cushman 1982; Marcus and Fischer 1986; Mascia-Lees, Sharpe, and Cohen 1989; Murray 1991; Rabinow 1977, 1986; Ricoeur 1979; Roof and Wiegman 1995; Searle 1995; and Tyler 1992.

Discussions with Michael Dorris (1945–1997) also added to my understanding of how and why anthropologists expropriate Native stories and traditions; his supportive advice influenced my choice of a fully collaborative method.

3. For a more detailed account of this controversy, see the epilogue and appendix C (ex-cerpted from Horne 1980).

4. Linguists, psychologists, and anthropologists whose work has led me to consider the issues of the integrated quality of writing versus the more fragmented nature of speak-ing include Alverson and Rosenberg 1990; Chafe 1982; Chafe and Tannen 1987; Cicourel 1985; and Stubbs 1983.

5. Formal (tape-recorded) interviews were conducted with Esther Horne's two daugh-ters, Yvonne Barney, now deceased, on June 14, 1987; and Dianne Kjelbertson on June 28, 1991. Her nephew Mike Cutler was interviewed on June 8, 1987. Rev. George Schul-enberg, former pastor of Samuel Memorial Episcopal Church in Naytahwaush, Minne-sota, was interviewed on June 11, 1987. Longtime Chippewa friends Rev. Doyle and Mary Turner, and Brent and Gayle Gish were interviewed on June 15, 1987. Ralph Erdrich and Rita Gorneau Erdrich, friends and teachers who worked with Esther Horne at the Wah-peton Indian School, were interviewed on July 15, 1988. Mildred Graff, friend and former housekeeper (1940–1944), was interviewed on June 18, 1992. John Gwinn (White Earth Chippewa), a former student and friend, was interviewed on June 27, 1992.

Frequently, the most telling insights into who Essie is were not revealed in formal in-terviews, but in casual conversation. Rita Erdrich, for example, said, "You can't *really* know Essie until you've seen her in the classroom. That is where she shines the brightest." I realized that as much as I know about this woman, I will never see this side of her, even though I have frequently observed her interactions with students of many ages.

I've also had numerous informal discussions with former students and other friends of Esther Horne. They all described her as a nonjudgmental confidant, a pillar of strength in hard times, and a woman to emulate—their Yoda. She was never too busy to spend time with them, listen to them, and give them her love and understanding. These include Sue Beithon, Joyce Melk Burr, Leroy and Janice Chief, Carol Crissler, Norma and Ed Estey, Dr. Joseph Gacusana, Karen Starr Gilles, Dennis Hastings, Sally Hausken, Rev. Harvey Henderson, Edna Hermes, Sampson Hill, Leonard Hudgkins, Rev. Frank Love, Jeanette Munson, Theresa Olsen, Beverly Peterson, Patricia Stuen, Debra Wallwork, and others who have touched and enriched her life and she theirs.

6. Autobiographical and ethnological memory have been of interest to behavioral scientists for many years. From the early works of Sir Francis Galton (1879a, 1879b), to Franz Boas's skepticism (1943), scholars have focused on the relationship between history and memory, and between memory and one's personal and cultural significance. Recent analyses of these topics which relate to both individual and collective memory include: Adams 1990; Anderson 1991; Appleby, Hunt, and Jacob 1994; Bauman 1982; Bolles 1988; Connerton 1989; Fussell 1975; Goleman 1985; Gusdorf [1956] 1980; Hobsbawm and Ranger 1983; Kammen 1991; Langer 1991; Le Goff 1988; Lowenthal 1985:185–259; Personal Narratives Group 1989; Rappaport 1990; Rousso 1991; Rubin 1986; and Thelen 1989.

7. Wilson provides a glossary of Hidatsa words but does not comment on any of the editorial decisions made in the production of the text, *Waheenee*. Linderman notes his difficulty in communicating with Native women. He states, "I have found Indian women diffident and so self-effacing that acquaintance with them is next to impossible" ([1932] 1972, 9). Other than this, he reveals little about the collection of Pretty-shield's life history except that it was processed "through an interpreter laboring to translate Crow thoughts into English words" ([1932] 1972, 11). Linderman says that his knowledge of sign language permitted him to follow this Crow woman's story and to guard against obvious divergences on the part of the interpreter.

Each of Michelson's narratives provides different types of relevant information for the reader interested in editorial decision making. The Fox autobiography (1925) includes the full text in English and in Fox syllabary (collected and transposed by a Native-speaking interpreter). Michelson adds, "No attempt was made to influence the informant in any way; so that the contents are things which seemed of importance to herself." He also adds that "a few sentences have been deleted" (1925, 295). His rationale for this erasure is that the content is too "naive" and frank for European tastes; he infers in a footnote that sexual taboos and/or "immoral" behaviors were the subject of the deleted section (1925, 342). Extensive ethnological and linguistic notes are included in this Fox narrative.

Truman Michelson's Southern Cheyenne (1932) and Arapaho (1933) narratives stand in marked contrast to his first collection. They are brief; they include limited footnotes, and they were collected by interpreters and intermediaries hired by Michelson. He probably did not make many changes to the English versions that he received, although it is possible that Michelson requested intimate details about marriage and childbirth.

8. The preface to *Mountain Wolf Woman* provides the reader one of the first backgrounds on the methods used to collect and edit autobiographical material. Lurie reveals that the story was recorded in Winnebago *and* in English on a tape recorder. She uses dashes in the text of the narrative to indicate where materials from notes or from the shorter version of Mountain Wolf Woman's autobiography are inserted. Her extensive use of footnotes (thirty-two pages of them) also allows the reader to understand the story in its cultural and historical contexts. Lurie's explanations of traditional Winnebago culture, the effects of government policies, and Mountain Wolf Woman's personal reflections add considerable depth to this life history.

9. Blackman's work with Davidson and Neakok is an important contribution to chronicling the lives of elder Indian women. However, at a time when anthropologists and Native people alike are questioning the methods and the very foundations of the anthropological endeavor itself, Blackman reveals little about the actual process of editing the oral tapes. I have, however, come to understand through my own work, through conversations with Margaret Blackman, and through my teaching of a life history writing course that the editing decisions which one makes are difficult to document. They involve countless decisions that require the writer to exercise judgment, flexibility, and intuition. It is to Blackman's credit that both Davidson and Neakok reviewed, and eventually approved of, the final manuscripts prior to publication. Horne's and my task was made less problematical (and more time-consuming) by our choice of a totally collaborative model, that is, one where the production of every chapter, page, and sentence was a joint effort.

10. In her scholarly work, Cruikshank has elaborated on the way that Native American women use oral tradition to enlarge our "understanding of the past, particularly in areas where written documents are biased by the circumstances under which they were produced" (1990a, 3). This oral history connection may also prove to be a valuable device in comparing the lives of Native American women with one another. As controversial as Essie's insistence that Sacajawea lived to be an old woman is to many people, her opinions contribute to our understanding of her sense of self, as well as to how important the writing of her story is to the continuity among generations.

11. Other recent books about Native American women's life stories include *Madonna Swann* (St. Pierre 1991); *Messengers of the Wind* (Katz 1995); *Molly Spotted Elk* (McBride 1995); *Their Example Showed Me the Way* (Minde 1996); and *When Nickels Were Indians* (Hilden 1995).

There are also many professional Native American women writers whose autobiographical works deserve mention. Recent examples of this genre include "The Auto-biography of Confluence" (Allen 1987); *The Blue Jay's Dance* (Erdrich 1995); *Claiming Breath* (Glancy 1992); *The Halfbreed Chronicles* (Rose 1985); "Ordinary Spirit" (Harjo 1987); *Sáanii Dahataal: The Women Are Singing* (Tapahonso 1993); *Storyteller* (Silko 1981); *Talking Indian: Reflections on Survival and Writing* (Walters 1992); and "The Two Lives" (Hogan 1987).

12. Many scholars have evaluated how and why people seek or create metaphors to give meaning to their experiences. Cassirer 1944, Clifford 1978, Lakoff and Johnson 1980, Olney 1972 and 1980, Ricoeur 1977, Smith 1987, Spengemann and Lundquist 1968, and Vecsey 1988 all examine this phenomenon in the context of life histories, autobiographies, and other personal narratives.

13. The conventional wisdom about Bureau of Indian Affairs and/or church-sponsored Indian boarding schools is that they were brutal, oppressive institutions which proceeded on the assumption that Indians were "savages" who had to be "civilized." The belief was that separation from family, community, and Indian values was the only way to assimilate these youth into white society. Recent publications on the boarding schools, however, paint a more complex portrait of how the boarding school experience was interpreted by the generations of Indians who attended these schools. The following recent manuscripts provide useful perspectives: D. W. Adams 1995, Coleman 1993, Gould 1997, Haig-Brown 1988, Hyer 1990, Johnston 1988, Littlefield 1989, Lomawaima 1994, McBeth 1983a, Mihesuah 1993, and Trennert 1988.

14. While the word "master" is masculine, it is the term that Essie uses to describe the culmination of her teaching expertise. There is no appropriate alternative term in the English language for the feminine form.

15. For references to these educational strategies see Cazden and John 1971 and Kasten 1992.

16. A few references to the importance of the hermeneutical approach, especially as it relates to autobiography and life history, can be found in Gadamer 1976 and 1979; Giddens 1982; Gunn 1982, 55–89; Peterson 1986; and Ricoeur 1979.

17. The complexities of Indian women's roles in their cultures and with white society are beginning to be explored. A few general recent articles, books, and bibliographies include Albers and Medicine 1983; Allen 1986; Green 1975, 1980, 1983, 1992; Kidwell 1992; La Framboise, Heyle, and Ozer 1990; Lurie 1972; and Mihesuah 1996.

18. See Henze and Vanett (1993) for an insightful critique of the metaphor "to walk in two worlds." Clifton's frequently cited and often criticized edited collection *Being and Becoming Indian* (1989) contains interesting biographical essays on individuals whom some would label as "marginals." General information on the concept of mixed-bloods can be found in Bieder 1980, Gould 1992, and Peterson and Brown 1984. Horne and McBeth both hold that individuals should retain the right to identify themselves.

Wallace Stegner's (1955, 50) reflection on the dominant society's perceptions of Indians and mixed-bloods in the early twentieth century bears repeating. It indicates the underlying racism that many Western white citizens felt toward families like Essie's. Stegner writes, "Their [his parents] behavior was an explicit reflection of local attitude: that an Indian was a thieving, treacherous, lousy, unreliable, gut-eating vagabond, and that if anything a halfbreed was worse."

19. I was looking through some of Essie's memorabilia and found a note from Duke Wellington, former superintendent of the Wahpeton Indian School. He wrote: "To the best instructor I have ever known in the BIA. She taught Indian children the way they should be taught. Learn all you can from the white man's books and ways, but always be proud of your Indian heritage." I asked Essie what this revealing and supportive quote meant to her. She said simply, "That is what I always tried to do—combine both worlds."

I. MY RELATIONSHIP TO SACAJAWEA

1. Mildred Large (1890–1971) was Esther's Shoshone mother. Fincelious Burnett Jr. (1877–1922) was her white father. See chapter 2 for further elaboration on their relationship.

2. For a more complete and balanced historical discussion of Toussaint Charbonneau see "Toussaint Charbonneau, A Most Durable Man" (Ottoson 1976).

3. The word "Snake" is another name for the Shoshone people and is a term commonly used in early historical accounts.

4. Chief Washakie (ca. 1804–1900) had become a prominent leader of the Shoshones by 1837. Shoshone oral tradition asserts that Sacajawea and Washakie were contemporaries and that Sacajawea assisted Washakie in his efforts to accommodate his people to life on the Wind River Reservation in Wyoming (cf. Wright 1980).

5. The Jefferson Peace Medal was a gift given by Lewis and Clark to various Indian dignitaries during the expedition of 1804–6. Meriwether Lewis records in his journal entry of August 17, 1805: "Cameahwait [Sacajawea's brother] pointed out two others whom he said were Chiefs. We gave him a medal of the small size with the likeness of Mr. Jefferson the President of the U' States in releif [sic] on one side & clasp hands with a pipe and tomahawk on the other" (Thwaites 1904, 2:363).

Horne believes that Sacajawea was presented with the same medal in recognition of her services to the Lewis and Clark expedition. The medal was said to be in the possession of Bazil. Doane Robinson (1924a, 80–81) believes that Bazil's medal does not provide proof that the woman said to have been buried in 1884 was Sacajawea. He says, "The medal said to have been in the possession of Bazil is urged as testimony in support of the identity of Sac-a-jawe and Sa-kaka-wea. It has no such significance. The Shoshoni did receive five medals from Lewis and Clark; that one of them should come down to Bazil has no significance so far as the identity of his mother is concerned. It is said he had it from his father.

There is no record and little probability that Lewis and Clark gave a medal to Charbonneau."

6. Fincelious Burnett Sr., Rev. John Roberts, and agents James Irwin and James Patten were non-Indians whose recollections supported the Shoshone oral traditions of Sacajawea's presence at Fort Washakie on the Wind River Reservation from around 1871 until her death in 1884.

7. Most historians question whether this conveniently missing document, compiled by Mrs. Sarah Irwin, ever existed. The problem of mysterious missing documents is a common one in historical research.

8. Excerpts from *The Oral Tradition of Sacajawea* (Horne 1980) are reprinted in "Appendix C: Memories of Sacajawea."

2. EARLY LIFE AT HOME

1. Fincelious (Finn) Burnett Sr. (1844–1924) was agricultural agent at Fort Washakie (Wind River Reservation) from 1871–1877. A somewhat romanticized account of his life was written by Robert Beebe David (1937). This biography includes a final chapter that details the relationship between Burnett and Sacajawea.

2. The 1868 Treaty of Fort Bridger granted the Wind River Reservation to the Eastern Shoshone.

3. While Horne suggests that neither the white nor Indian sides of the family approved of the couple's engagement, the practice of intercultural marriage was well established among Eastern Shoshones by the early twentieth century. Elopements were also a part of the cultural system (Lowie 1909, 210), as were migrations from Wyoming to Idaho (Hultkrantz [1961] 1974, 8).

4. Friends of Essie delight in teasing her about her fear of green worms. A friend chided, "Sacajawea went over hill and dale, forged rivers, climbed mountains, guided explorers through the untamed west, fearless—until she saw the army worms—then turned back, never to complete her destiny."

5. Nimimbe (nynymbi; nunum Bi; nïnïmbi) are one of the few traditional Shoshone spirits mentioned in Horne's narrative, and so they deserve some additional explanation. Shoshone memories of the nimimbe are tenacious, perhaps because their stories were repeated so often that no one questioned their existence. Trenholm and Carley (1964, 9, 33) and Hultkrantz (1987, 48) describe the nimimbe as frightening dwarfs who shoot invisible arrows of misfortune into anyone displeasing them. These malevolent descriptions suggest that these evil elfkin roam the dark recesses of the mountains and can cause their victims to hemorrhage in the lungs. In this century, they have sometimes been held responsible for the many cases of tuberculosis among the Shoshones.

Many written and oral sources, however, describe the nimimbe as more like leprechauns, who when captured can bring luck and success. Sarah Olden (1923, 6–18) collected nimimbe stories from Rev. John Roberts. Her descriptions attribute irresponsible behaviors to the "pigmies" but also portray them as skilled at procuring food and hide clothing. Shoshones described them as looking something like Santa Claus because they were clad in goatskins and always carried a large quiver of arrows on their backs. The stories recounted by Horne reflect a more beneficent characterization of these little people, more akin to leprechauns than evil yeomen.

6. Gene Stratton Porter was a popular fiction writer whose books were read by millions in the early decades of this century. One of her biographers writes that "the popularity, appeal, and worth of Gene Stratton Porter can best be understood by realizing that—at least for thousands of her readers—she was the right writer for her time. The change from an agrarian to an industrial and metropolitan society had almost been completed, but there remained a large portion of the country that was essentially rural. Her novels will be viewed as escapist for these people in that they helped ease the strain of a life which was rapidly becoming too mechanical" (Richards 1980, 10). *A Girl of the Limberlost* was published in 1909 by Doubleday. Its theme, like much of Porter's fiction, was overcoming obstacles through goodness and determination.

7. A milk separator is a machine that separates the milk proper from the cream.

3. WYOMING AND THE HASKELL INDIAN INSTITUTE

1. The Teapot Dome scandal (early 1920s) involved the secret leasing of federal oil reserves by Secretary of the Interior Albert B. Fall. Warren Harding was president at the time. In 1921 Fall secretly granted exclusive rights to the Teapot Dome (Wyoming) reserves to Harry F. Sinclair of the Mammoth Oil Company. In return for his approval of the leases, Fall received large cash gifts and no-interest "loans" from the oil producers. The conspiracy was exposed in the late 1920s (Werner and Starr 1959).

2. Established in 1884, Haskell Institute is among the oldest government-supported schools in the United States. It was located in Lawrence, Kansas, and was a typical off-reservation industrial training school. The last high school class graduated in 1965, and in 1970 the school became Haskell Indian Junior College. In 1993 the former United States Indian Industrial Training School became Haskell Indian Nations University, a four-year accredited college.

3. Screened sleeping porches, with long rows of cots, were used by the students in all but the coldest weather. It was believed that the fresh air was healthy and conducive to a good night's rest.

4. Uncle Charlie and Uncle Roy were two of Esther's mother's (Mildred Large) brothers. Carlisle Indian School (Carlisle, Pennsylvania) was the first off-reservation boarding school established by Col. Richard Pratt under the auspices of the United States government. Jim Thorpe (1888–1953), Sauk and Fox, attended both Haskell Indian School and the Carlisle Indian School. While playing football for Carlisle, Thorpe was

chosen as halfback for the All American Team in 1911 and 1912. He won the decathlon and pentathlon in the 1912 Olympic Games in Stockholm but was deprived of his medals in 1913 when it was discovered that he had played semiprofessional baseball in 1909 and 1910. The medals were restored to his family in 1983. Thorpe was a gifted athlete, and he excelled not only in football and baseball but also in basketball, boxing, lacrosse, swimming, and hockey.

5. Much has been written about the military discipline at boarding schools. Adams (1975, 121) writes, "The military atmosphere of the boarding school was more than a mere tribute to pomp and circumstance. It fit into the purposes for which the boarding school was designed. It was a particularly useful means of getting at the problem posed by the Indian's disregard for time and obedience to authority." Hyer (1990, 12) adds, "School administration used military drill to break down tribal values of group solidarity and to encourage competitiveness among students. Student officers were chosen as reward for good schoolwork and approved behavior."

6. WAC stands for Women's Army Corps; WAVE is a slang term for women in the navy.

7. Margaret Szasz (1977, 373) notes that "at Haskell Institute in Lawrence, Kansas," each hour of vocational training was matched by three hours of routine industrial work on campus."

8. Essie also says of the belt line, "But I wouldn't want any of my children to have to go through a belt line!" Other former boarding school students have stated how much they objected to being held responsible for punishing their classmates. Some said that if they did not become as involved in the whipping as the disciplinarian required, they were then sent down the belt line, thereby ensuring their compliance to this form of discipline.

9. Grace Thorpe was the younger sister of Jim Thorpe (see chap. 3, n. 4).

10. The Osage and Quapaw tribes of Oklahoma received large per capita payments for oil on their reservation lands in the 1920s.

11. Poor student health as a result of the inadequate diets of the boarding schools was one of the areas highlighted in the Meriam Report of 1924 (Meriam 1928).

12. A transom is a small hinged window above a door or another window.

13. Extracurricular activities included such things as band, orchestra, choir, girls and boys glee clubs, YWCA, YMCA, Normal Training Club, Officer's Club, Commissioned Officers Club, Businessgirls Club, Home Economics Club, Agricultural Club, Civic Club, Traders Club, Florence Nightingale Club, Sacajawea Library Club, Roosevelt Literary Club, Junior College Club, and Dramatic Club.

14. Rose La Framboise was a Turtle Mountain Chippewa from Belcourt, North Dakota.

15. Louise Breuninger (married name Peake) was a Cherokee from Oklahoma and a longtime friend of Essie.

16. Ella Cara Deloria (b. 1888 or 1889; d. 1971), a Dakota Sioux, was born on the Yank-

ton Indian Reservation in South Dakota. She studied at Oberlin College in Ohio from 1911 to 1913, then transferred to Teachers College, Columbia University. She received her B.S. in 1915. In 1923 she accepted a position at the Haskell Indian School in Lawrence, Kansas, as a teacher of physical education and dance.

In 1927 she resigned her teaching position at Haskell to devote herself to the scholarly study of the Dakota language. She worked with Franz Boas and Ruth Benedict, well-known anthropologists affiliated with Columbia University. Her publications include *Dakota Texts* (1932), *Dakota Grammar* with Franz Boas (Boas 1941), *Speaking of Indians* (1944), and *Waterlily* (posthumous, 1988). Raymond DeMallie says of her scholarship: "Ella Deloria's studies provide some of the best material ever recorded on Dakota culture and are the fullest accounts in the native language. Her work is also unique in emphasizing an understanding of the culture from the woman's perspective, a perspective lacking in most studies of Native American peoples" (1980, 184).

Ruth Muskrat Bronson (1897–1982), a Cherokee, was born in eastern Oklahoma in the Delaware district of the Cherokee Nation. She studied at the University of Oklahoma for a year and graduated from Mount Holyoke College in 1925. In that same year she became an employee of Haskell Institute as an instructor in English literature. From 1931 to 1943 she worked for the Brookings Institute of Washington DC, and for the Bureau of Indian Affairs. Her charge was to survey colleges and other institutions of higher education to determine what opportunities were available to Indians in the United States. Later in her life she worked for the United States Public Health Service, the National Congress of American Indians, and the Save the Children Federation.

She spoke out publicly against the termination policy (Bronson 1994, 492–94) and published a popular book, *Indians Are People, Too* ([1944] 1979). Vine Deloria (Ella Cara Deloria's nephew) and C. Lytle described her as "a brash young Cherokee girl" when, in 1924, she delivered the recommendations of the Committee of One Hundred (a group of Indian and non-Indian activists promoting New Deal reform for Indian people) to President Coolidge (Deloria and Lytle 1984, 43).

17. The giveaway is a ceremonial and public distribution of goods that embraces the native values of reciprocity and sharing. Gift giving is a way of showing appreciation to the community and of honoring someone's success. It has always been a traditional means of establishing family status and gaining prestige. It is a socially motivated giving (cf. Grobsmith 1981, 53–60).

Essie explains the giveaway in this way: "What goes around comes around. Our Indian values of generosity require that we not be greedy, but give back to our communities in a reciprocal exchange. It is good to give. It brings us pride in who we are and who we were. Honoring with gifts is a long-standing cultural tradition because it shows our respect for and generosity toward others. There are no people as generous, even with what little we have, as we Indian people." Generosity may be the single most important value of Essie's life and culture.

18. The date for the Haskell play was May 31, 1927. Essie still has the program and a single pressed rose (1965) from Ella Deloria. She also has her marked copy of the play from which she prepared.

19. Giving nicknames is very common among Indian people; the names are usually affectionate ones. Essie says, "Indian people are notorious for the nicknames they bestow on each other. I've lived up here on the White Earth Reservation since 1965, and there are people whose real names I don't even know, because they always go by their nicknames."

20. The "outing system" (begun at Haskell by 1888 or earlier) was an apprenticeship program instituted by a number of Bureau of Indian Affairs nonreservation Indian boarding schools. This system, designed to promote the already well-established assimilationist policies of these schools, had a two-fold purpose: to encourage children not to return to their home reservations and communities during the summer (or on weekends where and when that was possible) and to place children in intimate contact with "civilized" white American society. A third purpose began to surface in the early 1900s when boarding school–educated Indian youth became the providers of cheap, controllable, and menial labor for wealthy white families (Trennert 1983).

4. EUFAULA, OKLAHOMA, AND MARRIAGE

1. Robert Starr Horne, a Hoopa Indian from California, attended the Sherman Indian School in Riverside, California, before he transferred to Haskell. He and Esther met at Haskell and eventually married in 1929, raised two daughters, and lived together until Bob's death in 1974.

2. *Ramona*, published in 1884 (Roberts Brothers) is a romantic novel written by Helen Hunt Jackson. It is the story of a mixed-blood (California Indian and Scottish), orphaned young woman who falls in love with an Indian man from the village of Temecula, located in Southern California. There are interesting parallels to Essie Horne's mixed-blood status and Bob Horne's Hoopa (northern California) tribal affiliation.

5. THE WAHPETON YEARS

1. These young Indian employees included dormitory matrons, advisers, custodial personnel, and of course, a teacher and a power plant fireman.

2. Esther Burnett Horne is about five feet tall.

3. *Music of the American Indian* was recorded and edited by Willard Rhodes in cooperation with the Bureau of Indian Affairs, Washington DC. The Library of Congress Division of Music Recording Laboratory, Archive of American Folksong.

4. The Dust Bowl is a section of the Great Plains including parts of Colorado, Kansas, New Mexico, Texas, Oklahoma, Nebraska, the Dakotas, and surrounding areas. The

plains and prairie grasslands were plowed heavily during the 1920s in order to grow wheat. The years of overcultivation and poor land management took their toll in the 1930s (1930–35) when a severe drought hit and high winds carried off the topsoil. Dust storms blocked out the sun and piled the dirt in drifts. Thousands of families were forced to leave the region at the height of the Great Depression in the early and mid-1930s. The wind erosion was gradually brought under control, with federal aid, by the early 1940s (Bonnifield 1979).

5. Bilingual readers such as *The Hen of Wahpeton* (in Lakota, *Unjincila Wahpetun Etanhan Kin He*), n.d.; *The Pine Ridge Porcupine* (in Dakota, *Wazi ahanhan p'ahin k'un he*) (1941) by Ann Nolan Clark; and *There Are Still Buffalo* (in Lakota, *Nahanhci pte yukcanpi*) (1942), written by Ann Nolan Clark and illustrated by Andrew Standing Soldier, became more commonly used in boarding schools at this time. All were publications of the Education Division, U.S. Office of Indian Affairs (Lawrence ᴋѕ: Haskell Institute Printing Dept.).

6. Maria Martinez and her husband Julian Martinez were active potters in the traditional polychrome style of San Ildefonso prior to the time that Julian worked out the famous matte black-on-black style in about 1919. Their revival of the black-on-black style made the Martinez family famous. Early in their careers, Maria and Julian were encouraged by a trader to sign their pieces.

7. Ruth Murray Underhill (1884–1984) was born in New York. She attended Vassar College, the London School of Economics, and the University of Munich. Underhill also studied anthropology at Columbia University under Franz Boas and Ruth Benedict. She completed her Ph.D. degree in 1937 and did fieldwork with the Papago (now Tohono O'odham) and Mojave Indians prior to her many years of work with the United States Indian Service (1936–1947). In the Indian Service she lectured to and conducted workshops with teachers of Indian children. Following her government employment, she was professor of anthropology at the University of Denver for five years (1947–1952) until her retirement.

8. These works are *Quill and Beadwork of the Western Sioux* (1940) by Carrie A. Lyford, associate supervisor of Indian Education. U.S. Department of the Interior, Bureau of Indian Affairs, Education Branch, ed. W. W. Beatty; and *American Indian Beadwork* (1951) by W. Ben Hunt and J. F. "Buck" Burshears (Milwaukee: The Bruce Publishing Company).

9. Louis Brewer, a Sioux from Pine Ridge, was the boys' adviser at the Wahpeton Indian School.

10. I had the privilege of being hosted by the students of the Wahpeton Indian School in this small dining room in October 1983. The experience was indeed a special one for me. The students were very proud of their abilities to organize a meal in this setting and to socialize with members of the community.

11. Flandreau Indian School, a Bureau of Indian Affairs off-reservation boarding school, is located in Flandreau, South Dakota. It is still in operation under bureau auspices.

6. EVENTS OF THE 1950S AND 1960S

1. Russell Reid of the State Historical Society of North Dakota (Reid 1950) and Will G. Robinson of the State Historical Society of South Dakota (Poole 1964, 11; Robinson 1956) do not believe that the woman buried by Rev. John Roberts at Fort Washakie in 1884 was Sacajawea. They both agree that Sacajawea died and was buried at Fort Manuel Lisa in 1812. In fact, in the 1956 *Monthly Bulletin* of the South Dakota Historical Society, Robinson sets forth twenty-two points that counter "Mrs Horne's theory taken from her own investigation and the reports of Hebard and Eastman" (1956, 2).

2. Maria Tallchief (and her sister Marjorie) are renowned ballerinas. They are now retired; their tribal affiliation is Osage.

7. RETIREMENT AND THE 1960S THROUGH 1990S

1. Ed McGaa is an enrolled member of the Oglala Sioux tribe. Lawyer, lecturer, and writer, McGaa (Eagle Man) writes primarily about Native American spirituality for non-Indians.

Gerald Vizenor (b. 1934) is a prolific author. Much of his writing draws upon his experiences as a mixed-blood Anishinabe. His tribal affiliation is White Earth Chippewa/Ojibwa.

Fritz Scholder (b. 1937) is of French, English, German, and Luiseño (Mission) descent. He is an accomplished and commercially successful contemporary Indian painter. His highly original style portrays the Indian in a dramatic and strongly expressionistic manner. Essie knew Fritz Jr. when he was a young boy in Wahpeton—they were next-door neighbors. Scholder's father, Fritz Sr., was employed at the Wahpeton Indian School.

2. The Gallup Ceremonial is an annual intertribal Indian rodeo, powwow, and arts and crafts exhibit held every August in Gallup, New Mexico.

3. The responses to Blanche Schroer's article, "Is Sacajawea Really Buried at Fort Washakie?" in the *Wyoming State Journal*, February 9, 1978, pp. 1, 6, 7, continued into July of that same year. Essie and her sister Bernice convinced the Lander paper (*Wyoming State Journal*) to reprint their testimony. In addition, many individuals, including Milward L. Simpson, former governor and cousin of Essie's; Ida Burnett Greene, Essie's aunt; Louise Breuninger Peake, Cherokee, Essie's friend from Haskell; Dr. Ruth Arrington, Creek, Communications professor at Northeastern State University in Tahlequah, Oklahoma, and an old friend of Essie's; and others responded during the spring and summer of 1978. Mrs. Gladys Roberts Graham, daughter of Rev. John Roberts, sent a letter and supporting documents that were printed in the *Wyoming State Journal* on July 3, 1978 (Pioneer Days section, pp. 6, 7).

4. Esther Burnett Horne's seven-page testimony is recorded in a Congressional Report of February 24, 1982. For the full reference see U.S. Senate Select Committee on Indian Affairs 1982.

8. RETROSPECTIVE

1. Dennis Banks and George Mitchell emerged as leaders of an Indian patrol in Minneapolis, Minnesota, in 1968. The intent of the patrol was to control harassment and brutality that the police force directed at Native Americans in the Twin Cities. Mitchell, Banks, and other Native Americans decided to organize formally. They called themselves the American Indian Movement (AIM).

2. Leonard Peltier (b. 1944; Lakota/Ojibwa) was convicted in 1977 of killing two FBI agents in a 1975 South Dakota shoot-out. He is serving two consecutive life sentences in Marion Prison in Illinois. Many believe that he is not guilty and is a political prisoner. Peltier was active in the American Indian Movement (cf. Matthiessen 1983).

3. Leroy Chief, Indian Education Coordinator in the Park Rapids, Minnesota, schools and former superintendent of the Wahpeton Indian School (1972–1992), and his wife, Janice, are old friends of Essie. In 1995 Essie sent me a copy of the Peltier interview from the *Circle*, a Native American current issues magazine published in Minneapolis (Dunn 1995). I immediately called her on the phone and confronted her with this omission from the life history. I had no idea that Leonard Peltier had been one of her students. Her reply was, "Oh, didn't I mention to you that he was one of my fourth-grade students?"

4. Essie's grandson, Shawn Barney, and his wife, Sarah, have a son, Sam, and a daughter, Madison—Essie's great-grandchildren. Her granddaughter, Debra Kjelbertson Baker, and Debra's husband, Douglas, have one child, Cody. Her other granddaughter, Jennifer Kjelbertson Van Berkom, is married to Brien Van Berkom.

Works Cited

Abu-Lughod, Lila. 1993. *Writing women's worlds: Bedouin stories*. Berkeley: University of California Press.

Adams, David Wallace. 1975. *The federal boarding school: A study of environment and response, 1879–1918*. Ed.D. diss., Indiana University, Bloomington.

———. 1995. *Education for extinction: American Indians and the boarding school experience, 1875–1928*. Lawrence: University Press of Kansas.

Adams, Timothy Dow. 1990. *Telling lies in modern American autobiography*. Chapel Hill: University of North Carolina Press.

Albers, Patricia, and Bea Medicine, eds. 1983. *The hidden half: Studies in Plains Indian women*. Washington DC: University Press of America.

Allen, Paula Gunn. 1986. *The sacred hoop*. Boston: Beacon Press.

———. 1987. The autobiography of confluence. In *I tell you now*, ed. Brian Swann and Arnold Krupat, 141–54. Lincoln: University of Nebraska Press.

Allport, Gordon. 1942. *The use of personal documents in psychological science*. Social Science Research Council Bulletin 49, New York.

Alverson, Hoyt, and S. Rosenberg. 1990. Discourse analysis of schizophrenic speech: A critique and proposal. *Applied psycholinguistics* 11:167–84.

Ambler, Marjane. 1995. History in the first person. *Winds of change* 10 (4): 82–86.

Ambrose, Stephen E. 1996. *Undaunted courage*. New York: Simon and Schuster.

Anderson, Benedict. 1991. *Imagined communities: Reflections on the origin and spread of nationalism*. London: Verso.

Anderson, Irving W. 1970. J. B. Charbonneau, son of Sacajawea. *Oregon historical quarterly* 71 (3): 247–64.

———. 1973. Probing the riddle of the Bird Woman. *Montana* 23 (4): 2–17.

———. 1976. Fort Manuel: Its historical significance. *South Dakota history* 6 (2): 131–51.

———. 1978. Sacajawea, Sacagawea, Sakakawea? *South Dakota history* 8 (4): 303–11.

———. 1980. A Charbonneau family portrait. *The American West* 17 (2): 4–13.

Appadurai, Arjun. 1992. Putting hierarchy in its place. In *Rereading cultural anthropology*, ed. George Macus, 34–47. Durham NC: Duke University Press.

Appleby, Joyce, L. Hunt, and M. Jacob. 1994. *Telling the truth about history*. New York: Norton.

Atkinson, Paul. 1990. *The ethnographic imagination: Textual constructions of reality*. New York: Routledge.

Basso, Keith H. 1984. Stalking with stories: Names, places, and moral narratives among the Western Apache. In *Text, play and story*, ed. Edward M. Bruner. Proceedings of the American Ethnological Society, 1983, 19–55. Prospect Heights IL: Waveland Press.

Bataille, Gretchen M., and Kathleen Mullen Sands. 1984. *American Indian women: Telling their lives*. Lincoln: University of Nebraska Press.

Bauman, Zygmunt. 1982. *Memories of class*. London: Routledge and Kegan Paul.

Bell, Tom. 1989. Testimony of Edmo Le Clair. *Wind River mountaineer* 5 (1): 6.

Bell, Tom, and Beatrice Cofts. 1987. The Reverend John Roberts/Sacajawea. *Wind River mountaineer* 3 (2): 25–26.

Bertaux, Daniel, ed. 1981. *Biography and society: The life history approach in the social sciences*. Beverly Hills CA: Sage.

Biddle, Nicholas, and Paul Allen. [1814] 1902. *History of the expedition under the command of captains Lewis and Clark . . . 1804–5–6*, ed. James K. Hosmer. 2 vols. Chicago: A. C. McClurg.

Bieder, Robert E. 1980. Scientific attitudes toward Indian mixed-bloods in early nineteenth-century America. *Journal of ethnic studies* 8 (2): 17–30.

Blackman, Margaret B. 1982. *During my time: Florence Edenshaw Davidson, a Haida woman*. Seattle: University of Washington Press.

———. 1989. *Sadie Brower Neakok: An Iñupiaq woman*. Seattle: University of Washington Press.

Blackman, Margaret B., ed. 1992. The afterlife of the life history. Special issue, *Journal of narrative and life history* 2 (1): 1–79.

Bloodworth, William. 1978. Varieties of American Indian autobiography. *Melus* 5 (3): 67–81.

Boas, Franz. 1943. Recent anthropology II. *Science* 8 (2546): 334–37.

Boas, Franz, and Ella Deloria. 1941. Dakota grammar. *Memoirs of the National Academy of Science XXIII*. Washington DC: Government Printing Office.

Bohannan, Paul. 1995. *How culture works*. New York: Free Press.

Bolles, Edmund Blair. 1988. *Remembering and forgetting: An inquiry into the nature of memory*. New York: Walker.

Bonnifield, Paul. 1979. *The dust bowl*. Albuquerque: University of New Mexico Press.

Brackenridge, Henry M. 1816. *Journal of a voyage up the River Missouri performed in eighteen hundred and eleven*. 2d ed. Baltimore: Coale and Maxwell.

Brave Bird, Mary. 1993. *Ohitika woman*, with Richard Erdoes. New York: Harper.

Brodzki, Bella, and Celeste Schenck, eds. 1988. *Life/lines: Theorizing women's autobiography*. Ithaca NY: Cornell University Press.

Bronson, Ruth Muskrat. [1944] 1979. *Indians are people, too*. New York: Friendship Press.

———. 1994. Ruth Muskrat Bronson (Cherokee) criticizes the proposed termination of federal trusteeship, 1955. In *Major problems in American Indian history*, ed. A. L. Hurtado and P. Iverson, 492–94. Lexington MA: D. C. Heath.

Brumble, H. David, III. 1981. *An annotated bibliography of American Indian and Eskimo bibliographies*. Lincoln: University of Nebraska Press.

———. 1987. Sam Blowsnake's confession: Crashing Thunder and the history of American Indian autobiography. In *Recovering the word: Essays on Native American literature*, ed. Brian Swann and Arnold Krupat, 537–51. Berkeley: University of California Press.

———. 1988. *American Indian autobiography*. Berkeley: University of California Press.

Bruner, Edward. 1986. Ethnography as narrative. In *The anthropology of experience*, ed. V. W. Turner and E. M. Bruner, 139–55. Urbana: University of Illinois Press.

Bruss, Elizabeth. 1976. *Autobiographical acts: The changing situation of a literary genre*. Baltimore: Johns Hopkins University Press.

Campbell, Maria. 1973. *Halfbreed*. Lincoln: University of Nebraska Press.

Cassirer, Ernst. 1944. *Essay on man*. New Haven CT: Yale University Press.

Cazden, Courtney, and Vera P. John. 1971. Learning in Indian children. In *Anthropological perspectives on education*, ed. M. Wax, S. Diamond, and F. Gearing, 252–72. New York: Basic Books.

Chafe, Wallace. 1982. Integration and involvement in speaking, writing, and oral literature. In *Spoken and written language: Exploring orality and literacy*, ed. D. Tannen, 171–84. Norwood NJ: Ablex.

Chafe, Wallace, and Deborah Tannen. 1987. The relation between written and spoken language. *Annual review of anthropology* 16:383–407.

Chandler, Milford G. 1969. Sidelights on Sacajawea. *The masterkey* 43 (2): 58–66.

Child, Brenda J. 1993. A bitter lesson: Native Americans and the boarding school experience, 1890–1940. Ph.D. diss., University of Iowa, Iowa City.

Chuinard, E. G. 1976. The actual role of the Bird Woman. *Montana: The magazine of western history* 26 (3): 18–29.

Cicourel, Aaron V. 1985. Text and discourse. *Annual review of anthropology* 14:159–85.

Clark, Ella E., and Margot Edmonds. 1979. *Sacagawea of the Lewis and Clark expedition*. Berkeley: University of California Press.

Clifford, James. 1978. "Hanging up looking glasses at odd corners": Ethnobiographical prospects. In *Studies in biography*, ed. Daniel Aaron, 41–56. Cambridge MA: Harvard University Press.

————. 1983. On ethnographic authority. *Representations* 1 (2): 118–46.

Clifford, James, and George E. Marcus, eds. 1986. *Writing culture*. Berkeley: University of California Press.

Clifton, James A., ed. 1989. *Being and becoming Indian*. Chicago: Dorsey.

Coleman, Michael C. 1993. *American Indian children at school, 1850–1923*. Jackson: University Press of Mississippi.

Connerton, Paul. 1989. *How societies remember*. Cambridge MA: Cambridge University Press.

Cook-Lynn, Elizabeth. 1996. American Indian intellectualism and the new Indian story. *American Indian quarterly* 20 (1): 57–76.

Coues, Elliott, ed. 1893. *History of the expedition under the command of Lewis and Clark*. 4 vols. New York: Francis P. Harper.

Crapanzano, Vincent. 1977. The life history in anthropological fieldwork. *Anthropology and humanism quarterly* 2 (2–3): 3–7.

Crawford, Helen. 1927. Sakakawea. *North Dakota historical quarterly* 1 (3): 2–15.

Cronon, William. 1992. A place for stories: Nature, history, and narrative. *The journal of American history* 78 (4): 1347–76.

Crow Dog, Mary. 1990. *Lakota woman*, with Richard Erdoes. New York: Harper.

Cruikshank, Julie. 1990a. *Life lived like a story*. Lincoln: University of Nebraska Press.

————. 1990b. Getting the words right: Perspectives on naming and places in Athapaskan oral history. *Arctic anthropology* 27 (1): 52–65.

David, Robert Beebe. 1937. *Finn Burnett: Frontiersman*. Glendale CA: Arthur H. Clark.

Deloria, Ella Cara. 1932. *Dakota texts*. Publication of the American Ethnological Society, vol. 14. New York: G. E. Stechert.

————. [1944] 1979. *Speaking of Indians*. Vermillion SD: Dakota Press.

————. 1988. *Waterlily*. Lincoln: University of Nebraska Press.

Deloria, Vine, Jr., and Clifford Lytle. 1984. *The nations within*. New York: Pantheon Books.

DeMallie, Raymond J. 1980. Ella Cara Deloria. In *Notable American women: The modern period*, ed. Barbara Sicherman, 183–85. Cambridge MA: Harvard University Press.

————. 1993. "These have no ears": Narrative and the ethnohistorical method. *Ethnohistory* 40 (4): 515–38.

De Voto, Bernard. 1954. Sacajawea: Inspirational Indian maid. *Montana magazine of history* 4 (4): 61.

Dollard, John. 1935. *Criteria for the life history*. New Haven CT: Yale University Press.

Dongoske, Kurt, Leigh Jenkins, and T. J. Ferguson. 1993. Understanding the past through Hopi oral history. *Native peoples: The journal of the Heard Museum* 6 (2): 24–31.

Dunn, Anne M. 1995. Peltier recalls influence of early years. *Circle* 16 (10): 11.

Dye, Eva Emery. [1902] 1936. *The conquest: The true story of Lewis and Clark*. Chicago: C. McClurg.

Eastman, Charles A. 1925. *Report to the commissioner of Indian affairs (Investigation of Sacajawea's final burial place)*. Letter dated March 2, 1925. United States Department of the Interior, Office of Indian Affairs, Washington DC.

Erdrich, Louise. 1995. *The Blue Jay's dance*. New York: Harper-Collins.

Fabian, Johannes. 1983. *Time and the other*. New York: Columbia University Press.

Flannery, Regina. 1995. *Ellen Smallboy: Glimpses of a Cree woman's life*. Montreal: McGill-Queen's University Press.

Foucault, Michel. 1972. The discourse on language. Appendix in *The archaeology of knowledge*, 215–37. New York: Pantheon.

Frazier, Neta Lohnes. 1967. *Sacajawea: The girl nobody knows*. New York: David McKay.

Fussell, Paul. 1975. *The great war and modern memory*. New York: Oxford University Press.

Gadamer, Hans-Georg. 1976. *Philosophical hermeneutics*. Berkeley: University of California Press.

———. 1979. The problem of historical consciousness. In *Interpretive social science: A reader*, ed. P. Rabinow and W. Sullivan, 103–60. Berkeley: University of California Press.

Galton, Francis. 1879a. Psychometric experiments. *Brain* 2:149–62.

———. 1879b. Psychometric facts. *Nineteenth century* 5:425–33.

Geertz, Clifford. 1986. Making experiences, authoring selves. In *The anthropology of experience*, ed. V. Turner and E. Bruner, 373–80. Urbana: University of Illinois Press.

———. 1988. *Works and lives*. Stanford CA: Stanford University Press.

Geiger, Susan N. G. 1986. Women's life histories: Method and content. *Signs* 11 (2): 334–51.

Giddens, Anthony. 1982. Hermeneutics and social theory. In *Profiles and critiques in social theory*, 1–17. Berkeley: University of California Press.

Gilbert, B. Miles. 1972. Sacajawea: A problem in Plains anthropology. *Plains anthropologist* 17 (56): 156–60.

Glancy, Diane. 1992. *Claiming breath*. Lincoln: University of Nebraska Press.

Gluck, Sherna. 1977. What's so special about women?: Women's oral history. *Frontiers* 2 (2): 3–17.

Gluck, Sherna Berger, and Daphne Patai, eds. 1991. *Women's words: The feminist practice of oral history*. New York: Routledge.

Goleman, Daniel. 1985. *Vital lies, simple truths: The psychology of self-deception*. New York: Simon and Schuster.

Gould, Janice. 1992. The problem of being "Indian": One mixed-blood's dilemma. In *De/Colonizing the subject*, ed. Sidonie Smith and Julia Watson, 81–87. Minneapolis: University of Minnesota Press.

———. 1997. "I am putting my mind to learn": Indian boarding school literacy and literature, 1880–1929. Paper presented in February to the faculty and students at the University of Northern Colorado, Greeley.

Green, Rayna. 1975. The Pocahontas perplex: The image of Indian women in American culture. *Massachusetts review* 16:698–714.

———. 1980. Native American women: A review essay. *Signs* 6 (2): 248–67.

———. 1983. *Native American women: A contextual bibliography*. Bloomington: Indiana University Press.

———. 1992. *Women in American Indian society*. New York: Chelsea.

Gridley, Marion E. 1974. *American Indian women*. New York: Hawthorn.

Grobsmith, Elizabeth S. 1981. *Lakota of the Rosebud*. New York: Holt, Rinehart and Winston.

Gunn, Janet Varner. 1982. *Autobiography: Toward a poetics of experience*. Philadelphia: University of Pennsylvania Press.

Gusdorf, Georges. [1956] 1980. Conditions and limits of autobiography. In *Autobiography: Essays theoretical and critical*, ed. James Olney, 28–48. Princeton NJ: Princeton University Press.

Haig-Brown, Celia. 1988. *Resistance and renewal: Surviving the Indian residential school*. Vancouver: Tillacum Library.

Harjo, Joy. 1987. Ordinary spirit. In *I tell you now*, ed. Brian Swann and Arnold Krupat, 263–70. Lincoln: University of Nebraska Press.

Haviland, John B. 1991. "That was the last time I seen them, and no more": Voices through time in Australian aboriginal autobiography. *American Ethnologist* 18 (2): 331–61.

Hebard, Grace Raymond. 1907. Pilot of first white men to cross the American continent. *Journal of American history* 1:467–84.

———. 1933. *Sacajawea*. Glendale CA: Arthur H. Clark.

Henze, Rosemary, and Lauren Vanett. 1993. To walk in two worlds—or more?: Challenging a common metaphor of Native education. *Anthropology and education quarterly* 24 (2): 116–34.

Hilden, Patricia Penn. 1995. *When nickels were Indians: An urban, mixed-blood story*. Washington DC: Smithsonian Institution Press.

Hobsbawm, Eric, and Terence Ranger, eds. 1983. *The invention of tradition*. Cambridge MA: Cambridge University Press.

Hodge, Frederick Webb. 1910. Handbook of American Indians north of Mexico. 2 vols. Smithsonian Institution, Bureau of American Ethnology Bulletin 30, Washington DC.

Hoffman, Leonore, and Margo Culley, eds. 1985. *Women's personal narratives: Essays in criticism and pedagogy*. New York: Modern Language Association.

Hogan, Linda. 1987. The two lives. In *I tell you now*, ed. B. Swann and A. Krupat, 231–49. Lincoln: University of Nebraska Press.

Hopkins, Sara Winnemucca. 1883. *Life among the Piutes*, ed. Mrs. Horace Mann. New York: G. P. Putnam's Sons.

Horne, Esther Burnett. 1980. Oral tradition of Sacajawea. Unpublished manuscript adapted and excerpted in appendix C of this book.

Howard, Harold P. 1971. *Sacajawea*. Norman: University of Oklahoma Press.

Howard, Helen Addison. 1967. The mystery of Sacagawea's death. *Pacific Northwest quarterly* 58 (1): 1–6.

Hultkrantz, Äke. [1961] 1974. The Shoshones in the Rocky Mountain area. In *Shoshone Indians*, ed. David Horr, 173–40. Reprint New York: Garland.

———. 1971. Yellow Hand, chief and medicineman among the Eastern Shoshoni. In *Proceedings of the 38th international congress of Americanists*, vol. 2, 293–304. Stuttgart-München, 1968.

———. 1987. *Native religions of North America*, 37–84. San Francisco: Harper and Row.

Hyer, Sally. 1990. *One house, one voice, one heart: Native American education at the Santa Fe Indian School*. Santa Fe: Museum of New Mexico Press.

Jackson, Donald, ed. 1962. *Letters of the Lewis and Clark expedition with related documents, 1783–1854*. 2 vols. Urbana: University of Illinois Press.

Jelinek, Estelle C. 1986. *The tradition of women's autobiography: From antiquity to the present*. Boston: Twayne Publishers.

Johnston, Basil. 1988. *Indian school days*. Norman: University of Oklahoma Press.

Kammen, Michael. 1991. *Mystic chords of memory*. New York: Alfred A. Knopf.

Kasten, Wendy C. 1992. Bridging the Horizon: American Indian beliefs and whole language learning. *Anthropology and education quarterly* 23 (2): 108–19.

Katz, Jane. 1995. *Messengers of the wind*. New York: Ballantine.

Kidwell, Clara Sue. 1992. Indian women as cultural mediators. *Ethnohistory* 39 (2): 97–107.

Kingston, C. S. 1944. Sacajawea as guide: The evaluation of a legend. *Pacific Northwest quarterly* 35:3–18.

Kluckhohn, Clyde. 1945. The personal document in anthropological science. In *The use of personal documents in history, anthropology, and sociology*, ed. L. Gottschalk, C. Kluckhohn, and R. Angell, 78–173. Social Science Research Council Bulletin 55, New York.

Krupat, Arnold. 1985. *For those who came after: A study of Native American autobiography*. Berkeley: University of California Press.

———. 1992. *Ethnocriticism: Ethnography, history, and literature*. Berkeley: University of California Press.

——. 1994. Collaborative Indian autobiographies. In *Dictionary of Native American literature*, ed. Andrew Wiget, 176–78. New York: Garland.

——. 1996. *The turn to the native: Studies in criticism and culture*. Lincoln: University of Nebraska Press.

La Framboise, Teresa D., Annaliese M. Heyle, and Emily J. Ozer. 1990. Changing and diverse roles of women in American Indian cultures. *Sex Roles: A Journal of Research* 22 (7–8; April): 455–76.

Lakoff, George, and Mark Johnson. 1980. *Metaphors we live by*. Chicago: University of Chicago Press.

Landsman, Gail H. 1992. The "other" as political symbol: Images of Indians in the woman suffrage movement. *Ethnohistory* 39 (3): 247–84.

Lange, Robert E. 1986. N. Dakota's Sakakawea. *We proceeded on* 12 (4): 32–33.

Langer, Lawrence L. 1991. *Holocaust testimonies*. New Haven: Yale University Press.

Langness, Lewis L. 1965. *The life history in anthropological science*. New York: Holt, Rinehart, and Winston.

Langness, Lewis L., and Gelya Frank. 1981. *Lives: An anthropological approach to biography*. Novato CA: Chandler and Sharp.

Laut, Agnes C. 1905. What the Portland Exposition really celebrates. *Review of reviews* 31:428–32.

Lavender, David. 1958. *Land of giants*. Garden City NY: Doubleday.

Lawless, Elaine. 1991. Women's life stories and reciprocal ethnography as feminist and emergent. *Journal of folklore research* 28 (1): 35–60.

Le Goff, Jacques. 1988. *History and memory*. New York: Columbia University Press.

Liljeblad, Sven. 1958. Footnotes to history: Dr. Liljeblad's comment. *Idaho Yesterdays* 2 (2): 35.

Linderman, Frank. [1932] 1972. *Pretty-shield*. Lincoln: University of Nebraska Press.

Littlefield, Alice. 1989. The B.I.A. boarding school: Theories of resistance and social reproduction. *Humanity and society* 13 (4): 428–41.

Lomawaima, K. Tsianina. 1994. *They call it prairie light: The story of Chilocco Indian School*. Lincoln: University of Nebraska Press.

Lowenthal, David. 1985. *The past is a foreign country*. Cambridge MA: Cambridge University Press.

Lowie, Robert H. 1909. The Northern Shoshone. *Anthropological papers of the American Museum of Natural History* 2 (2): 165–306.

——. 1924. Notes on Shoshonean ethnography. *Anthropological papers of the American Museum of Natural History* 20 (3): 105–324.

Lurie, Nancy Oestreich. 1961. *Mountain Wolf woman, sister of Crashing Thunder: The autobiography of a Winnebago Indian*. Ann Arbor: University of Michigan Press.

———. 1972. Indian women: A legacy of freedom. In *Look to the mountaintop*, ed. Charles Jones. San Jose CA: Gousha Publishers.

Luttig, John C. 1920. *Journal of a fur-trading expedition on the Upper Missouri, 1812–1813*, ed. Stella M. Drumm. St Louis: Missouri Historical Society.

McBeth, Sally. 1983a. *Ethnic identity and the boarding school experience of West-Central Oklahoma American Indians*. Washington DC: University Press of America.

———. 1983b. Indian boarding schools and ethnic identity: An example from the southern plains tribes of Oklahoma. *Plains anthropologist* 28 (100): 119–28.

———. 1984. The primer and the hoe. *Natural history magazine* 93 (8; July): 4–12.

———. 1989. Collaboration. In *Day in, day out: Women's lives in North Dakota*, ed. B. Benson et al., 64–67. Grand Forks: University of North Dakota Press.

———. 1993. Myths of objectivity and the collaborative process in life history research. In *When they read what we write: The politics of ethnography*, ed. Caroline Brettell, 145–62. Westport CT: Bergin and Garvey.

McBeth, Sally, and Esther Burnett Horne. 1996. "I know who I am": The collaborative life history of a Shoshone Indian woman. In *Unrelated kin: Race and gender in women's personal narratives*, ed. G. Etter-Lewis and M. Foster, 71–85. New York: Routledge.

McBride, Bunny. 1995. *Molly Spotted Elk*. Norman: University of Oklahoma Press.

Mandelbaum, David G. 1973. The study of life history: Gandhi. *Current anthropology* 14 (3): 177–96.

Maracle, Lee. 1990. *Bobbi Lee: Indian rebel*. Toronto: Women's Press.

Marcus, George, and Dick Cushman. 1982. Ethnographies as texts. *Annual review of anthropology* 11:25–69.

Marcus, George E., and Michael M. Fischer. 1986. *Anthropology as cultural critique*. Chicago: University of Chicago Press.

Mascia-Lees, Frances E., Patricia Sharpe, and Colleen Cohen. 1989. The postmodernist turn in anthropology: Cautions from a feminist perspective. *Signs* 15 (1): 7–33.

Matthiessen, Peter. 1983. *In the spirit of Crazy Horse*. New York: Penguin.

Meriam, Lewis. 1928. *The problem of Indian administration*. Institute for Government Research. Baltimore: Johns Hopkins University Press.

Michelson, Truman. 1925. *The autobiography of a Fox Indian woman*. Smithsonian Institution, 40th Annual Report of the Bureau of American Ethnology, Washington DC.

———. 1932. The narrative of a Southern Cheyenne woman. *Smithsonian miscellaneous collections* 87 (5): 1–13.

———. 1933. Narrative of an Arapaho woman. *American Anthropologist* 35:595–610.

Mihesuah, Devon A. 1993. *Cultivating the Rosebuds: The education of women at the Cherokee Female Seminary, 1851–1909*. Urbana: University of Illinois Press.

———. 1996. Commonality of difference: American Indian women and history. *American Indian quarterly* 20 (1): 15–27.

Miller, David Reed. 1981. Review of Sacagawea of the Lewis and Clark expedition, Ella Clark and Margot Edmonds. *Western historical quarterly* 12 (2): 186–87.

Minde, Emma. 1996. *Their example showed me the way: A Cree woman's life shaped by two cultures*, trans. and ed. F. Ahenakew and H. C. Wolfart. Calgary: University of Alberta Press.

Mintz, Sidney W. 1989. The sensation of moving while standing still. *American ethnologist* 16 (4): 786–96.

Misch, George. 1951. A history of autobiography in antiquity. Trans. E. W. Dickes. Cambridge MA: Harvard University Press.

Moulton, Gary, ed. 1983. *Atlas of the Lewis and Clark expedition*. Lincoln: University of Nebraska Press.

Murray, David. 1991. *Forked tongues: Speech, writing and representation in North American Indian texts*. Bloomington: Indiana University Press.

Nelson, Margaret, and M. Frances Walton. 1982. *Ohoyo Ikhana: A bibliography of American Indian–Alaska Native curriculum materials*. Wichita Falls TX: Ohoyo Resource Center.

Olden, Sarah Emilia. 1923. *Shoshone folk lore*. Milwaukee: Morehouse.

Olney, James, ed. 1972. *Metaphors of self: The meaning of autobiography*. Princeton NJ: Princeton University Press.

———. 1980. *Autobiography: Essays theoretical and critical*. Princeton NJ: Princeton University Press.

———. 1988. *Studies in autobiography*. New York: Oxford University Press.

Ortiz, Alfonso. 1974. Some concerns central to the writing of "Indian" history. Commentary presented at a symposium on the writing of history, American Historical Association Meetings, Chicago.

Ortiz, Simon. 1977. Indian oral history: A sacred responsibility. In *The great Sioux nation: Sitting in judgment on America*, ed. Roxanne Dunbar Ortiz, 14–15. American Indian Treaty Council Information Center. Berkeley: Moon Books.

Osgood, Ernest Staples, ed. 1964. *The field notes of Captain William Clark, 1803–1805*. New Haven CT: Yale University Press.

Ottoson, Dennis R. 1976. Toussaint Charbonneau: A most durable man. *South Dakota history* 6 (2): 152–85.

Patai, Daphne. 1988. *Brazilian women speak: Contemporary life histories*. New Brunswick NJ: Rutgers University Press.

Patten, James I. 1926. Buffalo hunting with the Shoshone Indians, in 1874 in the Big Horn Basin, Wyoming. *Annals of Wyoming* 4 (2): 296–302.

Personal Narratives Group. 1989. *Interpreting women's lives: Feminist theory and personal narratives*. Bloomington: Indiana University Press.

Peterson, Jacqueline, and Jennifer Brown. 1984. *The new people: Being and becoming Metis in North America*. Lincoln: University of Nebraska Press.

Peterson, Linda H. 1986. *Victorian autobiography: The tradition of self-interpretation*. New Haven CT: Yale University Press.

Poole, Edwin A. 1964. Charbono's "Squar." *Pacific northwesterner* 8 (1): 1–13.

Porter, Clyde. 1961. Jean Baptiste Charbonneau. *Idaho yesterdays* 5 (3): 7–9.

Powers, Alfred. 1935. *History of Oregon literature*. Portland OR: Metropolitan Press.

Pratt, Richard Henry. 1897. *Annual report of the United States Indian school at Carlisle, Pennsylvania, 1897*. Washington DC: Government Printing Office.

Qoyawayma, Polingaysi (Elizabeth Q. White). 1964. *No turning back*. Albuquerque: University of New Mexico Press.

Rabinow, Paul. 1977. *Reflections on fieldwork in Morocco*. Berkeley: University of California Press.

———. 1986. Representations are social facts: Modernity and post-modernity in anthropology. In *Writing culture: The poetics and politics of ethnography*, ed. J. Clifford and G. Marcus, 234–61. Berkeley: University of California Press.

Radin, Paul, ed. [1926] 1983. *Crashing Thunder: The autobiography of an American Indian*. Lincoln: University of Nebraska Press.

Rappaport, Joanne. 1990. *The politics of memory: Native historical interpretation in the Colombian Andes*. Cambridge Latin American Studies series, no. 70. New York: Cambridge University Press.

Rees, John E. 1958. Footnotes to history. *Idaho yesterdays* 2 (2): 34–35.

Reid, Russell. 1950. *Saka'kawe'a: The Bird Woman*. Bismarck: State Historical Society of North Dakota.

Remley, David. 1982. Sacajawea of myth and history. In *Women and Western American literature*, ed. Helen Winter Stauffer and Susan J. Rosowski, 70–89. Troy NY: Whitston.

Richards, Bertrand F. 1980. *Gene Stratton Porter*. Boston: Twayne Publishers.

Ricoeur, Paul. 1977. *The rule of metaphor: Multi-disciplinary studies of the creation of meaning in language*. Toronto: University of Toronto Press.

———. 1979. The model of the text: Meaningful action considered as a text. In *Interpretive social science: A reader*, ed. Paul Rabinow and W. M. Sullivan, 73–101. Berkeley: University of California Press.

Robinson, Doane. 1924a. Sac-A-Jawe vs. Sa-Kaka-Wea. *South Dakota historical collections* 12:71–81.

———. 1924b. The name of the Bird Woman. *South Dakota historical collections* 12:82–84.

Robinson, Will G. 1956. Sa ka ka wea—Sa ca ja wea. *The Wi-Iyohi: Monthly bulletin of the South Dakota historical society* 10 (6): 1–8.

Ronda, James P. 1984. Lewis and Clark among the Indians. Lincoln: University of Nebraska Press.

Roof, Judith, and Robyn Wiegman, eds. 1995. *Who can speak?* Urbana: University of Illinois Press.

Rosaldo, Renato. 1980a. Doing oral history. *Social analysis* 4:89–99.

———. 1980b. *Ilongot headhunting, 1883–1974*. Stanford CA: Stanford University Press.

Rose, Wendy. 1985. *The halfbreed chronicles*. San Raphael CA: West End Press.

Rosenwald, George C., and Richard L. Ochberg, eds. 1992. *Storied lives: The cultural politics of self-understanding*. New Haven CT: Yale University Press.

Rousso, Henry. 1991. *The Vichy syndrome*. Cambridge MA: Harvard University Press.

Rubin, David C. 1986. *Autobiographical memory*. Cambridge MA: Cambridge University Press.

Ruoff, A. LaVonne Brown. 1990. *American Indian literatures*. New York: Modern Language Association.

Saindon, Bob. 1988. Sacakawea Boat-Launcher: The origin and meaning of a name . . . maybe. *We proceeded on* 14 (3): 4–10.

St. Pierre, Mark. 1991. *Madonna Swan: A Lakota woman's story*. Norman: University of Oklahoma Press.

Sanford, Martha Cobb. 1905. Sacajawea, the Bird-Woman. *Woman's home companion*, June issue, p. 5.

Sarris, Greg. 1993. *Keeping Slug Woman alive: A holistic approach to American Indian texts*. Berkeley: University of California Press.

Schroer, Blanche. 1978. Sacajawea: The legend and the truth. *Yesterday in Wyoming*, Winter issue, pp. 22–28, 37–43.

———. 1980. Boat-Pusher or Bird Woman? Sacagawea or Sacajawea? *Annals of Wyoming* 52 (1): 46–54.

Searle, John R. 1995. *The construction of social reality*. New York: Free Press.

Shaul, David L. 1972. The meaning of the name Sacajawea. *Annals of Wyoming* 44 (2): 237–40.

Shaw, Anna Moore. 1974. *A Pima past*. Tucson: University of Arizona Press.

Shaw, Bruce. 1980. Life history writings in anthropology: A methodological review. *Mankind* 12 (3): 226–33.

Shimkin, Demitri. 1947. *Wind River Shoshone ethnogeography*. University of California Anthropological Records, vol. 5, no. 4.

Silko, Leslie Marmon. 1981. *Storyteller*. New York: Arcade.

Simonelli, Richard. 1995. Bridging anthropology and Native people. *Winds of change* 10 (4): 70–73.

Smith, Sidonie. 1987. *A poetics of women's autobiography: Marginality and the fictions of self-representation*. Bloomington: Indiana University Press.

Smith, Sidonie, and Julia Watson, eds. 1992. *De/Colonizing the subject: The politics of gender in women's autobiography*. Minneapolis: University of Minnesota Press.

Snyder, Gerald S. 1974. The girl of history who became a woman of fable. *Westways* 66 (3): 36–39, 71–74.

Spengemann, William C., and L. R. Lundquist. 1968. Autobiography and the American myth. In *The American culture: Approaches to the study of the United States*, ed. Hennig Cohen, 92–110. Boston: Houghton Mifflin.

Spring, Agnes Wright. 1941. Recognition that Sacajawea died in Wyoming is sought (from Sacajawea: A symposium). *Annals of Wyoming* 13:168–83.

Stegner, Wallace. 1955. *Wolf Willow*. New York: Viking.

Stewart, Irene. 1980. *A voice in her tribe: A Navajo woman's own story*. Ballena Press Anthropological Papers, no. 17. Socorro NM: Ballena Press.

Stubbs, Michael. 1983. *Discourse analysis*. Chicago: University of Chicago Press.

Szasz, Margaret Connell. 1977. Federal boarding schools and the Indian child: 1920–1960. *South Dakota history* 7 (4): 371–84.

Taber, Ronald W. 1967. Sacagawea and the suffragettes. *Pacific Northwest quarterly* 58 (1): 7–13.

Tapahonso, Lucy. 1993. *Sáanii dahataal: The women are singing*. Sun Tracks series, vol. 23. Tucson: University Press of Arizona.

Thelen, David, ed. 1989. *Memory and American history*. Bloomington: Indiana University Press.

Thomas, William I., and Florian Znaniecki. 1918–1920. *The Polish peasant in Europe and America*. 5 vols. Boston: R. G. Badger.

Thwaites, Reuben Gold. 1904. *Original journals of the Lewis and Clark expedition, 1804–1806*. 8 vols. New York: Arno Press.

Trenholm, Virginia Cole, and Maurine Carley. 1964. *The Shoshonis*. Norman: University of Oklahoma Press.

Trennert, Robert. 1983. From Carlisle to Phoenix: The rise and fall of the Indian outing system, 1878–1930. *Pacific historical review* 42 (3): 267–91.

———. 1988. *The Phoenix Indian School: Forced assimilation in Arizona, 1891–1935*. Norman: University of Oklahoma Press.

Trouillot, Michel-Rolph. 1995. *Silencing the past: Power and the production of history*. Boston: Beacon Press.

Tyler, Stephen. 1992. On being out of words. In *Rereading cultural anthropology*, ed. George Marcus, 1–7. Durham NC: Duke University Press.

Udall, Louise (as told to). 1969. *Me and mine: The life story of Helen Sekaquaptewa*. Tucson: University of Arizona Press.

Underhill, Ruth. [1936] 1979. *Papago woman*. New York: Holt, Rinehart and Winston.

U.S. House. 1886. Annual report of the commissioner of Indian affairs to the secretary of the interior. In *House executive documents*, 49th Cong., 1st sess., September 28, Serial Set 2467.

U.S. Senate Select Committee on Indian Affairs. 1982. *Closing of off-reservation boarding schools*. Bureau of Indian Affairs Proposal to Close Three Off-Reservation Boarding Schools, 97th Cong., 2d sess., February 24.

Vander, Judith. 1988. *Songprints: The musical experience of five Shoshone women*. Urbana: University of Illinois Press.

Vansina, Jan. 1965. *Oral tradition: A study in historical methodology*. Chicago: Aldine.

Vecsey, Christopher. 1988. *Imagine ourselves richly: Mythic narratives of North American Indians*. New York: Crossroad.

Vizenor, Gerald. 1989. A postmodern introduction. In *Narrative chance: Postmodern discourse on Native American Indian literatures*, ed. G. Vizenor, 3–16. Albuquerque: University of New Mexico Press.

Voget, Fred W. 1995. *They call me Agnes*. Norman: University of Oklahoma Press.

Walters, Anna Lee. 1992. *Talking Indian: Reflections on survival and writing*. Ithaca: Firebrand Books.

Watson, Lawrence. 1976. Understanding life history as a subjective document. *Ethos* 4:95–131.

Watson, Lawrence, and Maria-Barbara Watson-Franke. 1985. *Interpreting life histories: An anthropological inquiry*. New Brunswick NJ: Rutgers University Press.

Weintraub, Karl. 1978. *The value of the individual: Self and circumstance in autobiography*. Chicago: University of Chicago Press.

Werner, M. R., and John Starr. 1959. *Teapot Dome*. New York: Viking.

Willis, Jane. 1973. *Geneish: An Indian girlhood*. Toronto: New Press.

Wilson, Gilbert L. [1927] 1981. *Waheenee*. Lincoln: University of Nebraska Press.

Winnie, Lucille (Jerry). 1969. *Sah-Gan-De-Oh: The chief's daughter*. New York: Vantage Press.

Wong, Hertha D. 1987. Pre-literate Native American autobiography: Forms of personal narrative. *Melus* 14 (1): 17–32.

———. 1992. *Sending my heart back across the years*. New York: Oxford Press.

Wright, Peter M. 1980. Washakie. In *American Indian leaders*, ed. R. David Edmunds, 131–51. Lincoln: University of Nebraska Press.

Zimmerman, Larry J. 1995. We do not need your past! In *Beyond subsistence*, ed. Philip Duke and Michael Wilson, 28–45. Tuscaloosa: University of Alabama Press.

Zitkala-Sa (Gertrude Bonnin). [1921] 1985. *American Indian stories*. Lincoln: University of Nebraska Press.

Index

In the American Indian Lives series

I Stand in the Center of the Good
Interviews with Contemporary Native American Artists
Edited by Lawrence Abbott

Authentic Alaska: Voices of Its Native Writers
Edited by Susan B. Andrews and John Creed

Chief: The Life History of Eugene Delorme, Imprisoned Santee Sioux
Edited by Inéz Cardozo-Freeman

Winged Words: American Indian Writers Speak
Edited by Laura Coltelli

Life, Letters and Speeches
By George Copway (Kahgegagahbowh)
Edited by A. LaVonne Brown Ruoff and Donald B. Smith

Life Lived Like a Story: Life Stories of Three Yukon Native Elders
By Julie Cruikshank in collaboration with Angela Sidney, Kitty Smith, and Annie Ned

Essie's Story: The Life and Legacy of a Shoshone Teacher
By Esther Burnett Horne and Sally McBeth

Song of Rita Joe: Autobiography of a Mi'kmaq Poet
By Rita Joe

Catch Colt
By Sidner J. Larson

Alex Posey: Creek Poet, Journalist, and Humorist
By Daniel F. Littlefield Jr.

Mourning Dove: A Salishan Autobiography
Edited by Jay Miller

John Rollin Ridge: His Life and Works
By James W. Parins

Singing an Indian Song: A Biography of D'Arcy McNickle
By Dorothy R. Parker

Crashing Thunder: The Autobiography of an American Indian
Edited by Paul Radin